Critical Muslim 1

The Arabs Are Alive

Critical Muslim 1, January-March 2012

Editors: Ziauddin Sardar and Robin Yassin-Kassab
Deputy Editor: Samia Rahman
Publisher: Michael Dwyer
Managing Editor: (Hurst Publishers): Daisy Leitch
Cover Design: Fatima Jamadar

Associate Editors: Abdelwahhab El-Affendi, Muhammad Idrees Ahmad, Iqbal Asaria, Michael Muhammad Knight, Vinay Lal, Hassan Mahamdallie, Ehsan Masood

Contributing Editors: Waqar Ahmad, Merryl Wyn Davies, Iftikhar Malik, Parvez Manzoor, Usama Hasan

International Advisory Board: Karen Armstrong, William Dalrymple, Farid Esack, Anwar Ibrahim, Arif Mohammad Khan, Bruce Lawrence, Ebrahim Moosa, Ashish Nandy

Critical Muslim is published quarterly by C. Hurst & Co (Publishers) Ltd on behalf of and in conjunction with Critical Muslim Ltd and the Muslim Institute, London.
All correspondence to Muslim Institute, CAN Mezzanine, 49–51 East Road, London N1 6AH, United Kingdom
e-mail for editorial: editorial@criticalmuslim.com

C. Hurst & Co (Publishers) Ltd.,
41 Great Russell Street, London WC1B 3PL

ISBN: 978-1-84904-190-4
ISSN: 2048-8475

To subscribe go to www.musliminstitute.org/critical-muslim
Or call +44 20 7250 8068, or write to the above address.
A one year subscription, inclusive of postage (four issues), costs £50 (UK), £65 (rest of Europe) and £75 (rest of the world).

Cover © Taus Makhacheva from her series of photographs 'Affirmative Action'.
Cover design © Fatima Jamadar

OUR MISSION

Critical Muslim is a quarterly magazine of ideas and issues showcasing ground-breaking thinking on Islam and what it means to be a Muslim in a rapidly changing, increasingly interconnected world.

We will be devoted to examining issues within Islam, and Muslim societies, providing a Muslim perspective on the great debates of contemporary times, and promoting dialogue, cooperation and collaboration between 'Islam' and other cultures, including 'the West'. We aim to be innovative, thought-provoking and forward-looking, a space for debate between Muslims and between Muslims and others, on religious, social, cultural and political issues concerning the Muslim world and Muslims in the world.

What does 'Critical Muslim' mean? We are proud of our strong Muslim identity, but we do not see 'Islam' as a set of pieties and taboos. We aim to challenge traditionalist, modernist, fundamentalist and apologetic versions of Islam, and will attempt to set out new readings of religion and culture with the potential for social, cultural and political transformation of the Muslim world. Our writers may define their Muslim belonging religiously, culturally or civilisationally, and some will not 'belong' to Islam at all. *Critical Muslim* will sometimes invite writers of opposing viewpoints to debate controversial issues.

We aim to appeal to both academic and non-academic readerships; and emphasise intellectual rigour, the challenge of ideas, and original thinking.

In these times of change and peaceful revolutions, we choose not to be a lake or a meandering river. But to be an ocean. We embrace the world with all its diversity and pluralism, complexity and chaos. We aim to explore everything on our interconnected, shrinking planet—from religion and politics, to science, technology and culture, art and literature, philosophy and ethics, and histories and futures—and seek to move forward despite deep uncertainty and contradictions. We stand for open and critical engagement in the best tradition of Muslim intellectual inquiry.

CM1
January–March 2012

CONTENTS

REVIEWS

ET CETERA

CONTRIBUTORS

Muhammad Idrees Ahmad, journalist and critic, is finishing a PhD at the School of Applied Social Sciences, University of Strathclyde. ● **Saffi-Ullah Ahmad**, a social activist, is contemplating his future. ● **Anne Alexander**, Buckley Fellow at the Centre for Research in the Arts, Social Sciences and Humanities, University of Cambridge, works on new media and political change in the Middle East. ● **Rose Aslan** is a doctoral student in religious studies at the University of North Carolina at Chapel Hill and specialises in narratives of pilgrimage, ritual and sacred space in Muslim traditions. ● **Merryl Wyn Davies**, writer and anthropologist, is Director of the Muslim Institute and author of *Introducing Anthropology* amongst other books. ● **Abdelwahab El-Affendi** is Reader in Politics, Centre for the Study of Democracy, University of Westminster. ● **Fadia Faqir's** latest novel is *My Name is Salma*. ● **Naomi Foyle** co-founded British Writers In Support of Palestine upon her return from the Gaza Freedom March in Cairo (Dec 2009). ● **Rachel Holmes** is finishing her latest book, a biography of Eleanor Marx. ● **Robin Yassin-Kassab's** only novel is *The Road From Damascus*. ● **Jamal Mahjoub's** novels include *The Drift Latitudes* and *Travelling with Djinns*. ● **Taus Makhacheva** is an artist based in Moscow, Dagestan and London. ● **S. Parvez Manzoor** is a critic based in Stockholm. ● **Ehsan Masood** is editor of Research Fortnight and author of *Science and Islam: a history*. He tweets occasionally: @EhsanMasood. ● **Aasia Nasir** is a Member of the National Assembly in Pakistan. ● **Nizar Qabbani** was the most accessible pioneer of Arabic modernism. ● **Ayat al-Qormezi** currently resides in a Bahraini prison cell. ● **Samia Rahman**, who is writing her first novel, is Deputy Director of the Muslim Institute. ● **Jasmin Ramsey** is a freelance journalist, writer and editor. ● **Jerry Ravetz**, a well-known philosopher of science, is the author of *The No-Nonsense Guide to Science* and other books. ● **Ziauddin Sardar's** latest book is *Reading the Qur'an*. ● **Shadia Safwan** is a Syrian blogger. ● **Abu al-Qasim al-Shabi's** verses inspired the Tunisian revolution ● **Ashur Shamis** was involved with the Front for the Salvation of Libya for several years. ● **Bilal Tanweer** is writing his first novel. ● **Tawfiq Zayyad** was the Communist Mayor of Nazareth, and is an important figure in modern Arabic poetry.

THE ARABS ARE ALIVE

THE BRITISH MUSEUM

Discover the Islamic World at the British Museum

From early scientific instruments to contemporary art, explore how Islam has shaped our world through objects for centuries

britishmuseum.org
Great Russell Street
London WC1B 3DG
⊖ Holborn, Russell Square

Mosque lamp. Enamelled glass.
Syria, c. AD 1330–1345.

SURPRISE, SURPRISE!

Ziauddin Sardar

Lord Naritsugu is a terrifying, sadistic ruler. He enjoys grotesque violence and kills and rapes at will. He treats his citizens as private property, as his personal inheritance and fortune. He is a law unto himself, and no one can touch him. Elegant and insane, and always with a slightly suppressed smile, Lord Naritsugu does more than simply rape and kill his victims. He humiliates them. He plays football with their heads. He chops the hands and legs of those he rapes. Fear and terror stalk the land, and the dignified citizens have only two choices: submit to his brutality or commit suicide.

In Japanese director Takashi Miike's *13 Assassins*, Naritsugu personifies the extreme decadence of despotic power. He has a romantic notion of his own power and prestige. But things are about to change. The Edo feudal period (1603–1868) during which the film is set, when Japan was ruled by a single shogun family, is about to end. The Meiji restoration is around the corner. The change is to be speeded up by the thirteen assassins of the title, noble unemployed samurai who know well that times are changing and their own profession is about to be written out of history. The team, led by the aging and decorated samurai, Shinzaemon, with the supernatural hunter Kiga amongst them, set out to confront Naritsugu and his army, and end his reign of terror.

For the past half century, the Arab world has been steeped in comparable terror. Like Lord Naritsugu, the tyrants who ruled various Arab lands treated their people with similar contempt. The Arab world resembled feudal Japan, ruled by ruthless warlords who gloried in humiliating their own people. These despots regarded the state as their personal property, to use, abuse and loot as they wished, and as private inheritance to be passed on to their progeny. The main commodity they traded in their mafia states was violence—meted out to the citizenry by the triad over which they had total control: the police, the secret service and the military. With an exaggerated notion of their own power and importance, the regimes of the Arab world, some of history's most oppressive totalitarian systems, reduced their citizens to abject poverty and despair. The Arab world was shrouded in utter fear as societies stagnated, religious establishments rotted, sectarianism flourished, and slums overspilled. The Arabs had no option but to submit to their oppression. Political conversations frequently ended with a raising of the brows and gritty rehearsals of the saying *al-'arab jarab*: 'the Arabs are scabies'.

As in *13 Assassins*, the trigger for change in the Arab world was a suicide. In the small town of Sidi Bouzid in Tunisia, a poor vegetable vendor named Mohammad Bouazizi suffered a humiliation too far. Bouazizi lost his father when he was three and had been supporting his family from the age of ten. He was prevented from setting his stall in front of a government building by a municipal inspector called Fadia Hamdi, who had a reputation for strictness. Whether Hamdi slapped Bouazizi, as some have alleged, is beside the point. The fact is that on 17 December 2010, Bouazizi, a young man of twenty six, frustrated by being constantly pushed around and unable to make a viable living, set himself on fire. It was an act borne of intense dissatisfaction with authoritarian rule.

And it had all the poignancy and symbolism of the opening scenes of *13 Assassins*. The film opens with a dignified man seated alone in a large courtyard, his face displaying all the pain of humiliation and hopelessness. We see nothing but his face—but can hear the knife plunging. We learn later that the noble man committed *seppuku* to protest the barbarity of Lord Naritsugu. Bouazizi's act was a protest against the ornate excesses and brutality of the Tunisian President Zine El Abidine Ben Ali, who came to power in November 1987 and who ruled the country, along with his wife and family, with an iron grip. Just as in *13 Assassins*, the suicide set off a chain reaction.

Riots followed. They were suppressed with the usual violence and brutality. But the revolt spread, first to the surrounding cities, and then to Tunis, where students gathered in Kasbah Square, in front of the Prime Minister's office. They protested against a host of injustices ranging from rising prices and unemployment to the lack of political freedom and democracy, rampant corruption, the extravagant lifestyles of the ruling clique, and authoritarian rule. The students were joined by labour unions, lawyers, and other civil society groups. There were more symbolic suicides. But after twenty eight days of riots, demonstrations and civil disobedience, the people of Tunisia forced the dictator Ben Ali into exile.

The speed with which the uprising spread and its final outcome was a total surprise. Something happened in Tunisia that few had predicted, not many understood, and most commentators, experts and policy makers struggled to grasp. That something was the evaporation of fear. For decades the Tunisian people had lived in fear—fear of their lives, fear of being tortured, fear of the police and the secret service, fear of losing their jobs, fear for their families, fear of speaking out. But once the revolution had been set in motion the fear dissolved like salt in water. And there were yet more surprises to come.

What the people of Tunisia could do, the Egyptians could do as well. And the Libyans, the Yeminis, the Syrians, and the citizens of Bahrain. A revolutionary wave of protests, demonstrations, and uprisings spread with astonishing speed throughout the Arab world.

The uprising in Tunisia was dubbed the 'Jasmine Revolution'. For some strange reason recent revolutions have been colour coded, with a hint of the scent of flowers. There was a yellow revolution in the Philippines, which may have started the ball rolling, way back in 1986. The noughties saw the orange revolution in Ukraine, the tulip revolution in Kyrgyzstan, and the rose revolution in Georgia. With the April 2005 cedar revolution in the Lebanon we move to the Middle East. The Iranian election protests that began in 2009 came to be known as the green revolution. Another yellow revolution is on its way in Malaysia.

This colour coding has been problematic; the colours have often been more meaningful to the Western spin doctors who promoted these brands than to the people involved in the actual revolts. In Tunisia, the term 'Jasmine Revolution' was also used to describe Ben Ali's rise to power in 1987, so the Tunisians prefer to call theirs the Sidi Bouzid revolt. Green is the colour of Islam and could equally be used for the Islamic Revolution of Ayatollah Khomeini. There are also limitations to how many sensible colours we can use. The Lotus is not a very common flower in Egypt so describing the Egyptian uprising as the Lotus revolution does sound a bit odd. The mind boggles when the demonstrations in Kuwait are referred to as the blue revolution; and the restoration of democracy in Iraq is painted in all shades of purple. The Yemenis are, of course, colourless, so we move on to seasons: the revolutions in the Middle East came to be known collectively as the 'Arab Spring'.

But these terms, whatever their merits, are trying to emphasise an important factor. These are predominantly non-violent uprisings, involving the entire spectrum of the population. Often led by students and young people, they rely on demonstrations, strikes, civil disobedience and sometimes the occupation of the main squares of major cities. They aim to restore democracy, accountability, and the rule of the law; to stamp out corruption, cronyism and the accumulation of wealth in fewer and fewer hands; and to end the brutality of the police and the savagery of the secret services.

All of these features are evident in the Egyptian revolution. 'You know', Robin Yassin-Kassab writes so perceptively in 'Tahrir Square', 'that something rare and powerful is occurring, something all-encompassing, not limited to a political or intellectual elite, when even a mobile nuts-and-seeds stall has "Social Justice" stencilled on its side'. Rare indeed. For the first time in the modern history of the Arabs, popular revolutions are toppling one dictator after another. And it was all achieved, without the aid of religious obscurantism or nativist romanticism, by ordinary people. They all came together: the coalition of workers, the alliance of non-governmental organisations, students and youth groups, the middle and upper classes, even the Islamists, to smash the idol of the police state and remove the hated dictators along with their families and cronies. Where failure had been the norm, here was glittering success. Despair and despondency were now replaced by euphoria and high expectations.

Of course, not all the uprisings in the Middle East have succeeded. The June 2009 green uprising in Iran, described by Jasmin Ramsey, mobilised opposition and civil society, leading to mass demonstrations, but ultimately left the despotic theocracy in power. But where they have succeeded, as in Egypt and Tunisia, the success has been spectacular. The bloodshed (hundreds were killed in Tunisia and nearly a thousand in Egypt) has largely been limited to countries with tribal or sectarian leaders protected by their tribe or sect and supported by the military. Muammar Gaddafi's support comes largely from his powerful Qadhadfa tribe of the Sirte region in Northwestern Libya, who run into hundreds of thousands. As Ashur Shamis notes in the thrilling account of his life fighting the Colonel, Gaddafi systematically 'raised his relations and members of his tribes to high ranks in the army and gave them key appointments in the political and economic power structures of the country' to consolidate his control on all levers of power. Bashar al-Assad, who comes from the minority Alawi sect, was a bit more inclusive sharing power between Sunni, Christian, Druze, and Alawi elites. Perhaps this is why he still has support from members of all communities.

The entrenched despots of Libya, Syria and elsewhere may have encouraged development in the initial stages, but by meeting protests with bullets they proved their loathing for democracy. Indeed, in their contempt for their people, their megalomania, their delusional sense of self-importance and self-belief in the divine right to rule they resemble Lord Naritsugu all too closely. Like Naritsugu, all the Arab dictators, both deposed and yet to be deposed, have tried to strip the Arabs of their innate dignity. Naritsugu describes his people as 'mountain monkeys'. Gaddafi compares them to drink and drug-crazed 'greasy rats'. 'Their ages are seventeen. They give them pills at night, they put hallucinatory pills in their drinks, their milk, their coffee, their Nescafe', he tells anyone who will listen. Assad says they are all sedition obsessed 'conspirators'. The protestors, he announced, are led by a Saudi-Salafist plot, the Syrian Muslim Brotherhood, the fanatics of al-Qaeda.

Naritsugu sees himself as a natural born leader. 'Ruling is convenient but only for the ruler', he declares; and people 'must live to serve'. The citizens have only one function: to obey their political master. 'If servants are spoiled, then one day they forget their duty to serve…and make light of their master and revolt'. Thus, 'punishment is a master's duty', and if servants revolt they must be suppressed brutally. Both Gaddafi, who has been in power for 43 years, and Assad, whose family has ruled Syria for 40 years, see themselves as indispensable, with god-like powers. Only 'God, Syria, and Bashar!', Assad has his 'parliamentarians' chant. 'God, Gaddafi and Libya' shout the colonel's supporters. With God on their side, the Arab despots, like Naritsugu, have no need to worry about accountability and restraint. They can shed blood with impunity.

'Dying for one's master is a servant's duty', declares Naritsugu, who thinks violence is 'magnificence', 'something wonderful'. He kills so his servants can appreciate life: 'With death comes gratitude for life'. In his 30 March 2011 speech to the parliament, Assad thanks his citizens for their 'willingness to sacrifice yourselves for your president'. Gaddafi has frequently declared that his people will die for him. Both glory in death and violence. Gaddafi used aircraft, tanks and foreign mercenaries against his own people and wanted Misrata to be obliterated and the 'blue sea turned red' with blood. He even gave Viagra to his soldiers to encourage them to rape, the chief prosecutor for the International Criminal Court has claimed. Assad, like his father before him, sent his troops—tanks and air-craft—in an attempt to raze Hama to the ground. Syrian troops first entered Darra in south-western Syria, and then cities all over the country and shot civilians of all ages. Pictures of Syrian forces, taken with mobile phones, shooting demonstrators, and killing women and children freely, have filled television screens across the world. Even Syrian dissidents living in Britain have been threatened.

Naritsugu and his supporters believe that the universe is structured around him; the ruling order will collapse without him. Gaddafi thinks Libya will descend into chaos and extremists will take over if he hands over power. Al-Qaeda will turn Libya into an Islamic state, he warned in a speech on 24 February 2011. 'The most important element in the regime narrative', notes Shadia Safwan in her lament on Syria, 'is the lack of an alternative to the Assads. Syrians themselves, it is claimed, as much as the West, need the ruling clique firmly in control, otherwise the entire region risks being destabilised'.

Lord Naritsugu repeatedly asserts that his actions bring glory to the samurai tradition. Ditto the despots of the Arab world. Assad claims he has built 'strong foundations of freedom, solidarity and engagement' for Syria, and increased her standing in the world. Gaddafi believes he has 'brought glory to his land, the whole world looked up to Libya'. Like Naritsugu, both Gaddafi and Assad are totally divorced from reality. Gaddafi thinks 'the Libyan people are free'. Assad imagines that his people not only sup-port him en masse but are also ready to 'embrace the state' and are willing to work 'hand in hand' with 'the army, the security personnel, the police'. Naritsugu wants to die the noble death of a samurai in the cause of the ruling shogun family. 'I'll die a martyr', Gaddafi screams. 'Muammar is the leader of the revolution till the end of time'. The president is ready, shouts Assad 'to sacrifice himself for his people and homeland'. 'We will win. Victory is ours. As long as our Lord is safe', declare Naritsugu's men. Both the 'Brother leader' (aka 'King of Kings', 'Figurehead of a Thousand African

Nations') of Libya and the 'Brother and Comrade' of Syria see a glorious future ahead. 'We can crush the enemy', Gaddafi roars. 'If we are forced into a battle, so be it', Assad yells. The 'future is full of hope'.

There are a couple of obvious differences between Naritsugu and the Arab autocrats. Naritsugu speaks in short, cryptic sentences. Gaddafi and Assad give rambling, incoherent and excruciatingly long speeches. Naritsugu knows he has chosen a foolish path because 'it's more fun that way'. It is not clear whether Gaddafi and Assad feel the evil of their deeds.

The revolutionary samurais in *13 Assassins* are forced to act because tyranny has reached its apex. Did the Arab populations simultaneously rise against their totalitarian leaders for the same reason? The Arabs have known for decades that these tyrants have no limits, there is nothing they will not do to keep their hold on power. So why have the Arabs been quiet for so long? Why do we have an 'Arab Spring' now?

There is something specific about this moment in history that has enabled the uprisings to gain momentum and spread so quickly and so far. Elsewhere I have characterised the contemporary period as 'postnormal times', an historic moment of accelerating change, a realignment of power, and an upheaval in which events move and multiply in geometric fashion. This is a specific characteristic of a deeply interconnected world of the Internet, Facebook, Twitter, 24-hour news channels, quick and easy globetrotting, instant information and networks. But the world is more than just a network of vast networks, all interconnected and interdependent, it is also complex. Everything we have to deal with, from fixing global financial problems to climate change, is complex. Complexity is a natural by-product of the fact that most of our problems have a global scale. And globalisation itself enhances complexity. Combine complexity with networks and you get positive feedback: things change rapidly and often happen simultaneously leading to chaos.

Chaotic behaviour is evident all around us. Remember how quickly the markets collapsed in the economic meltdown of 2009. Pandemics spread in chaotic ways: swine flu became a major threat overnight. Notice how quickly the crisis at Rupert Murdoch's News Corporation, one of the most powerful media empires in the world, reached chaotic proportions. The phone hacking scandal had been simmering for years. Then, when the revelations began to multiply, people started to demand that advertisers

boycott *News of the World*. The boycott snowballed, driven by angry consumers who used Twitter and Facebook to put pressure on brands to
respond in real time. Many did; and cancelled their advertising with the
News of the World. Each of the major advertisers was targeted by consumers
and had a mini-social media crisis of their own. By the time it was discovered that *News of the World* journalists had hacked into the mobile phones of
terror victims, bereaved families of soldiers and the family of Milly Dowler
(the teenager who was abducted on 21 March 2002 and subsequently
murdered), it was the beginning of the end for News Corp. Events acceler-
ated unpredictably and in geometric proportion, leading to the closure of
the *News of the World*, and an almighty crisis in the Murdoch empire. Postnormal times are an epoch of accelerating change where predictability is
rare, and small events can rapidly lead to big consequences

The 'Arab spring' displays many postnormal characteristics. It would
not have been possible without networks of unions and workers, NGOs,
and young, technologically savvy people promoting the uprising via the
Internet, Facebook and Twitter. Tahrir Square, writes Anne Alexander in
her scintillating account of the role of the digital media in the Egyptian
revolution, 'was one of the most self-consciously "mediated" spaces I have
ever entered. Everywhere you looked, there were people with mobile
phone cameras recording video and pictures'. The communication technologies generated positive feedback, multiplying the demonstrations in
geometric progression, leading rapidly to chaotic behaviour which the
despots found difficult to control and manage—even when they used
extreme violence. It is important that the uprisings had no leaders. In
classical revolutionary situations, leaders are the first target, and once they
are removed, killed or co-opted, revolutionary fervour evaporates. But
networks have no central leaders, which is their main strength. They do,
however, have a powerful ability to self organise autonomously and spontaneously. Self-organisation is a basic feature of chaotic systems. In the case
of the Arab uprisings, it is a demonstration of a mode of expression of a
wise and competent people capable of organising autonomously.

Every individual member of the network is as important as everyone
else. As everything is linked up and networked with everything else, a
breakdown anywhere has a knock-on effect, unsettling other parts of the
network, even bringing down the whole network. Individual social respon-

sibility and accountability is thus paramount for collective action as well as the survival of the whole process. It is worth noticing how responsibly the individual actors behaved in the uprisings in Tunisia, Egypt and Libya. While networks need no leaders, they do need a symbolic action that triggers the chaotic process. This is where small, apparently insignificant, initial conditions come in: the flapping of the butterfly's wings in the Amazon that causes a storm in North America. The Tunisian uprising began with the self-immolation of Mohammad Bouazizi, a vegetable vendor. In Egypt, Khalid Said, a twenty-eight-year old blogger who was beaten to death by the police on 6 June 2010, came to represent the savagery of a brutal regime. A Facebook page, 'We are all Khalid Said' was created and he became the focal point of the revolution. Later another blogger, Wael Ghonim, who worked for Google, was hailed as a hero, a figure of hope and change. Ghonim was arrested on 27 January 2011, and went missing. After his release, he broke down and wept live on Dream TV when he was shown images of some of those who died in the uprising, which galvanised the revolution. Hamza al-Khatib, a small boy of thirteen from the village of al-Jizah near the southern city of Deraa, became the symbol of the Syrian revolution. He was picked up by the security forces on 29 April 2011 and brutally tortured. His badly mutilated body was returned to his family on 27 May. Within minutes he came to symbolise all innocent Syrian victims of the Assad regime. Earlier, Neda Agha-Soltan, the young woman who was shot dead in the street protests in Tehran after the disputed June 2009 presidential elections, came to symbolise the struggle in the 'Islamic Republic'.

In postnormal times, individuals are not powerless. The torture or death of a protestor does not go unnoticed. Nothing can be hidden as there is no real hiding place. In a complex, interconnected world, despots and dictators have little control over chaotic processes. However, while communication technologies are an important postnormal tool, they are not an end in themselves. Nothing can be achieved, as Alexander notes, without the will of 'the people who were able to defeat the state' in pitched battles.

'The people', that homogeneous group that is often seen as a problem or reduced to mere consumers, came into their own in these uprisings. The nebulous 'Arab street' proved itself to be—temporarily at least—in the driving seat. The people showed that they were not irrelevant. They had greater relevance, greater power, than anyone dared to imagine. And they had a renewed sense of dignity. Egyptians cleaned their streets up. Syrians decided they would no longer put up with police brutality. 'The Syrian people won't be humiliated!' they chanted. Poor Yemen and rich Bahrain rose against their respective tyrannies. The Arabs were not scabies after all.

'The people', however, were not a standardised lot. They came from different backgrounds and subscribed to different outlooks. Diversity and pluralism are the hallmark of the 'Arab spring'. In Tahrir Square, tradition-alists, liberals, secularists, mystics, modernists, postmodernists, believers as well as agnostics and atheists, all came together to demand freedom from tyranny. They chanted their slogans, engaged in running battles with the state apparatus, and then, when it was time to pray, all those who wanted to prayed together in the Square.

While Islam was always present in the background—after all we are talking about Muslim nations—these were not Islamist revolutions. They could not be more different, for example, from the 'Islamic revolution' in Iran. As Jamal Mahjoub says in the case of Sudan, the 'older, traditional parties bound to Islamic sects' have had their day. They have 'all tried and failed in the past to provide the kind of unity, vision and leadership the country desperately needs'. Indeed, Islam or the creation of the legiti-mately feared 'Islamic state' is not the goal of these revolutions. Rather, they are motivated by something altogether different: the aspirations of all segments of society, believers and non-believers alike, for freedom, social justice and accountable governance.

Moreover, those usually labelled as 'Islamists', those seen as advocates of 'political Islam', used frequently to scare little children and liberal demo-crats alike, have turned out to be more sensible than they might otherwise have been. Indeed, as Abdelwahab El-Affendi points out in his contribution to this issue, during the Egyptian Revolution the Muslim Brotherhood 'worked seamlessly with everybody else and remained almost invisible'. Indeed, the Brotherhood has no interest in taking power in Egypt. They had declared this, El-Affendi tells us, as long ago as 1985, but who was listen-ing? The Brotherhood's 'espousal of democracy' was as sincere as, given the circumstances, it was unavoidable. To drive the point home further, Mohammad Mursi, a spokesman for the Brotherhood, spelled out the policy of the movement on 8 February 2011 in the pages of the *Guardian*: 'We aim to remove all forms of injustice, tyranny, autocracy and dictatorship, and we call for the implementation of a democratic, multi-party all-inclusive political system that excludes no one'. All the Brotherhood wants, and fully deserves, says El-Affendi is 'equal opportunity to work for the prosperity of Egypt'.

The bogey of an 'Islamist' takeover has served both the despots and the West well. If the uprisings are not an Islamist nor an al-Qaeda plot, then they are an Iranian-Shia plot. In Bahrain Sunnis and Shias marched together for freedom, not for a Shia theocracy, but the Bahraini regime—which demolishes Shia mosques, fires on Shia religious ceremonies, and confers nationality on any foreign Sunni who serves in the security forces—cast the democrats as the front line of an Iranian-Shia conspiracy. In Syria the regime cast its democrats as the vanguard of a Saudi-Salafist plot. It blamed the Syrian Muslim Brotherhood—which has a history of sectarian terrorism and is despised by the country's secularists and minorities—for the protests, and warned of sectarian war even as it did its best to promote one. The Saudis, who not only despise the Shia but regard them as outside the 'House of Islam', are forever denouncing Iranian-Shia conspiracies. Mubarak, Gaddafi and Ali Abdullah Saleh of Yemen also raised the spectre of an Islamist takeover. But the 'Arab spring' is not, and can never be, about sectarianism. Its goal is as clear as those of the *13 Assassins*: to remove the terrifying, sadistic despots. The people, in all their mindboggling diversity, have worked, and are working, together to realise this ambition.

Let us not forget that over half 'the people' are women. As Fadia Faqir points out, 'some of the bravest Arabs battling for a democratic future are women', who are making an 'energetic and inspiring' contribution to the uprisings. The Orientalist image of the 'silent and oppressed Arab woman' was totally shattered when the 20-year-old Bahraini poet Ayat Al-Qormezi read her poem in Pearl Square. It was an amazing act of courage and defiance. She called for King Hamad Al-Khalifa's resignation and openly challenged his oppressive rule':

> We don't want to live in a palace, nor do we desire the presidency
> We are a people who slays humiliation and assassinates misery
> We are a people who demolishes injustice at its base
> We are a people who doesn't want to continue this catastrophe.

While the Arab people are courageously changing the reality on the ground, the West has continued in its historic role, with the accent firmly on hypocrisy. Most of these dictators, from Mubarak to Ben Ali and Saleh, ruled with more than active support from the US and Europe. The Arabs, western powers have frequently argued, were not ready for democracy; strong authoritarian rulers were not only good for business but also necessary for a culture historically steeped in turmoil and despotism. But now there was a dilemma: the Arab people themselves were standing up for, and demanding, democracy. Beyond all the talk of supporting the 'Arab street', the policy of self-interest continued. When the Mubarak regime was crumbling, President Barack Obama's special envoy to Egypt, Frank Wisner, was infuriated with the protestors. 'President Mubarak's continued leadership is crucial', he declared, 'it is his chance to write his own legacy'. There were attempts to impose acceptable leaders—most notably Omar Suleiman, a former general.

When it came to 'humanitarian intervention' to save civilian lives, the hypocrisy came right to the fore. It was acceptable to intervene in one oil rich country, Libya, but not in another, Bahrain, where Saudi troops marched in under the Gulf Cooperation Council's banner, saving the Khalifa monarchy and the US Fifth Fleet from democracy. It was fine to denounce, and abandon, the autocratic ruler in Yemen but not in Saudi Arabia. The fact is that Western governments are not really interested in justice and the aspirations of the Arab people. What motivates the elites of Europe and the US is self interest. Notice how Britain had declared that it was not in her interest to intervene in the Bosnian war; and actively prevented the international community and the US from coming to the aid of the government of Bosnia-Herzegovina. The then foreign secretary, Douglas Hurd, refused to lift the international arms embargo on the former Yugoslavia: 'it would create a level killing field' he declared. The policy deprived lightly armed Bosnians of the chance to defend themselves against the well-equipped Serbs, and led to the Srebrenica massacre. Whether Britain intervenes in a particular country is decided not on the basis of humanitarian concerns, but naked self interest. US policy towards the Middle East is dictated not by any notions of democracy or human rights, but, as Wikileaks reveal and Muhammad Idrees Ahmad outlines, by its concerns for Israel and its oil supplies. The principal aim of the US is to encourage the Arabs to join an alliance with Israel against Iran. The Americans will support and prop up ruthless dictators if necessary to achieve their goal.

The Arabs may be liberating themselves, but the West still sees them through the lens of Orientalism. The Arabs are so stupid that they had to be taught how to access the Internet and use Facebook and Twitter by an American. The chap in question, Gene Sharp, a retired Professor of Political Science at the University of Massachusetts Dartmouth, is also credited with teaching non-violent resistance to Arab people (indeed he seems to have invented it, Gandhi notwithstanding). The fact that Arabs (or anyone outside the US) had never heard of him was, of course, neither here nor there. The civilising mission is alive and well.

The praise heaped on various members of the despotic families educated in the West, or with some western connections, is truly astonishing. Before he revealed his true colours, the London School of Economics-educated Saif al-Islam Gaddafi was seen as an ultra cool, charming 'moderniser'. The half Welsh Suzanne Mubarak, who loves fur, goes shopping with Carla Bruni, France's first lady, and sits on the board of the Arabian version of *Sesame Street*, was a 'modernising' influence on her husband. 'The fragrant, London-born first lady of Syria', Asma al-Assad, 'who graced the glossies', as the *Sunday Times* (3 April 2011) has it, was 'a reformer in the police state'. These despotic elites invoke all the allure of Orientalism. They represent 'Us' in a land that is remote, chaotic and, let's face it, largely incomprehensible to our constructive ignorance of their language, culture and history. They don't only speak *pukka* English, they speak our political language, a language we can relate to. The presence of such figures is welcomed in the West as it provides a curious affirmation of the theory of Oriental Despotism. The assumption is that despotic dynastic politics is virtually *sui generis* to Arab nations.

Conventional revolutions against despotic rulers do not emerge spontaneously. They are bloody affairs that sometimes take years to plan. And once the violence is over, one dictator is replaced by another, even if the new one is seen in a more benevolent light. The Arab spring, however, is not a once-and-for-all conclusive event. The uprisings in the Middle East do not follow the historic models of the French or Russian revolutions, nor the more recent revolution in Iran. These revolts do not seek a single transformation of power after a single event. The Arab street, one hopes, has no intention of replacing one despotic ruler with another. The Arab people understand the deep malaise of their societies very well. What they seek is not just political transformation to democracy but a positive change in the economic, social and cultural dimensions of society. These changes cannot be introduced by a simple transformation of political power. They need to be ushered in over a prolonged period, with the constant vigilance of the people.

There are, of course, counter-revolutionary tendencies. The military top brass, the secret services and the police will work, we can take it for granted, to preserve as much of the status quo as possible. The Western powers will try to perpetuate the client status of the Arab nations. And a crony capitalist class which benefited from and became vastly enriched under despotic regimes will try to hold on to its ill-gotten wealth. It is hardly surprising then that both in Tunisia and Egypt the revolutions have stalled. These revolutions, successful in their initial aims of removing the dictators and their immediate circles, have now moved into another phase, in which people are bound to come into conflict with counter-revolutionary forces. In Tunisia, the army was needed after the uprising to maintain order, and elections were postponed a number of times. But elections alone will not provide employment for the vast majority who are unemployed, nor will they improve education, health and welfare provision, redistribute wealth and provide more freedoms. There is also the all important question of ejecting Ben Ali's cronies from their entrenched power holds. In Egypt, Mubarak was replaced by the Supreme Council of the Armed Forces (Scaf). The army tried to preserve the power structures Mubarak had left behind. But the people objected; and a civilian prime minister was installed, albeit with hardly any powers. The police continued to behave as they had always done; but now they had also become the main instrument of counter revolution. Attempts to tax income acquired by speculation were blocked. And so it went on. The revolutions may have triumphed but they did not immediately solve many of the intrinsic problems left behind by departing dictators.

Shinzaemon, the noble samurai trusted to lead the revolt against the vile Naritsugu in *13 Assassins*, knows that sacrifice alone is not enough. Success demands a carefully thought out strategy. After much discussion he settles on a plan to ambush Naritsugu on his long journey home from Edo. A village on his route is picked for the ambush, and the villagers are persuaded to collaborate in the scheme. The village is transformed into a labyrinthine mousetrap, with strategically placed weapons and camouflaged fortifications. Spontaneously generated and autonomous organisations of the people do not have the luxury of such detailed planning. But it is essential for those involved in the uprising to have an appreciation of what is needed to usher in genuine reforms. In almost all cases, new constitutions that recognise multiparty political systems, freedom of expression, assembly and criticism, gender equality and rights of minorities, are required. Systems for managing natural resources and social productions are needed. National independence has to be secured from foreign powers and global corporations. These are big asks; and need planning every bit as detailed and thorough as that of Shinzaemon.

Perhaps the Turkish experience with democracy could provide a useful model. Turkey, as Parvez Manzoor argues, 'has chosen to follow the modern path', but it has redefined modernity to suit its own 'authentic political existence' which synthesises a secular constitution, a democratic way of life with religious aspirations. Postnormal times demand synthesis: taking the best that is on offer to create something new that is much more than the sum of its individual ingredients.

The second half of *13 Assassins* is one long, kinetic battle scene. There are surprises even before the battle begins. Shinzaemon's warriors discover they are outnumbered even more heavily than originally anticipated: Naritsugu is protected by 200 soldiers, not the seventy they were expecting. Sometimes the best laid plans prove inadequate. So one has to be prepared for uncertainty and surprises, which are more important in postnormal times than ever before. A particular 'wild card' is the evaporation of the revolutions' original aspirations. As Jerry Ravetz points out, this is something that was understood by Ibn Khaldun, the great fourteenth century historian and sociologist. In Ibn Khaldun's vision, 'the ideology that enabled a conquest becomes progressively less relevant as the conquerors settle down. The conqueror's quality, the warrior's life in the saddle, becomes irrelevant for his son the king, and finally seems ridiculous to his grandsons raised in the palace. That was the pattern in pre-modern times; now, even if there is an explicit benevolent ideal that led to the initial seizure of power, it suffers the same sort of fate when new generations want no more than a peaceful and prosperous life, or new leaders want the privileges of the old. That has been the sad fate of nearly all twentieth-century revolutions'. The Arab spring is in danger of repeating the cycle. Ravetz suggests that emphasis on quality is needed to avoid the trap. Poor or total lack of quality is not simply a question of bad or weak people. 'It is a systemic pathology of a social order'. Quality is thus an essential cordon that the revolutions need to protect their futures.

The Arab uprisings are not as simple an affair as the revolt in *13 Assassins*, which is based on a true incident in 1844. Once Shinzaemon and his men had accomplished the almost impossible task of beating Naritsugu's battalion of Akashi soldiers, peace and justice was resumed. Shinzaemon fulfils his promise: 'I will do what I must for my people'. The people of the Middle East now need to do what they must do to ensure the continuing success of their revolutions. There is, as yet, no end point to these uprisings. They are an on-going phenomenon that will unfold over a lengthy period of time. A few Lord Naritsugu clones have fallen. Others will follow.

Seasons change. After spring comes summer. But the changes ushered in by the Arab uprisings are here to stay.

TAHRIR SQUARE

Robin Yassin-Kassab

Cairo felt different. Tahrir Square, of course, carried a new set of meanings. The traffic, the pollution, the Stalinist gloom of the Mugamma building—these had shrunk, and revolutionary graffiti, redignified national flags, and the endlessly various Egyptian people now dominated the eye. Neither did it feel the same to walk over the Qasr el-Nil bridge, not after the glorious battle of 28 January. (I kept trying to work out where the police van was burnt.) And the streets were in fact cleaner, in central Cairo at least. In ritual overcompensation for the years of filth, people had been observed during the revolution's eighteen days scrubbing the pavements with toothbrushes. A man in a café called Ali Jabr explained it to me: 'The

Egyptians used to hate their country just as they used to hate themselves. Anywhere you went in the world, the people thought the Egyptians were rubbish. And the Egyptians agreed. After the revolution we know we aren't rubbish, so we pick our rubbish up from the streets'.

You know that something rare and powerful is occurring, something all-encompassing, not limited to a political or intellectual elite, when even a mobile nuts-and-seeds stall has 'Social Justice' stencilled on its side.

I visited in late March and early April. My plane to Cairo was a quarter full at best. The airport was almost empty.

The immigration guard peered long at me and asked if I was originally Iranian, prompting me to wonder if anything had changed at all. There were no pictures of Mubarak on the walls. That was a change.

Then the driver who took me into town. He addressed the revolution immediately. 'Tell me congratulations!' he grinned. I did so. 'We've finished with him!' he exulted. 'We're free!' Pictures of some of freedom's martyrs swung from the rear-view mirror.

I asked who he wanted for president now.

'Whoever proposes the best programme. The personality isn't important. The ideas are important, the policies. I'll judge on that'.

Most of Egypt considered itself a potential winner, but the losers were visible too. There was the burnt-out frame of the National Democratic Party headquarters for a start, hulking over the river like a man shamed in the stocks. And the police, who I was told 'are sulking'. Certainly fewer patrolled than when I had last been here, and those who did certainly seemed less sure in their swagger, as if they'd recognised themselves at last—poorly trained, underemployed, unloved.

The news on the cab radio as we drove from the airport: the Ministry of the Interior was burning, the fire blamed on police officers protesting outside for a pay rise and the prosecution of their corrupt commanders. But their undeclared demand was for respect. I saw a poster pasted anonymously to Nile-side walls pleading for trust to be restored in the police 'on the basis of mutual love, not insult... for there are many noble men in the police force'.

During the revolution, Mubarak's interior minister Habib al-Adli (currently on trial) ordered the police to withdraw from duty at the same time as he ordered the prisons to be emptied. This was the regime's *après-moi-*

le-deluge card, to demonstrate just how awful post-regime chaos would be. Marauding thugs, some with agendas but mostly opportunists, poured through the prison doors, picked up or were handed weapons, and swarmed the city's neighbourhoods. The people formed Neighbourhood Committees in response, and defended their homes. As a side-effect to the restoration of order, there was a degree of vigilante injustice. Egyptian journalist Sarah Carr, who writes for al-Masry al-Yowm and blogs at www. inanities.org, observed ten men beating up a fifteen-year-old, a suspect miscreant.

As well as withdrawing on orders, the police were often driven from the streets. Policemen begged residents in the towered apartment blocks around Tahrir for civilian clothes, and dumped their uniforms in order to flee. Police stations burnt all over the country. Even after Mubarak's fall, a policeman was thrashed in Ma'adi, south Cairo, and his vehicle burnt, for brandishing his gun pre-revolution style at a man who'd transgressed traffic regulations. On 5 March the dreaded State Security Intelligence buildings were stormed.

Which meant Egypt had changed at street level. Authority in general was open to question.

A friend in Ma'adi detected several resulting, and contradictory, trends. The previously snooty, he noted, were now treating their social inferiors with exaggerated respect. Uncovered women were moving more proudly than usual, as if they felt they owned the moment. Salafis appeared all over the place, comfortably frowning, as if they'd been hidden before.

The army was gently enforcing the curfew, from midnight to six in the morning when I arrived, and then put back to two. I contravened it once, taking too long in a downtown café. Armed personnel carriers blocked some main roads, but side roads were open. It was easy to take a taxi to my hotel.

I was there during a period of calm, but still the universities were demonstrating for the dismissal of pro-Mubarak teaching staff; still outside Maspero, the state TV and radio building, activists and media workers were protesting against an anti-protest law and demanding the sacking of compromised officials. 'Sarkhet Namla' or 'An Ant's Scream' was showing at the cinema, a film whose plot eerily anticipates the revolution: filming finished in October 2010. At the Talee'a theatre 'A Ticket to Tahrir' was playing, billed as an 'improvised documentary' of recent events. Zamalek's galleries displayed pictures of crowds and fists, flags and blood. The city was fuller than usual of intense discussion, and an atmosphere of disbelief, of expectancy. It was a healthy time.

And Egypt, lest we so suddenly forget, had been seriously sick. It had seemed so stuck in its sickness that it would never get well. The sickness was political, economic, cultural and social. The country that had been the undisputed leader of the Arab world, the home of Um Kulsoom, Naguib Mahfouz, Saad Zaghloul and AbdulNasser, the seat of al-Azhar, had become a tragi-comedy. Tiny Qatar demonstrated more political pluck. At least a third of Egyptians were illiterate. Half lived in extreme poverty. The clerical establishment issued unintentionally amusing fatwas and justified the construction of an underground wall on the Palestinian border. Pollution,

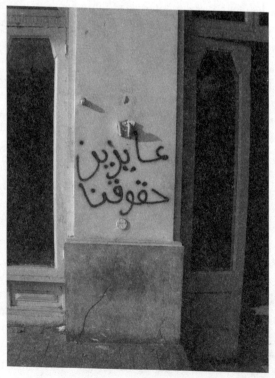

'We want our rights'

sectarian hatred and sexual harassment were rising inexorably. The buildings collapsed, the trains caught fire, the ferries sank. Egypt was stagnant, the stagnant heart of a stagnant Arab world. That's how it looked from the outside, and to many on the inside too.

And then the revolution.

'...revolution in Egypt always began unexpectedly, ... a ferment went on beneath the Egyptians' calm surface, which made them, at the very moment they seemed to give in to oppression, erupt suddenly in revolution'.

Alaa al-Aswany

Nobody expected the uprising, but in retrospect everybody agrees that Egypt in the months before was breathing a political atmosphere in ferment.

Journalist and blogger (at the indispensable www.arabawy.org) Hossam Hamalawi suggests precedents which paved the way for 2011, starting with mass protests in support of the Palestinian Intifada (2000) and against the invasion of Iraq (2003). 'The regional is local here', he told Al-Jazeera, describing how protestors marvelled at the contradictory weakness of the regime with respect to Israeli and American assaults on the region on the one hand, and its enormous, unreasoning strength when dealing with peaceful Egyptian activists on the other. By 2004, demonstrators had begun to chant explicitly against the president.

From 2005 on Mubarak sought American approval for his son Gamal's proposed succession to the presidency by pleasing America's Israel lobby as much as he possibly could. Egypt went far beyond the Camp David peace treaty to strictly enforce the siege on Gaza, to scupper any attempt to reconcile Palestinian factions, and to sell underpriced oil, gas and cement to Israel (while obstructing concrete shipments to demolished Gaza). These policies represented another assault on Egyptian dignity, national now as well as personal. Hence the descriptions during the revolution of Mubarak as an 'agent', and such slogans as *kalamu bil-abri, ma byafham arabi*—Speak to Him In Hebrew, He Doesn't Understand Arabic. The Palestinian tragedy had become once again a symbol of everything wrong with the domestic order, especially in Egypt, where the nation's status as client state rankled deep in people's hearts.

Then there were the workers, inspired by AbdulNasser but left to rot on starvation wages during the Sadat and Mubarak decades even as a new gangster-capitalist class flaunted its wealth. Their revolt had many precedents, most importantly the strike and street battles in the textile city of Mahalla al-Kubra in April 2008 (three killed by police, hundreds arrested). The young activists who coordinated the 25 January revolution called themselves the Sixth of April Movement in tribute. On that date the idea of a nationwide general strike gained ground, for better working conditions, higher wages, and the right to form independent unions. Industrial activism spread throughout the country over the next three years.

Add in to the mix the well-educated but unemployed (or underemployed) young people, the brain drain generation, who stereotypes informed us wanted nothing more than to flee their homeland for burger-merchandising careers in the West. It turns out they wanted nothing more than freedom, and were finally prepared to bleed in the streets in order to achieve it.

Many were galvanised by the murder of Khaled Said, a blogger from Alexandria who uploaded videos of policemen conducting drugs deals. Khaled was punished for this in June 2010, when police dragged him from a cybercafe and beat him to death on the pavement outside. Police torture was endemic and systemic, and murders not uncommon, but this one was as effectively publicised by activists as it was clumsily mishandled by the state media. The 'We Are All Khaled Said' Facebook group was one of the most visible motors of the 25 January protests.

Texts, tweets and status updates. Social media was certainly a useful weapon against an ossified dictatorship whose stalwarts had been formed in an earlier technological age. Obviously the Internet, like satellite TV, renders state control of print and broadcast media irrelevant, and obviously it provides a means of organising. But its role has been exaggerated by some Western commentators who optimistically assume that technology-savvy means culturally-Western. The telephone also played a role—no-one would claim that telephone users share an ideology or attitude. And Mubarak's teargas also came from the West.

Torture. Poverty. Illiteracy. Capitulation to foreign powers. Universal corruption. Egypt's social fabric was being ripped apart. During the 2006 Eid holiday a mass of young men groped and ripped clothes from women walking through downtown Cairo. The assault—against the covered and the uncovered, the old and the young, the accompanied and the unaccompanied—continued for four hours. The police, who would stave a man's skull just for thinking wrong thoughts, were nowhere to be seen.

On New Year's Day 2011 a bomb attack on an Alexandrian church killed tens of worshippers.

Commentator Issandr el-Amrani (of www.arabist.net) sums up the causes of the revolution thus: 'a general moral crisis, with the state's institutions in a condition of advanced necrosis'.

'The time has come for us to leave our seats in the auditorium and create the next scene ourselves'.

Alaa al-Aswany.

How then did the dam burst?

'It was a perfect storm', says Max Rodenbeck. 'Egypt was definitely moving towards a revolutionary moment, with the whole system built

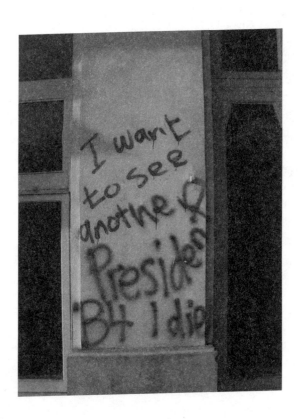

around the aging president. But serendipity was a large part of it. The government made a series of mistakes. If Mubarak had made the concessions at the start that he made later on, he could have deflected it'.

Rodenbeck is Middle East correspondent for the Economist and an engaging host. He's lived in Cairo for thirty years, written a history of the city, and knows the place inside out. 'There were 1,800,000 people in the security apparatus', he told me. 'Egypt had the world's most formidable riot police, and they were beaten. They were overcome by people's bravery. That was impossible to predict'.

The precursor was Tunisia. Tunisia showed that the nebulous 'Arab street' had greater potential, greater power, than most Arabs dared dream. When Ben Ali flew out of Tunis on 14th January, a celebratory protest erupted outside Cairo's Tunisian embassy. The people chanted:

Thawra thawra hatta an-nasr; thawra thawra fi shawarea masr! 'Revolution, Revolution Until Victory! (the old PLO slogan)/ Revolution, Revolution in the Streets of Egypt!'

For the love of irony, the revolutionaries planned their first big protest for Police Day, 25 January. Activists marched from various densely-populated areas of the city, calling up to the flats for people to join them. The different marches congregated downtown and pushed their way into Tahrir. At nightfall the riot police swept the square clean in fifteen minutes. But the day had broken the fear barrier. Around the country, over a million had gone out— representing the whole people, of all ages and classes. Open mouthed Egyptians gazed at their screens and discovered at last that they were not alone, that their compatriots were marching in every major city, that change was therefore possible. In retrospect the revolution looks prophesied—in novelist Alaa al-Aswany's comments, in the poetry of Fuad Ahmed Negm, in the grumbles and eye-rollings of countless Egyptians—it seems almost inevitable, but until 25 January nobody believed the moment could actually come. Nobody expected it. In that sense the revolution was entirely unplanned. It was an unprefigured confluence of events, an act of God or fate.

On the 28th, the Friday of Anger, Egyptians reclaimed their streets. In every region, they swarmed from the mosques after prayers. Christians began their marches from the churches. The Muslim Brothers finally gave the protests their blessing, and they proved indispensable organisers and fighters. For the first time, the people vastly outnumbered the police, and they met their bullets with rocks. In some remarkable instances they diminished violence simply by telling the police to not be scared. They fought their way back onto Tahrir, and held it thereafter. From Friday on the square was liberated territory. In the streets, popular sovereignty had already replaced the regime.

At this point the police were withdrawn, the prisons emptied, and the Neighbourhood Committees leapt into the vacuum. According to Max Rodenbeck, 'the urban middle class expected the rabble to destroy everything. When that didn't happen, the bourgeoisie joined the revolution. It was their participation which tipped the balance'.

Google executive Wael Ghonim's tearjerking interview helped too. On Muna Shazli's popular show (on privately-owned Dream TV) this bourgeois young man wept for those killed and insisted the revolutionaries were not Hezbollah operatives or Iranian provocateurs (as Mubarak's sectarian, anti-resistance propaganda had claimed) but patriotic Egyptians like him. The protests swelled the day after the interview.

The assault on Tahrir by plainclothes thugs is known in Cairo as 'the day of the camels'—for there as here the day was distilled by its most striking TV image. Most Egyptians experienced the revolution primarily through the media, judging the battle between state TV (and Saudi-owned channels) and the rest, led by Al-Jazeera. That channel's English broadcasts were watched in the White House, while the Arabic station relayed images of Tahrir to the crowd in Tahrir. And when the Internet went down—a world first for Mubarak, quickly seconded by Gaddafi—the media's absence became as much a part of the story as its presence.

Glimpses of history from those eighteen days of continuous revolutionary struggle. The arrival of the military to chants of 'The People and the Army—One Hand!' The officers raised on the revolutionaries' shoulders. Mubarak's three speeches—an unperturbed, rubber-masked godfather addressing his children. Intelligence chief Omar Suleiman, with at least a metaphorical gun to his head, curtly announcing Mubarak's resignation. The army's communiques. The military spokesman's salute to the martyrs.

More than 800 people died. Thousands are still missing.

The military's role is murky. Most probably the high command did give orders to fire on protestors, but the rank and file refused. The possibility of revolution within the army spurred the top ranks to action. There are whispers of an assassination attempt against Omar Suleiman, Mubarak's last-minute vice president. Significantly, the military's Communique Number One was issued a day before Suleiman declared Mubarak's resignation.

But the coup saved Egypt from civil war. Like the army in Tunisia, but unlike in Libya, Bahrain, Yemen or Syria, the military stood as one with the people against the president. Or, more cynically, the body of the regime sacrificed its head so as not to lose absolutely everything.

Alongside its appointed left/liberal caretaker cabinet, the Supreme Council of the Armed Forces (SCAF) rules until the September elections, and will continue to wield great influence afterwards. The army represents a huge sector of the economy. It owns land and businesses, receives vast amounts of American aid, and therefore, at the high command at least, it wants the status quo preserved as far as possible.

The SCAF responds flexibly if reluctantly to popular pressure, removing prime minister Ahmad Shafeeq, arresting Mubarak and sons, announcing that provincial governors will be replaced—but there has been no systematic rupture with the old regime. Unlike in post-revolutionary Tunisia, where three major commissions were rapidly appointed, Egypt has no clear programme for truth and reconciliation. Cases against former officials are dumped randomly on the public prosecutor.

So the people are forced to push to achieve their further aims, yet as they do so they are conscious they might provoke the military too far. A crackdown could erase all the progress made. And even if the military could be pushed aside, what would replace it?

Cairo felt like a held breath. It was the turning point of spring and summer. There was an air of reflection, of taking stock, and of puzzled expectation, of humility before the forces of history.

'In Egypt today most people are concerned with getting bread to eat. Only some of the educated understand how democracy works'.

Naguib Mahfouz

On the cab drive to Heliopolis I told the talkative national-chauvinist driver that the future belonged to China. He said no, it belongs to Egypt, obviously so. Egypt has diamonds and gas and the cleverest people. He clicked his fingers. 'Unlike the Libyans, who are stupid to a man. It's not their fault, of course. Gaddafi made them stupid. But Libya's not a real country. Egypt is the only real country in the Middle East'.

He drove through the busyness of Cairo—a city of crushing crowds, flyovers and underpasses, streets like ravines through which traffic surges five or six or ten lanes deep, walled by high inhabited stone, mammoth statist rectangles or French-era apartment blocks garlanded in Dickensian filth. Up to the curfew the downtown streets were as packed as ever, reflecting so much swing and bustle and sparkling light they made you want to burst out laughing.

Heliopolis, however, was relatively calm, reassuringly low-rise, radiating the atmosphere of an overcrowded seaside town. Here was the recently vacated presidential palace. Here, amongst pretty whitewashed commercial streets, was the Cilantro cafe. And here inside was Ethar Kamel el-Katatney, contributing editor for *Egypt Today*, winner of CNN's African Journalist of the Year, and author of a book recounting her Islamic studies in Yemen. She has an MBA and a Masters in Arts and Television. She's 24 years old.

Tens of thousands followed Ethar's tweets during the revolution. She's certainly not an organiser in the classic sense, but an informant, a news bearer, a connector.

She didn't go out on 25 January. She knew how it would end—in clouds of tear gas or in a police cell—and she didn't see the point. It was when the Internet was cut—on 26 January—that she realised the gravity of the moment. The next three weeks she described as ranging the full spectrum of human emotion, like Bollywood. 'Every event was followed by a reaction. The day of the camels swung the pendulum against Mubarak. The day the foreigners were attacked put a different slant on things again. And now everything is up in the air. No-one can predict the future. It's not an easy time'.

Ethar referred to 'Holes in the Conscience', a book by psychiatrist Ahmed Okasha. The argument goes like this: the Egyptian population, not used to taking decisions or bearing political responsibilities, not well-equipped to deal with change, now faces information overload and therefore profound confusion, a bewilderment as to what is to be done. And deep fear. Half the nation, she reminded me, lives on less than two dollars a day. Any disruption to this income means starvation.

Ali Gomaa, the Mufti and not a friend of the uprising, warned that revolutions tend to eat their children. There's a large receptive audience for the sentiment. 'The countryside isn't Tahrir', said Ethar. 'The people want money and security first of all'.

Or as Bill Clinton might say, it's the economy, stupid. People of all classes fear an economic collapse and the social consequences, which might not be very far distant. The tourists have been scared away. An enormous chunk of capital has fled overseas, a trend exacerbated by the popular hunt for corrupt officials. And the poor want justice soon—something the economy is unable to deliver. As well as fear, there's a potentially explosive discontent.

Take the man who worked the late shift at my nearest kiosk (his second job of the day). 'The revolution was in January', he told me. 'This is late March, and I'm living the same conditions. I can barely provide the basics to my wife and two children. This poverty is an insult to the people's dignity. Wasn't the revolution supposed to bring dignity? That's what they said it was for. So where's the dignity? I'm waiting'.

Revolutions, in Max Rodenbeck's words, are 'apt to be two-humped beasts'. France, Russia, Iran—first comes the bourgeois, democratic wave, then the second, something much more radical.

'The factor that brings about justice in any society is the application of the law against powerful people rather than against the small'.

Alaa al-Aswany

In Huda Shaarawi's old apartment, now the Garden City Club, Issandr el-Amrani told me that Egypt's GDP in 1945 was higher than Italy's. For the subsequent decline he blames the mismanagement of the 50s, Nasser's expensive adventurism, and US-backed crony capitalism in the Sadat and Mubarak eras.

'It leaves the country with serious structural problems. There are six and a half million civil servants. That's too many. But there is potential too. Egypt is a rich country full of poor people. It has resources: the unexploited minerals in the desert, the gold, the oil and gas, the Suez canal'.

'But Egypt has a mafia. People don't realise the extent of it because there's been a poor business media here. But the mafia is everywhere'. To illustrate his point, el-Amrani details the 'larceny' of the Israeli gas deal, the cuts and kickbacks.

Max Rodenbeck says, 'The economy is precarious. There's a huge national debt. The outgoing government, despite its corruption, was probably the best team of technocrats that Mubarak ever had. Now the competent people have been disgraced as much as the NDP fat cats. The present government, if clean-handed and friendly, is not particularly qualified to manage things. It's being forced to make the public happy by raising salaries and employing more workers. If it ends up printing money, there'll be hyper-inflation. It's very dangerous indeed'.

As decades' worth of resentment was all at once expressed, unrest bubbled in every economic sector. It was like the lid lifting off the proverbial pressure cooker: strikes against starvation wages, corrupt bosses, remembered insults. Schoolchildren even demonstrated for an easier curriculum.

Some suspected old regime involvement. The popular new prime minister Essam Sharaf saw in the strike wave 'an organised plan to destabilise Egypt'.

Such was the fearful context (in March) in which the SCAF drafted a law to ban those strikes and protests deemed to damage the economy, on pain of a one-year jail term. Protestors and rights groups condemned the law. The SCAF promised it would be temporary, only to be used when necessary, and that it was intended to assure stable change. The revolutionaries understood it as another move by the forces of counter-revolution— that is, disenfranchised Mubarak cronies, NDP apparatchiks, state security officers, and the tainted rich.

Ethar el-Katatney was reporting on a demonstration in support of dismissed prime minister Ahmad Shafeeq when she came across a bejewelled, lavishly coiffeured woman. She asked her why she'd come out to protest. 'I don't support Shafeeq', insisted the woman. 'I'm protesting against the dictatorship of Tahrir'.

'Egypt's history is replete with lost opportunities for democratisation'.
                                                            Alaa al-Aswany

On 9 March, soldiers and plainclothes thugs violently broke up a small protest camp in Tahrir. 170 protestors were taken to the army's base behind the Egyptian museum, where they were allegedly tortured. Amnesty International described as 'shocking' reports that female detainees were subjected to 'virginity tests'. In Egypt the allegations made less

'The people want to write their constitution'

of an uproar than they might have; they were covered by a couple of news-papers' online English-language websites, but not in print or anywhere in Arabic. According to someone who knows, the reason is simple: the SCAF ordered editors not to touch the story.

Hossam Bahgat's Egyptian Initiative for Personal Rights was the first organisation to speak out during the revolution against the army's involve-ment in detention and torture. Besides these problems, Bahgat was con-cerned by the army's excessive penchant for military courts where protestors and common criminals were being tried in five-minute sessions and in the absence of proper legal representation. The army was also leg-islating, for instance amending the penal code to increase sentences for sexual violence, including a mandatory death sentence for rape with intent. What bothered Bahgat was that such measures, arising from 'a mis-guided, short-sighted urge to show that the army is in control of domestic security', have been implemented without democratic consultation. And they are a typically military overreaction; there is no proof that sexual crime has increased since the collapse of the Interior Ministry.

As for the torture allegations, 'the SCAF now says they'll be examined. There have been no new allegations after 9 March. So we hope the army has got the message'.

We spoke on 3 April. On 8 April, the army opened fire on protestors breaking the curfew in Tahrir. As soldiers charged the crowd, they detained five uniformed officers who had 'joined the revolution' and denounced the SCAF from the stage. The two killed in the assault may have been mutinous officers.

The army's role has been increasingly questioned, and not only by rights activists and protestors in Tahrir. Another cab driver, a middle-aged, well-educated man who works as a state engineer in the mornings, an 'average Egyptian' of the sort not normally associated with Trotskyist thinking, spoke of the necessity for revolution within the army's ranks. 'What's the difference between Mubarak and (chief of staff) Tantawi?' he asked, then answered himself: 'Nothing'.

The SCAF oversaw the 19 March constitutional referendum, which limited presidential terms and ensured judicial supervision of elections yet left the bulk of the constitution untouched. Translator Muhammad Fouda, a supporter of Mohamed ElBaradei, explained why he'd voted no: 'The new parliament will write the next constitution, and will present it for referendum in one chunk, not article by article. There will be no discussion. A lot of the bad things will stay'.

Many revolutionaries also voted no because they feared the path towards elections was being rushed, that they needed more time to organise. The beneficiaries of quick elections would be those with known faces and organisation already in place—in other words the NDP in rebranded packages, and the Muslim Brothers, with their cell structure and social services network.

On the day, 40 percent of the electorate voted, tripling the participation of Mubarak-era 'elections'. 77 percent voted yes.

The Muslim Brotherhood had endorsed a yes vote. An article describing a 'yes' as a religious duty was taken down almost immediately after appearing on the MB website. But Salafi leaders were more forthright. Sheikh Muhammad Hasnain Yaqoub declared the referendum result 'a dramatic victory for Islam over non-Muslim voters', adding that those who didn't like it could migrate to the United States. He worried that a 'no' result would have allowed liberals to tamper with Article Two of the constitution, which declares sharia the major source of legislation. For the same reason, and because they dread the rapid empowerment of the Brotherhood, most Copts voted no. Thus the first exercise of the democratic era resulted in religious polarisation.

Nobody really knows why the silent majority voted yes. There are plenty of theories. Perhaps Egyptian voters were swayed by Islamist propaganda. Perhaps they consider an extended period of military rule the worst option, and so they voted for speed. The most likely explanation is that the silent majority is scared. It wishes the revolutionary process to stabilise soon before it swings onto more radical ground.

So parliamentary elections should be held by September, and presidential elections some months later. Max Rodenbeck again: 'The young revolutionaries include extremely sophisticated and bright elements. One would hope that these people are the future. Getting the people onto the streets and then organising the defence of Tahrir Square—these were impressive achievements. But electoral politics is a different game. More experienced and cynical forces will come into play. Violence and money will play their roles'.

Although most Egyptians live in cities, the countryside will dominate parliament. This means the choices made by rural notables—a freefloating element with money and influence but no obvious ideology—will be crucial in deciding the coming dispensation. In the past such people backed the NDP, the only horse running. Now they will gravitate towards whatever party looks like a winner, with the proviso that there is enmity between the notables and the Muslim Brothers.

If the revolution does swing into a second hump these rural potentates will become less relevant, but for the time being they have to be taken into serious consideration. Consistently hardnosed, Issandr el-Amrani thinks young liberals and leftists should be making contact with elements of the NDP, to use their expertise. Another friend, a former investment banker who's moved back home to participate, is educating himself more directly in rural opinion by making road trips out of Cairo. One of his ideas: the MB become known when they offer social services. So the liberals and leftists could do the same. Teach kids computer skills, for instance. Become a political force through practical engagement.

'I am fed up. After 62 years in public service, I have had enough. I want to go. If I resign now there will be chaos'.

Hosni Mubarak

The revolution was, famously, leaderless. It was too big for a leader. Which means that, at the time of writing, there was no obvious front-running party or presidential contender to define Egypt's new face.

There were candidates aplenty, including: former foreign minister and Arab League Secretary General Amr Moussa, experienced, widely respected, but too closely associated with the old regime; Sami Enan, the military's potential candidate; Ayman Nour, founder of the reformist Ghad Party, imprisoned under the Mubarak regime and injured during the revolution; Mohamed ElBaradei, a principled man distinguished by service as IAEA head, but also the victim of a partially successful Mubarak smear campaign which had him as a foreign national with an Israeli wife and a libertine daughter; and Judge Hisham al-Bastawisi, popular for explicitly contesting and detailing election irregularities in December 2005, and suffering the consequences—exile and a heart attack.

I asked Max Rodenbeck who he thinks would control the parliament. 'There are majorities against everything', he replied. 'Against the MB, the NDP, the Copts. It's more difficult to know what—or who—a majority is for'.

A great deal of business money will flow towards a competent liberal party as soon as an obvious candidate arises. Contestants include Baradei's National Association for Change, the Tahrir Revolutionaries Party, the Wafd Party—which dominated before the 1952 coup, but is at present a withered shadow, and the Social Democratic Party, which proposes 'market socialism'.

And what of the left? Ballooning strike action was perhaps even more crucial to the revolution's success than street protests. Yet the activism of the working class will not automatically translate into leftist electoral success. The best-known leftist party, the formerly tolerated Tagammu, has been marginalised by poor leadership and its compromises with the old regime. 73 leading party members resigned while I was in Egypt. New parties, such as the Popular Alliance, an umbrella group, are being formed.

But cold facts would obstruct a socialist programme. The Mahalla textile factory, for instance, doesn't make a profit. That's what Issandr el-

'Demands of the people'

Amrani told me in the Garden City Club. 'There is a strong idea of redistributive justice here, but it's impossible to implement hard left policies in present conditions. Egypt owes money. It has to obey external demands. It can't take risks or rock the boat. It's as simple as that'.

The left's strength is developing in movements rather than parties. Akram Youssef's Progressive Youth, for example, aims to popularise leftist ideas in Egyptian communities. And the Democratic Workers Party is looking a year ahead at least, to stage two, and is much more interested in building a country-wide workers' movement than in playing the electoral game. One of its declared intentions is to illuminate the class relations of military top brass versus rank and file.

'By the second Friday of the Revolution, Egyptians were reclaiming a legacy long appropriated by political Islam: the legacy of jihad, which means not blowing yourself up to bring down America but simply fighting the good fight. We all undertook jihad during the Revolution, many Muslim Brothers and some Salafis were with us,

not as Islamists but as Egyptians. We all practised jihad in Tahrir, but none of us were jihadis'.

Youssef Rakha

Will an al-Azhar unshackled from the sultan's whim reclaim its authoritative place in Islamic thought? Will the revolution therefore halt the ascendance of Saudi-Wahhabi influence? Will Egyptian Islam stop functioning as an escape from reality and begin to attend to real issues? Will clerics now address torture, poverty and social division as confidently as they've addressed issues of dress and personal hygiene in the past?

It remains to be seen to what extent political revolution will feed into a revolution in Islam. What is certain is that the Islamists of the Egyptian Muslim Brotherhood, a movement with an eighty-year history, will play an important role in shaping the next phase.

The Brothers still living can be divided into three generations, the first of which was formed in the 1950s and 60s, the AbdulNasser years. The MB supported the 1952 Free Officers' revolution, but in 1954 were charged with the attempted assassination of AbdulNasser (a charge they denied) and were banned and savagely repressed. Sayed Qutb is the most famous of the period's ideologues shaped by imprisonment and torture.

The second generation, shaped in the seventies and eighties, had an easier time of it. Chastened in the pursuit of its social justice and anti-imperialist targets, post-Nasserist Egypt employed Islamic symbolism in the political sphere more and more overtly. Using language previously alien to Egyptian statehood, Sadat described himself as a Muslim president of a Muslim country. To eliminate opposition to his pro-West, pro-business policies, Sadat had to eliminate those socialists and nationalists who still clung to the revolutionary implications of Nasserism. And so he entered an informal alliance with the Muslim Brothers against the nationalist left.

Once state persecution had eased, the Brothers renounced violence as a means of achieving an Islamic state, focusing instead on the steady Islamisation of society by persuasion and example. The founders of liberal breakaways from the Brotherhood belong to this generation. And, disgusted by the mainstream's rejection of violence, al-Gama'a al-Islamiyya also split from the Brothers in the 70s.

The third generation was formed from the 90s onwards, and fills the movement's often non-traditional youth wing. It has gleaned the dual experience of harsh repression, when Islamists of any stripe were blamed for violence against policemen and tourists in the 90s, and of semi-toleration, when Brothers were allowed to run in (rigged) parliamentary elections, albeit as independents.

The MB achieved 20 per cent of the vote in the 2005 elections. Their success prompted another regime crackdown. In future elections the Brothers seem assured of their 20 per cent base, a starting point which can be significantly improved upon. Nobody else has the mobilising capacity or the guaranteed finance (members dedicate a portion of their income to the movement). According to Max Rodenbeck, the Islamist trend from its right to its left represents perhaps 40 to 50 per cent of the electorate.

Yet for now, aware of the fears they provoke, the Brothers have modest expectations. Their new party, al-Hurriya wal-Adala, or the Freedom and Justice Party, aims to field candidates in only a half of parliamentary seats. And the MB won't contest the presidency.

I spoke to leading Muslim Brother Essam el-Eryan, who Sarah Carr tongue-in-cheek describes as 'a member of the Dark Force which is the Muslim Brotherhood, and who himself is jolly and almost always laughing and a bit cuddly'. I would not go so far as 'cuddly', but it was a pleasure to hear the man talk.

He spoke of Egypt's position at the heart of the Arab world, its leading role in both victory and defeat. 'Before 1952 Egypt was the beacon of enlightenment to the Arabs, during the Nasser years a stronghold of anti-colonial resistance, and after 1973 the trailblazer of normalisation with Israel and intimate relations with the United States. And now Egypt will lead in the age of democracy'.

I asked, 'And the Brothers don't want to take power in Egypt?'

'This is not a moment of power. No, this is the moment for building a new political order. We need five or ten years at least to build a democratic civil society'.

'And then?'

'Then there will be a democracy'.

He's a great politician, an expert in not answering the question, but el-Eryan is justifiably cautious. He's conscious of the success, domestic as much as external, of Mubarak's demonisation campaign, as well as unresolved debates within the movement and society at large on the role of religion in a pluralist democracy. The media, academia, the elite, and lots of working class Egyptians, are deeply suspicious of the Islamists. It's one reason why the old regime survived so long.

Ethar el-Katatney told me that most people supported the Brothers for the services they provided, services the state failed to provide—for economic reasons, in other words. And now people fear the economic ramifications of a Brotherhood majority, that it would frighten away Western investment, that tourists would stop coming.

Others, like a couple of men from Mahalla come to Cairo for the day (we met in a café), by no means opponents of the Brotherhood, wanted an MB minority in parliament on a sophisticated point of principle. 'Their job is to criticise, not to legislate. They should be in parliament to expose corruption and to protest when the state does something immoral. But they shouldn't make the government'.

In any case, the Brotherhood will not remain a unified force, despite Supreme Guide Mohamed Badie's decree that Brothers must not join parties other than Freedom and Justice. With the advent of freedom comes a dividing or a blossoming, depending on your perspective. Ex-Brother Ibrahim al-Houdaiby calls it 'the challenge of freedom'.

In the 70s the rifts were initiated by violent groups exasperated by the quietist line of the conservative mainstream. Today the splits are reformist-led, by Islamists who accept a greater separation of religious and political life, who (in contrast to the Brotherhood's official 2007 programme) are untroubled by the prospect of a Christian or female president.

The Wasat (Centre) Party split away in 1996, and was finally granted a licence a week after the revolution. Wasat stresses the equality of all citizens under the law irrespective of their religious origin. And now prominent Brothers Ibrahim al-Zaafarani, Haytham Abou-Khalil and Abdel Moneim Abou el-Fotouh have resigned from the Brotherhood and may be constructing the Nahda (Awakening) Party, which will probably be slightly less liberal than the Wasat party, and will focus on economic issues.

Essam al-Eryan was dismissive of the Nahda—'It's not a good idea. It won't be successful. It's a dream or a protest action, not a party'—and denied that the proliferation of parties was proof of division in the movement. But I remembered the reported words of the Prophet—'Difference of opinion in my community is a blessing'. In part due to the Brothers' efforts, Islamic ideas are current throughout society. In a democracy, there's no reason why one party should lay exclusive political claim to these ideas. Let right and left present their own interpretations, and let the people decide.

To the chagrin of the MB leadership, the youth wing—the troublesome third generation—seems to agree. The youth wing organised its own conference on 26 March. Among other things, it objected to the Supreme Guide's command to vote only for Freedom and Justice. Sameh al-Barqi's speech also encouraged internal reform in the movement, urging the empowerment of the elected Shura Council and arguing that the Guidance Bureau should execute the decisions of the Shura Council, not rule from the top. Other speakers called for a greater role in the movement for women and the young.

The MB cadres tend to be professionals. Salafis, on the other hand, are often recent migrants to the urban slums, living the full initial flush of alienation, or alternatively, people who migrated directly from the village to Saudi Arabia and back again. Permitted to preach by the old regime for their convenient doctrine of loyalty to even an unjust ruler (before the revolution they issued a fatwa against Baradei for opposing the 'wali al-amr'), Salafis are taking the fullest advantage of the new dispensation.

Although their sole legal political action since the revolution has been to distribute leaflets against 'kafir' democracy, up to five Salafi parties are currently brewing. As for illegal activities, in the brief time I was there these included cutting the ear off a Copt accused of renting a room to a prostitute, burning an ex-prostitute's furniture, provoking a village brawl by attacking a Copt's beer shop, and attempting to destroy Islamic shrines in Alexandria. This last action prompted some Sufi sheikhs to consider forming their own party to defend shrines and moulids.

The plot thickens inexorably. There were rumours too of clean-cut tele-preacher Amr Khaled's political ambitions. His position in March: he wouldn't rule out either forming a party or running for president if these options would help him realise Egypt's development goals.

'...the more important truth is that despotism will never protect anyone from religious extremism, because religious extremism is one of the symptoms of despotism'.
                                                                    Alaa al-Aswany.

The Mubarak regime dealt with its Islamist challenge in two ways: politically, it rigged elections ever more blatantly and persecuted its visible opponents; socially, it pandered to the most retrograde desires of Islamism (limiting the construction of churches, banning books) as well as doing its best to whip up petty chauvinism over the most ridiculous of pretexts (for instance the mutual football hooliganism of Egyptian and Algerian fans). And when sectarian fights enveloped villages, when churches or shops were burnt, the state failed to respond effectively. Its approach was through formal reconciliations, featuring financial compensation and hand shakes, but not resolving any underlying issues. There were never any prosecutions, and no rebuilding.

Yet the regime marketed itself as the protector of Christians, waving the Brotherhood bogeyman at home as it did to the West. In this Mubarak enjoyed the connivance of the Coptic Church, which Pope Shenouda—who supported Gamal Mubarak's succession to the presidency—ran like his own dictatorship. The Church instructed its followers not to participate in the revolution. (Of course many disobeyed.)

It was widely noted in Christian circles that no church was attacked in the days of looting, for every church was protected by neighbourhood committees, very often by Muslims. Clearly, the people in this democratic mood were a better guarantor of sectarian peace than the old regime had ever been. Many Egyptians now believe that the regime was behind the New Year's church bombing in Alexandria, that it was another clumsy ploy to scare Christians into loyalty.

But the sectarian hatred is real. Ethar el-Katatney warns, 'it's a recent phenomenon, but the idea of co-existence is being slowly and steadily removed. The Gulf invests in Salafis, their TV stations, and the approach appeals in Egypt because it's very one-plus-one-equals-two. It promotes itself as a curriculum, a way of life. And we have the problem of fake religiosity, when people enjoy neither the world nor the sweetness of faith, so they envy the people who are different, and turn on them easily. We need better-educated sheikhs. We need Muslim leaders to take responsibility for the problem'.

Essam el-Eryan could have been more reassuring on diversity. When I asked him if Turkey's Justice and Development Party was a model for the MB's Freedom and Justice, he answered no, Turkey's situation was completely different. Turkey wants entrance to the EU, and is a NATO member, unlike Egypt. And Turkey is a mosaic of peoples, Turks and Kurds, Sunnis and Alevis, while Egypt is homogenous.

A moment later he noticed his omission. 'Of course here we have Christians', he caught up, 'but they are citizens too'. As if the Alevis were not Turkish citizens.

Magdy Samaan is a journalist for *al-Shorouk* newspaper, and a Protestant. His religious community constitutes perhaps a million people, perhaps ten percent of Egypt's Christians. Here is his list of culprits for sectarian division: 'Hate speech in mosques, schools and the media, the old regime's manipulation of the problem, the absence of the rule of law, the current absence of security. These can be overcome by democracy. It's true that Salafis are proliferating, but they threaten the Sufis as much as they threaten the Christians'.

Christians, like their Muslim compatriots, await the future with hope and trepidation. Christian political impulses are diverse and nuanced, and the response to Islamism is not one of unanimous alarm. Rafiq Habib, for instance, an Anglican intellectual, is a key member of the MB-offshoot Wasat Party.

Yet the suspicion of difference is a deeply-flowing strain in Egyptian society. Sarah Carr, the proudly Egyptian daughter of an Egyptian mother and a British father, writes perceptively on the issue. Not surprisingly, she feels strongly about Article 75 of the Constitution, which disqualifies electoral candidates whose spouse or grandparents hold a foreign nationality. 'Imagine them doing that in Britain', Sarah urged me. 'It's nothing to do with security'.

For a couple of days during the revolution Cairo witnessed a string of attacks on Western foreigners, plus light-skinned Egyptians and anyone who looked 'different'—men with long hair, for instance, or women with short hair. The attacks followed state media propaganda to the effect that Israeli spies were posing as foreign journalists, and that foreigners stood behind the unrest (like so many pro-Zionists, Mubarak was an anti-Semite). Hossam Bahgat blamed the violence on straightforward brainwashing, arguing that dark-skinned foreigners are the more usual victims of Egyptian racism. Sarah Carr, who was collating incidents of anti-foreigner violence for Hossam's EIPR when I met her, thought it went deeper than that, that it's the result of Egyptians being second class citizens in their own country—to British, French, Albanians, Turks—for hundreds of years. This tradition, she asserted, was continued by the NDP, whose high ranks lived like colonists, residing in gated communities, educating their children in foreign languages and foreign universities, viewing the people as a threatening rabble.

Whether the 'other' is a Christian, a Shii Muslim, a white or a black, two visions of Egypt—as homogenous or plural—are in competition. Max Rodenbeck cast it as a 'battle of narratives, a battle of dreams, between 'the Islamic conquest' and 'national brotherhood''. Which side would win? 'Well, Egypt has thrived whenever it's welcomed diversity. One positive thing is the general aversion to *fitna*. Having a free press to air the issues is also very important, but it's a race against time'.

The fear is that Saudi Arabia is also running in the race, or at least seeking to trip up the 'plural' runner. Issandr el-Amrani reminded me that the Sauds are facing the end of their Arab supremacy, and are struggling desperately to retain influence. People worry that Chief of Staff Tantawi, who was Egypt's military attaché in Afghanistan, has very close ties to the Saud princes. Salafi-inspired chaos would be another obvious conduit of Saudi influence. (In May Salafis burnt a church in Cairo's Imbaba neighbourhood, causing the stock market to crash the next day.)

Magdy Samaan fears outside intervention of two types—from Saudi Arabia, either to support conservative Islamist rule or, via Salafis, to play spoiler, and from the US and Israel, to press the army into a permanently dominant role. 'But if the Egyptians are left alone', he continues, 'they'll build a functioning civil democracy. I'm very optimistic about this. In Tahrir I met ordinary people with an extraordinary level of political awareness, people learning very fast. The young, social-media-savvy activists are a minority of course, but they are a determined, active minority, and they'll be very influential in the wider society'.

'The people I saw in Tahrir Square were new Egyptians, with nothing in common with the Egyptians I was used to dealing with every day. It was as if the revolution had recreated Egyptians in a higher form... There was a deep feeling of solidarity and courteous conduct, as if the revolution had not only rid Egyptians of fear but also cured them of their social defects'.

Alaa al-Aswany.

There were a million revolutionary theatres—mosque plazas, village squares, factory floors—Tahrir Square iconises them all. It symbolises perfect democracy, in which freedom and responsibility are one, in which all participate and all difference is respected. Ethar el-Katatney sums it up as 'a sense of unity. No suspicion. It felt like Hajj. The different colours, the two genders, different social classes, all together'.

Revolutionary Tahrir provides the second icon of the century, separating 2011 from 2001, 25 January from September 11—an entirely different crowd scene this time, the crowd no longer signifying the victimised or manipulated herd. In Tahrir the crowd means power, the agency of positive change.

Tahrir generated symbols of harmonious pluralism. Muslims praying under the protection of Christians. Coptic mass held on the MB stage. A Qu'ran-bearing sheikh intertwined with a Bible-wielding priest, both surrounded by a crowd chanting 'One Hand! One Hand!'

First the revolution was televised; then it was commercialised. On my visit, I found the following on sale in the square: revolutionary T-shirts, key rings, flags, cards, posters. One poster shows the 'corruption team'—top Mubarak cronies photoshopped in football gear. As well as small businessmen, I could see Bedouin from the Sinai, the wives and mothers of political prisoners, street-tough boys posing in their vests, students wearing backpacks, families enjoying history in the making, the middle classes, the workers, the poor. Groups rippled through carrying enormous Egyptian flags, like ant work parties bearing outsize leaves. Free Libyan flags flapped among the Egyptian. At the edge of Qasr al-Nil Bahraini students displayed gruesome pictures of the repression in their country. Speakers on the stages (a plurality of makeshift stages, not a single stage or a single dragooned crowd) demanded an end to the Israel gas deal—'Who sells his resources under price to his enemy?'—and the trial of the 'heads of corruption', and for the anti-strike law to be cancelled, and for the people's right to debate and write their own constitution. 'We have broken the barrier of fear', called the man who talked on that stage. 'So there is no excuse not to continue until the goals of our revolution have been achieved. Whoever thinks the revolution has succeeded is making a fool of himself'.

This jumbled assembly of protests was gathered 'to rescue the revolution', and such was the general, unifying fear: that the revolutionary moment was coagulating, that the momentum for change was endangered.

One banner read: 'The bottom line: We will not be ruled by USA or EU anymore, despite our sincere love for their people'. Another declared the existence of the Popular Socialist Alliance Party (under construction). Leaflets called for workers to establish free trades unions, or for the citizenry to beware the army's true nature, or for the release of the prisoners (17,000 'Islamist' detainees still languish in desert camps. Most have not been tried or even charged with a crime. Because they are from the poor classes, Egypt very nearly forgot about them).

Passionate disputes enlivened clumps amid the swirl—Is the army a friend or enemy of the people? Do Islamists threaten democracy? The discussions quickly moved beyond mere rhetoric. People constructed arguments, offered evidence to back their points of view. It was a bit like Speakers' Corner in London's Hyde Park, minus the lunatics, plus a great deal of practical urgency. The crowd was more engaged, better informed, than any other crowd I've been a part of.

'The revolution was a breakthrough for the health of our society, but it hasn't solved all our ills in one go. We need to work. But now we have a chance. The oxygen had been sucked from our society for at least thirty years. Now we can breathe'.

Hossam Bahgat

The struggle for Egypt's future is being fought between religious, civil and military forces, between homogenising and pluralising urges, between those who desire revolutionary acceleration and those who fear sudden change. Regionally, the usual suspects will interfere, overtly and covertly. But the Egyptian people are still, for now, in the driving seat. Their achievement has rearranged the maps, shaken the earth—the Arab earth shakes from Bahrain to Libya, Yemen to Syria—and where all was stagnation, everything is in flux.

Sarah Carr again: 'Tahrir was wonderful, a mini-Utopia. I wish you could take the atmosphere there and put it in a jar. I wasn't harassed once. There was one Salafi who told me to wear my jacket around my waist while we were being attacked by thugs. I just looked at him. Is this the moment to be worrying about my waist? Worry about the Molotov cocktails. Apart from that incident, all I saw of the Tahrir people was intelligence and respect. But step out of Tahrir, and you were back in Egypt'.

Did anything last of it? 'Yes. It created a zest which didn't exist before'.

Or more than that. Not only a zest, but a contagion. Even in Libya and Syria—where the Allahu Akbars attain higher frequency with every massacre experienced—the people still chant One Hand and One People, injecting some Tahrir into dictator hell. There is an awareness abroad, amongst ordinary people from Maghrib to Mashriq, that rights matter, that everybody deserves to be treated with dignity and respect. The acuteness of the awareness marks a true generational—and historical—change.

Hossam Bahgat says, 'People have woken up. Previously apolitical people are interested now. People are engaged. This is the biggest guarantee for the future'.

GADDAFI AND ME

Ashur Shamis

Friday 11 April 1980. I was in Kuwait on a fundraising trip. After a hard day of rejections—I couldn't persuade anyone to support our welfare projects in Britain—I was ready for bed. The phone rang just as I was about to fall asleep. It was a friend from London. 'Muhammad has been killed', he said in a nervous, quivering voice. 'He was shot at point-blank range by two Libyans in the courtyard of the London Central Mosque in Regents Park, following Friday prayers'. 'Why?' I asked instinctively even before the news had sunk in. He could not answer. He simply said: 'Be careful and don't come back to London'.

Muhammad Mustafa Ramadan was one of my closest friends. I had known him since my school days in Tripoli. He came to London in 1966 to join BBC Arabic Radio and became a well-known newsreader. He was an independent, playful man, with razor sharp wit and a wicked sense of humour. Along with his countless listeners, I enjoyed listening to his merciless and pungent criticism of the ideologues of the Arab world. I admired his outlook on life and his ability to establish himself as an independent thinker motivated by social justice.

After the shock had subsided, things began to fall in place. I remembered talking to Muhammad in London a few days earlier. We were both concerned about Musa Kusa, the newly installed 'ambassador' in London for the newly launched 'state of the masses' (*jamahiriya*) of Libya. The *jamahiriya*, we were told, was a new concept in statecraft which Muammar Gaddafi was launching for the benefit of humanity, and Libya was going to have the privilege and the honour of being the first such entity in the world. When Kusa took over the Libyan embassy in London in September 1979, one of his first actions was to contact Muhammad. He wished to be introduced to Muslim organisations in Britain, he said. One particular organisation he was keen to visit was the Muslim Welfare House in London of which I was the Director. Muhammad felt we could not possibly refuse a Libyan ambassador's visit to our centre. The visit was arranged for 15 March 1980. Kusa, a tall awkward man who did not have the demeanour of an ambassador, arrived with two beefy gentlemen whom he did not bother to introduce. We chatted generally about our projects and the work of other Muslim organisations. He was taken on a tour of the Welfare House. As soon as he left, we breathed a sigh of relief and forgot all about it.

But in my hotel room in Kuwait, the visit took a completely different meaning. Was it a reconnaissance sortie? Were the two men accompanying Kusa assassins? Had they come to eye their target?

My friend Muhammad Ramadan had by then taken to writing open letters to Colonel Gaddafi. In the letters, he argued that while revolutionary and socialist thoughts have relevance in Islam, they should be focussed on promoting equality and social justice. He delivered these letters to Gaddaf ad-Dem, a cousin of the colonel, who was a military attaché at the embassy. He published some of these letters in the *al-Arab* newspaper in London between 1972 and 1977. His tone was always respectful but his advice was sincere and frank. He wanted to have an open debate with the colonel. Gaddafi's reply came in the form of a bullet. Muhammad's body was taken to be buried in Tripoli, but the authorities refused to receive it. The state-owned paper *The Green March* declared, 'the cemeteries of Libya reject the stinking corpses that befoul the air'. It was returned for burial in London.

I had to think fast. Was the next bullet meant for me? Two weeks before the assassination of Ramadan, Mahmud Nafea, a Libyan lawyer, was shot outside his office in South Kensington. Back in February of the same year, two Libyans were murdered in Italy and a well-known leader of the nationalist Baath party, Aamir Daghious, was killed in Tripoli. Clearly, the murder squads were hunting down Libyan opponents of the Gaddafi regime in the streets of Europe. The fact was confirmed by Musa Kusa himself. He unabashedly told the *Times*, 'we killed two in London and there are another two to be killed'. Adding: 'I approve of this'. I wondered if I should return to London or 'disappear' somewhere on the 'Arab street'. I had little choice and decided to return to Britain and go underground. I flew to Manchester and sought refuge with my dear and trusted friend Mohamed Elamin Osman, a Sudanese doctor who was living and practicing in Carmarthen, South Wales. He welcomed me to his home.

Upon my return, the British authorities and some friends with links to the Libyan embassy in London informed me that I was indeed on the same hit list. But why? How did I suddenly become an enemy of the state? I was not involved in any dissident activities. I had no link with the opposition. Indeed, I had not even said anything against the regime. Was it because of my friends? Was it because of my teachers? Was it because of my activities concerning the welfare of Muslims? Or was it my connection with the Muslim Brotherhood?

When Colonel Gaddafi overthrew Libya's monarchy in a military coup in September 1969, I was studying in England. I arrived in London on 29 October 1965, age eighteen, with a grant from the Libyan government to study aeronautical engineering. During the 1960s, British universities attracted the crème-de-la-crème of students from all over the Arab world as well as from Malaysia, Turkey, Iran, Pakistan and Nigeria. The country was buzzing with Islamic activists. The two most active organisations at the time were the Muslim Student Society (MSS) and the Federation of Student Islamic Societies (FOSIS). The first conducted all its activities in Arabic, aiming to attract Arabic speaking students, and was a constituent member of the second, FOSIS. The leading members of MSS were from the Muslim Brotherhood, from Egypt, the Sudan, Iraq and Syria. I was already familiar with the pan-Islamic movement.

I had arrived in London with a letter of introduction from Sheikh Fathullah Hawwas, a famous leader of the Muslim Brotherhood in Libya, addressed to Mohamed al-Magrief, another member of the Brotherhood. When he finished reading the letter, he put it aside. 'With or without the letter', he said, 'you are welcome. You have reached home'. I spent six rich and wonderful years with him until 1971, when he returned to Libya. He introduced me to the MSS and FOSIS and I became involved in their activities—organising conferences, winter gatherings and debates and discussions.

The 1960s and 1970s were exciting times for Muslim students in Britain. We dreamt of an imminent Islamic revival and spent a great deal of our time discussing the intellectual foundations of Muslim civilisation. But we did not acquire this passion in London; we brought it with us from our countries of origin. During my adolescence in Libya, I became aware of the distinction between the newspapers and magazines owned by the state and those owned privately. On the whole, the former told lies and perpetuated propaganda, while the latter told the truths that the state wanted to subdue. I realised that there was an undeclared war between the state and the independent newspapers such as *al-Ra'ad* (pathfinder), *al-Maydan* (battle-ground), *al-Haqiqah* (the truth), and *al-Balagh* (proclamation). There was also hostility between state-sponsored writers and independent thinkers. It was thus natural for independent thinkers to coalesce together. I acquired a close group of friends which included Mahmud Annakuo, Fath-allah Hawwas, and Ali Abu-Zied—young intellectuals like myself. And, like a moth to a flame, we were attracted towards the fiercely independent thinker and teacher Sheikh Mohammad Angudi, who introduced us to the works of a variety of Arab writers such as Taha Hussein, Ahmed Amin and Khalid Mohamed Khalid. He persuaded me to read some of the important Islamic reference books, such as *The Life of Muhammad* by Ibn Ishaq, *Commentary on the Qur'an* by Ibn Kathir, and *Revival of Religious Sciences* by Imam al-Ghazzali. With humour and erudition, Sheikh Angudi instilled in me the love of the *Qur'an*. I became attached to it as a source of solace and guidance in my life.

But the man who influenced us most was Sayyid Qutb. I would read each of his works many times, especially his magnificent commentary *In the Shade of the Qur'an*. (Later, I would translate it into English). I keenly followed his, and the Muslim Brotherhood's, confrontation with the Egyptian regime of Gamal Abdul-Nasser. Qutb was executed by Nasser for publishing his controversial work *Milestones*. Instantly he became a hero for young men like me opposed to colonialism and despotism in all its forms, be it that of the British aggression against Egypt, the French occupation of Algeria, or the totalitarian regimes which had sprung up in the Arab world—in Iraq, Syria, Egypt and Yemen. We were anti-socialist and anti-Communist. We argued for Arabism and Arab nationalism which we saw as parts of Islam in the sense that there was no Arabism without Islam. We saw Qutb as a devout Muslim who stood up to a despotic ruler, his words an instrument of resistance in the face of tyranny.

While I was clearly influenced by the Muslim Brotherhood, I was not a member. No one asked me to join the organisation. Or pay a subscription, or pledge allegiance. But I felt that I belonged to a group, a fraternity. In London, there was a certain distinct bond amongst us, members and non-members of the Brotherhood. But we were also independent spirits. When the Brotherhood attempted to create a British organisation in the early 1970s, its attempts were rejected. The very idea of belonging to an international branch of the Brotherhood became a bone of contention. Who were we supposed to give our loyalty to: to our homelands or some abstract notion of international brotherhood? What was more important, the region or the centre? And where was the centre anyway? Even the members of the Brotherhood made it clear that their primary loyalty was to their own country. And in some cases, for example Syria where three Muslim organisations were vying for supremacy, the problems were truly insurmountable. Moreover, students from different countries had different temperaments. The Iraqis, for instance, were more inclined to harshness and secrecy; the Sudanese were more easy-going and open; while the Egyptians shared aspects of both. All these problems exhausted the Brotherhood and they abandoned the idea of having a British movement.

The Libyan students in London had mixed feelings about the coup in Libya. The new regime had declared its loyalty to the 1952 military movement of Gamal Abdul-Nasser in Egypt under the slogan of 'Freedom, Arab Unity and Socialism'. We wanted freedom and Arab unity but were not sure about socialism. Some of us saw it as progress towards a new era. Others were filled with apprehension and foreboding. Most of us did not approve of Nasser and did not like the idea that the new regime was following in his footsteps. I was in Tripoli for my summer break during the coup. I returned loaded with photographs I had taken of popular demonstrations supporting the new regime.

The regime's true colours were first revealed in 1971 when Gaddafi introduced a law banning the formation of or participation in political parties. The punishment for contravening the law was death. The same year, at a 'Symposium on Revolutionary Thought' held in Tripoli, he made it clear that opposition to the regime would not be tolerated. This was followed by the so-called Cultural Revolution of 1973. It repealed the existing laws of the country. Gaddafi declared that he aimed to isolate and eradicate individuals with perverted, anti-Revolutionary and deviant minds and ideas. The bourgeoisie and bureaucracy would be crushed. And 'popular committees' would be set up to take the revolution forward. According to a member of Gaddafi's inner circle who was sitting next to him on the podium when he announced the 'cultural revolution', it was the first time anyone had heard of it. Within days, hundreds of university lecturers, lawyers, writers, civil servants, technocrats and journalists were arrested. Most of them were identified as Marxists, Ba'athists, secularists, Muslim Brothers, or intellectuals with political leanings at variance with the regime. The whole stratagem was aimed at those who so far had failed to identify with the politics of the regime. The detainees were held in prison without trial until December 1974.

During this period I counted Muhammad Ramadan and Amr an-Nami as my closest friends. We were in turn surprised, shocked, and angered by this turn of events. Muhammad started writing his open letters to Gaddafi. I first met Amr in London; he was studying at Cambridge. What really brought us together was that we were both sons of the Western Mountain, Jabal Nafusa, in Libya. We discovered that we shared the memories, the traditions and anecdotes of that area. Amr was a natural poet, a sensitive man whose poetry had a tinge of sadness. He was seen as one of Libya's leading men of letters. Disturbed by the events in Libya, Amr decided to return home.

Amongst the first victims of the Cultural Revolution, Amr was arrested and imprisoned in 1973. My other friends in Tripoli, Mahmud Annakuo, Fathallah Hawwas, and Ali Abu-Zied, were also arrested. They were accused of being members of the Muslim Brotherhood. But their interrogation made it clear that they belonged to no organisation, and they were all released in December 1974. Amr decided to go into self-imposed internal exile, and returned to the Western Mountain to tend his flock of sheep. He was pursued and arrested again in 1981—and has never been seen since. Ali Abu-Zied was brutally murdered in London in November 1995. What mattered to Gaddafi was not someone's membership in any particular organisation but their independent spirit.

In 1975, a member of Gaddafi's junta, Omar Mehaishi, led a coup against the colonel. It failed. Gaddafi used it as an excuse to tighten his grip on the army. He raised his relations and members of his tribes to high ranks in the army and gave them key appointments in the political and economic power structures of the country. But he went further to consolidate his power: he introduced the 'Revolutionary Committees' (RCs). The RCs consisted of armed civilians with a mission to protect the 'Revolution'—they were the *apparatchiks* of Gaddafi's power base. They were not part of the government, they acted above the law, and they answered to no one except Gaddafi. They immediately set about committing the worst of human rights abuses, and overran private businesses and properties, claiming impunity in the name of the Revolution.

Between April 1976 and April 1977, in what came to be known as the Students' Revolt, thousands of university students in Benghazi and Tripoli were expelled and prevented from completing their studies. The RCs arrested hundreds, torturing many. In the first political extra-judicial killing witnessed in Libya since the Italian occupation, four student activists were hanged by the RCs. For the first time ever, the hangings took place on university campuses. The RCs also targeted the private sector, claiming that the national wealth belonged to all the people. Death squads roamed the major cities liquidating the 'enemies of Revolution'.

In a menacing speech to the RCs in March 1979, a month before the murder of my friend Muhammad Ramadan, Gaddafi declared that anyone who acted against the Revolution from anywhere in the world, even if they were at the north or the south pole, would be a target of the RCs wrath. Such were the laws of war, he said. Whoever was against the principles of 'no landlords and no tenants', 'no wage-earners and no employers', and 'land and wealth belong to the people', would be considered an 'enemy of the revolution' and would be crushed.

For over a year after the assassination of Muhammad Ramadan I remained underground. But I could not stay in hiding forever. Life was becoming unbearable. I had to come out—whatever the risk. While I never appeared openly in public I started to move around, ever so carefully, always mindful of who was watching me, looking for a menacing presence. Any day out could be my last day. I gave up all my organisational responsibilities and started to withdraw from my Islamic activities. I wanted to do something to save Libya from Gaddafi. But I had no idea what to do.

Then something unexpected happened. The Libyan ambassador to India, Mohammed Yusuf Maghrief, suddenly announced that he was resigning. He was going to openly oppose Gaddafi's regime. I was asked to attend a meeting in May 1981 in Morocco to join a 'task force' that would work on creating a popular opposition to Gaddafi's rule. The 'task force' consisted of Mohammed Yusuf Maghrief; the noted writer and accomplished journalist Mahmoud Annakuo; diplomats Ahmed Ibrahim Ehwas, Mohamed Ramadan Hawissa and Ibrahim Sahad; university professors Aly Ramadan Abuzaakouk and Suleiman Abdullah Darrat; and myself. We organised a series of clandestine meetings to prepare the framework for the task ahead.

In our meetings, the team discussed various aspects of the work required. We did not identify with any political ideology or movement. Our goal was purely patriotic: to liberate Libya for constitutional democracy, genuine freedom and equal opportunity. Right at the outset, we decided to be open to all Libyans, inside and outside the country. We consulted widely and contacted Libyans in Britain, the United States and Egypt and sought private gatherings with businessmen, professionals and exiles in several countries. We wanted to create a coalition of talent, abilities and resources which appealed to a wide range of Libyan people. An urgency and burning desire was driving us forward, an overwhelming sense that something great had to be done, something far greater than any of us individually. The work of the task force culminated with the launch in the Sudan of the National Front for the Salvation of Libya on 7 October 1981.

The Front moved quickly to consolidate its work and enlist the participation and support of the majority of Libyans against the regime. We held rallies in London and various American cities. We contacted various countries that were willing to cooperate with us, and enlisted their logistical, media and security support, starting with those, such as Morocco, Sudan, and Egypt, who were hostile to the regime. We enrolled Libyan students' unions to our cause, established contact with opposition elements inside the country, and started a media campaign. We began publishing a magazine entitled *Inqadh* (Salvation) and acquired a radio station that broadcast our message. In less than two years, we had galvanized the Libyan exile community through persuasive hard work. The Front became known inside Libya and support began to grow.

The regime continued to divide the people into two categories: those with the revolution and those against. It carried on 'cleansing' the country and established training camps for the RCs. The camps were led by the notorious terrorist Carlos 'the Jackal' and run by other international terrorists, most notably the rogue Palestinians Abu Nidal and the CIA agent Ed Wilson. Outside Libya, events also turned nasty. During a demonstration organised by the Front outside the Libyan embassy in London, in which I took part, machine-gun rounds were fired at the protestors from inside a first floor window. Eleven Libyans were injured and a twenty-five-year-old British policewoman, Yvonne Fletcher, was killed in the line of duty.

We now came under immense pressure to take military action against the regime. We were not short on enthusiasm or dedication but our resources were modest. We were not ready for military operations; and some of us had severe doubts about fighting bullets with bullets. Nevertheless, the Front embarked on its first military engagement inside Libya in May 1984. It was an unmitigated disaster. Our small band of troops was insufficiently trained. We lost our top military leader Ahmed Ehwas, a dedicated, humble and courageous man, together with his select group of *fida'een*. It was a major blow to the Front.

The following year I was elected Chairman of the National Council of the Front during its second meeting held in Baghdad, Iraq. We were now presented with a second opportunity for military action. Algeria had invited the Front to train and prepare a paramilitary force on Algerian soil to be sent inside Libya clandestinely to participate in some kind of take-over bid. The Algerian proposal was terse and somewhat blurry, but the Front, despite the loss of its military leadership a year before, was quick to respond on the assumption that Algeria knew what it was doing. It put all its energy and resources into what came to be known as the Algerian Project.

Hundreds of our members attended training camps in Algeria. But a few months later, in November 1985, the project came to a grinding halt. The Algerian government got cold feet and pulled the plug. A Libyan officer and a cousin of Gaddafi called Hassan Eshkal was thought to be implicated in a takeover attempt to coincide with the Algeria project. He was shot dead while trying to meet Gaddafi at Bab el-Azzizyia, possibly to kill him. This was a signal that the project was off. The Front was left grappling with its aftermath.

Many of our members were angry and disappointed, some felt disillusioned, and a series of withdrawals and resignations were triggered for the first time in the Front's history. Whispers about divisions within the Front started spreading in Egypt, Britain and the USA. There was nothing we could do to alleviate the feeling of frustration amongst our members.

In late 1987, when the turmoil of withdrawal and resignations was spreading, the Front embarked on yet another military adventure. This time the invitation for military action came from Chad. Libya had invaded Chad in July 1980 in an attempt to overthrow the regime of President Hissene Habre. By 1983 Libyan troops occupied all of the country north of Koro Toro. But with the active support of the USA and France, Habre ended the Libyan occupation of Chad in 1987 and inflicted a heavy defeat on Gaddafi's forces. Chad also managed to capture many Libyan soldiers. We heard through the Chadian authorities that around 1,700 soldiers, lead by colonel Khalifa Hefter, were willing to defect to the Front. It was manna from heaven, an offer we could not refuse. The Chad project was going to make or break the Front. We threw ourselves into the project, establishing contacts, organising meetings, training and planning for the operation. But even after two years of effort the project still had not taken off. In November 1990 the regime of Hissene Habre was overthrown, marking the end of the Front's Chadian adventure. The Front had to evacuate Chad in a hurry and disperse her members to various countries.

By now it was obvious that the Front was not cut out for military action. The Chad project had exhausted our resources. It was becoming difficult for us to justify each failure with a worse failure. It was also clear that we had lost the support of the Libyan people, and that the leadership had lost its political will. From thousands of followers and supporters, the Front had now been reduced to a few hundred, mostly in the United States. It attracted no new activists from inside Libya and had no influence on Libya itself. Almost all the people associated with it were exiled. Some reconciled themselves with the Gaddafi regime, and one way or another, returned home.

I was associated with the National Front for the Salvation of Libya right from its inception. I was involved at all levels and was responsible for the most intimate decisions—from political to military, to media and social organisation. But now I was torn by many questions. Could I continue engaging in something that I did not believe in? How far could we continue pretending that military action was worth pursuing? Could we face our people after so many failures? Would my departure represent an act of betrayal of the Libyan people and colleagues and friends who had given their lives to rid Libya of Gaddafi's regime? I felt that the Front's failures were my responsibility.

I withdrew quietly in 1989. Other leaders—Aly Ramadan Abuzakuke and Mahmoud Annakou—had left the Front even earlier. Another wave of resignations came in 1994. Sharp arguments were rife among the Chad recruits and amongst Front members, as demonstrated at meetings in Cairo, Alexandria and London, and at numerous meetings in Washington, Lexington and Atlanta in the United States.

It took me some time to recover. I withdrew to concentrate on my personal affairs. I translated Nelson Mandela's autobiography *Long Walk to Freedom* into Arabic and Sheikh Ghazzali's concise seminal work *A Thematic Commentary on the Qu'ran* into English. Eventually, I managed to get some work from MBC and the BBC and started freelancing. But Libya and Gaddafi were never far from my mind.

I took time out to meet a new generation of Libyan activists. One movement I came to know well was the Islamic Fighting Group. I met the group's leaders who were exiled in London in 1994. It was a critical period in the group's evolution; their popularity was growing but they had not yet announced their existence. They had recently moved their armed struggle from Afghanistan to Libya, where things were heating up for them. Although the group was being associated in the Western media with 'Islamic terrorism', they are in fact far removed from terrorism. They were concerned largely with 'armed struggle' against Gaddafi within Libya. They were working hard on formulating and articulating their own Islamic identity in order to build a popular movement. My meetings with them were useful and invigorating, and I passed on the lessons learned from the failures of the Front.

My return to normal life received a jolt in June 1996. What started as a small squabble over standards of food and healthcare at Bou-Salim prison, about ten kilometres south of Tripoli, turned within hours into a massacre. Abdullah Senoussi, Gaddafi's notorious security chief and brother in law, led an all-out attack on unarmed prisoners with machine guns and heavy weapons. Within minutes 1270 prisoners were brutally murdered. They were buried in a mass grave sealed with cement. Their families were not informed and a policy of total silence was followed by the Gaddafi regime. No one knew what had happened inside Bou-Salim prison. It took five years for the brutal details to appear.

My conscience was stirred once again. We could not let such atrocities continue. Moreover, arrests, detention and torture were now the norm for the regime. Even worse, Gaddafi was now presenting a benign picture to the world and the international community, led by Britain, was normalising relations. We needed to make our voice heard and to find a way back towards active resistance.

But how? I consulted with a wide group of former colleagues inside Libya, in Europe and the United States. After many discussions we decided on a realistic and moderate line to be directed to the widest possible Libyan audience, including those loyal to the regime. Our main concern was the interests of our people and our country. We had to participate in preventing our country's political, economic and human disintegration. We found ourselves responding to calls of dialogue, debate and discussion from individuals, groups of professional elites and the intelligentsia on both sides of the divide. Instead of 'opposition' we opted for 'partnership' and positive engagement, presenting ourselves as catalysts for change and reform. We defused our relationship with the regime by emphasising that we were non-political and merely concerned with building civil society.

We started with an Internet newspaper that went live in October 2001: *Akhbar Libya* (Libyan News). It was to be our main instrument for fighting the Gaddafi regime. In addition to writing editorials and op-ed articles, we managed to form a clandestine network of highly-intelligent and well-placed contacts inside the country who would feed us with news stories, sensitive information and other reports and documents. We were critical of the regime, but not harshly so; we emphasised the importance of civil society and promoted alternatives to Gaddafi ideology and policies. Soon it became one of the most-visited Libyan Internet sites. The regime tolerated it but kept an eye on us.

When our message began to spread inside Libya, I received an unexpected invitation from Saif al-Islam, Gaddafi's eldest son. He had just enrolled for a PhD at the London School of Economics. Meetings between a Gaddafi and the opposition were very rare and I believe I was one of the very first to be approached. It took me a couple of days to consult and make up my mind. I thought it would be a chance to convey to him some of our ideas and concerns, and, in any case, we would have nothing to lose. Besides, if he was going to write a thesis on 'The role of civil society in the democratisation of global governance institutions: from 'soft power' to collective decision-making', he ought to know what the champions of civil society were actually saying and thinking.

We met in April 2002. It was a warm meeting. I found him receptive and engaging. I raised three issues his father's regime would have to address immediately: the release of all political prisoners, an open inquiry into the Bou-Salim prison massacre, and the disbanding of the Revolutionary Committees. No one had ever come to us from Gaddafi's side to talk on these terms. We also spoke about reform generally in Libya and what it meant. We identified political repression, lack of freedom of expression, draconian laws, and the security grip on the country as other priorities that the regime would have to tackle fairly quickly.

My meetings with Saif al-Islam Gaddafi continued over the next four years, up to the end of 2006. Other Libyans with expertise in oil, finance, and security participated in these meetings. The most prominent participant was the late Tarek Benhalim, a banker and a financial expert and the son of former Prime Minister, Mustafa Benhalim. He went back to Libya, after 36 years in exile, to advise on reforming the financial sector and the privatisation of Libyan banks. Our assessment was that Saif was coming out from the long shadow of his father to quietly stage a palace coup. We thought he responded positively on a number of issues. We engaged with him and gave him the benefit of the doubt but we also kept a safe distance—the assassination of Muhammad Ramadan was always fresh in my mind.

But towards the end of 2006 it became clear that our meetings with Saif al-Islam were not going anywhere. He was dithering and indecisive. Bizarrely, at one stage he announced he was withdrawing from politics altogether. It appeared that his reform programme had gone off the rails and he had lost credibility with the people who invested in him and expected him to lead Libya towards democracy. We saw him change his agenda to coincide more with his father's. He wanted to recruit people to be used as cannon fodder for his petty battles with some sections of the old regime. So we parted company.

The regime now resorted to heavy-handed and thuggish measures. It started attacking the *Akhbar Libya* website. Over the last few years it has destroyed the website no less than ten times. Every time we had to re-build it from scratch. The regime also found a round-about way to implicate me and the website in a defamation case brought against us in the High Court in London. The court action was first initiated on 28 March, 2007 but the case did not come to court until 3 July, 2008. The regime won the case but lost the battle over freedom of speech. The presiding judge, Mr Justice Eady, said in his judgement that I had been 'involved in campaigns for freedom of speech, political dialogue, reform, democracy and respect for human rights'. The *Akhbar Libya* website, he declared, 'was to provide a forum for discussion of political affairs and matters of controversy in Libya which would be outside the scope of censorship operating from that country'.

On Monday 21 February 2011, I caught Saif al-Islam Gaddafi on the news. After the bloodiest few days in Libya's modern history he had come out to defend his father. With a menacing posture and wagging his finger, he delivered a rambling speech full of fury and rage. As Gaddafi's security forces fired relentlessly into crowds of civilian protestors, he declared that the regime 'will fight to the last minute, until the last bullet'. The unrest, he said, was caused by tribal factions and drunken or drugged Islamists acting on their own agendas. All those killed, raped and tortured were victims of a 'planning error'. 'Rivers of blood' would flow if the uprising did not stop, he screamed, going on to lament the 'plot' against his father.

My plots against the Gaddafi regime have failed. But the people's uprising is succeeding. The *jamahiriyah* beast is being extricated from Libya, the country of peace and tranquillity, the country of my birth, and the abominable Gaddafi malignancy is, slowly but surely, being rooted out.

The story of the final unravelling is yet to be told.

A TRANS-ISLAMIC REVOLUTION?

Abdelwahab El-Affendi

One of the most gripping and revealing episodes of the popular Egyptian revolution that erupted on 25 January, 2011 was a scene in which a disoriented leader of the Egyptian Muslim Brotherhood explained to Al Jazeera news channel why he happened to be talking from a borrowed mobile phone outside a prison in the middle of the desert. He kept insisting that he and his colleagues had not escaped from prison, but were released from their cell by members of the public who smashed the door with stones, a process that took several hours. When they emerged from their incarceration, they found no prison guards or officials. 'We are looking for anyone in authority to notify him of our situation', he concluded.

According to their account, this group of thirty four top *Ikhwan* leaders, including seven members of the Guidance Council, the movement's executive body, had been rounded up by the security forces late at night on Thursday 27 January and deposited at a detention centre run by State Security in a western Cairo suburb. Disturbed by the lack of clarity on their legal status after more than a day in detention, they barricaded themselves in an area of the jail, and insisted on seeing a senior official from the Ministry of the Interior. The assistant to the interior minister finally arrived and promised to resolve the matter within hours. Later that day, the prisoners were informed that they were being taken to the Attorney General's Department where their cases would be reviewed. However, they were then blindfolded and driven for nearly a hundred miles north on the Cairo-Alexandria highway, where they were transferred to Wadi al-Natroun prison on the edge of the desert.

Arriving there late at night on Saturday, they were still no clearer about their status. Overnight, however, something mysterious happened. Just after midnight, a prison revolt apparently broke out, and the detainees heard tear gas and bullets being fired. By early morning, the prison guards gave up and fled. Still locked in, the *Ikhwan* prisoners called for assistance from the inmates outside, and someone threw them a mobile phone which they used to call for help. Others tried to break the door from outside. By midday, fellow prisoners, assisted by some locals, succeeded in breaking down the prison door, and the *Ikhwan* leaders were able to leave and engage in that famous interview outside the gates.

Apparently completely unaware of the transformation Egypt had under-gone in the space of their two days of incarceration, the released prisoners were still terrified of being accused of breaking out of jail, and were offer-ing, live on Al Jazeera, to hand themselves in. When you have lived in a police state all your life, the last thing you want to be accused of is being a fugitive. It is noteworthy that two of the best known prisoners of the radical Gama'a Islamiyya, Abboud al-Zumar and his cousin Tariq, refused to leave the Damanhur prison, where they had been incarcerated since 1981, even though every other inmate, including other members of the Gama'a, had escaped. The formerly jihadist group had in fact publicly distanced itself from the protests. Having experienced the might of the police state up close and personal, the incarcerated jihadists (of whom the pair mentioned had finished their jail terms many years before, and were now held under emer-gency laws) were by no means anxious for another confrontation.

Outside the Cave

Unbeknownst to the escapees, however, Egypt had ceased over that fateful weekend at the end of January to be a police state; or, more accurately, it had become a collapsed police state in the process of rapid and visible disintegration. It was probably the greatest transformation any country in the world has witnessed in the space of forty eight hours. As in the Qu'ranic parable of the 'People of the Cave', who slept for over 300 years and emerged to find themselves in a completely unfamiliar world, the *Ikhwan* leaders emerged, two days after being rounded up in the middle of the night by agents of one of the world's most formidable police states, to find themselves in a magically transformed environment. Since the group was formally banned in 1954 and six of its leaders were executed the fol-lowing year, Egyptian politics had been dominated by a fight between these two antagonistic political actors: the Muslim Brotherhood (the *Ikhwan*) on one side, and the intelligence services (the *Mukhabarat*) on the other.

The two 'parties' (neither was a party in any genuine sense of the term; they were 'secret' societies that were not secret at all) slugged it out as each tried to defend itself and its interests, with the *Ikhwan* bearing the brunt of this unequal contest. Until the early 1970s, all important Ikhwan figures were incarcerated or forced into exile, and quite a few died under torture or were killed in prison in disputable circumstances.

Revulsion against the torture and brutal maltreatment of detainees is often blamed for the rise of violent extremist Islamist groups from the late 1960s on. However, this narrative may need to be revised. The accepted story argues that Sayyid Qutb (1906–1968), the preferred ideologue of the radical groups, was shocked by the mistreatment of prisoners (including a massacre during a peaceful protest in Tura prison in June 1957) into writing his incendiary indictments of contemporary Islamic society as a recreation of pre-Islamic barbarism (*jahiliyya*). His ideas then appealed to a generation of alienated youths who had themselves experienced torture and humiliation. None of these assertions are true. To start with, Qutb in fact borrowed intellectually from the Pakistani leader of Jamaat Islami, Sayyid Abu'l Ala Maududi (1903–1979), who did not suffer torture when he expounded his ideas. Secondly, the young men who began to advocate violence had not gone through prison either. Most had no direct contact with the earlier generation of Islamists, and derived their ideas directly from re-interpretations of traditional authorities such as Ibn Taymiyya. In a supreme irony, the Nasser regime, in its own attempt to undermine Islamists, encouraged traditionalism and made a huge body of traditional religious works available to the public.

In the meantime, and even before the relative opening which saw the *Ikhwan* leadership released from jail in the early 1970s, the movement had publicly rejected the logic of Qutb's writings and distanced itself from groups inspired by him. At the time, those groups were more isolationist and quietist than violent. The so-called *Gama'at Islamiyya* (Islamic Groups) or, as the government media preferred to call them, the *Gama'at Diniyya* (Religious Groups), emerged in the 1970s, mainly in the universities of Upper Egypt, independently of the *Ikhwan*, whose leadership then skilfully engineered a take-over of sections of the Gama'at by co-opting some of their key figures (most prominent of whom were Esam al-Aryan, Abu al-'Ula Madi and Mukhtar Nuh). Many refused to join the Ikhwan, and later went on to form the Gama'a Islamiyya and its off-shoot, Islamic Jihad.

When he took over from Nasser, Sadat tried to use the Islamists to counter the then hegemonic Nasserist elite, well-entrenched in the state, the media and cultural institutions. He permitted the new movements some freedom, released *Ikhwan* leaders from prison, and permitted them to operate openly, although the movement was never formally legalised. The honeymoon with Sadat did not last long, however; Islamists again became a target when they refused to endorse the 1978 Camp David treaties with Israel. In his final years, Sadat condemned the *Ikhwan* and other Islamist figures, arresting many of them in a major sweep of opponents and critics in September 1981. A brief second honeymoon was witnessed in the early period of Hosni Mubarak's rule, but the regime still refused to grant the *Ikhwan* official recognition. When the group nevertheless managed to achieve electoral successes in alliance with other parties, the regime's stance hardened. It began to refer to the *Ikhwan* as the 'banned movement' and proceeded to harass and arrest its key activists. The most prominent and effective leaders were often hauled before military courts where heavy jail sentences were handed down.

So when Essam El-Arian was woken up by his wife at 2 am to be informed that the police had come for him, he recalled that this was the fifth time he had received such a nocturnal visit since the big sweep of 1981, the last being in January 2010. He had, in addition, been arrested twice at more civil hours, once in broad daylight in front of the Lawyers' Union in 2005, and once at dusk in 2009. It had become a way of life.

The regime's main complaint against the group was its popularity. President Mubarak consistently warned that any free elections in Egypt would bring the *Ikhwan* to power, a warning he kept sounding until his last day in office. The state also promoted the narrative that the violent groups which emerged in the 1970s and waged full scale war on the regime in the 1990s has emerged from 'under the cloak' of the *Ikhwan*. The Mubarak regime and its intellectual exponents argued (anticipating recent Western official positions on the terrorism/extremism nexus) that the difference between the *Ikhwan* and the violent Islamist groups was one of degree, with the former acting as the thin wedge of extremism.

The *Mukhabarat*, the real power in the country, concluded that the *Ikhwan* was the real enemy, and adopted a policy of containment which it hoped would eventually lead to the extermination or significant weakening of the movement. However, during the 1980s and early 1990s, when radical Islamist groups were in the ascendancy, the *Mukhabarat* relied heavily on the *Ikhwan* to contain, tame or sideline those groups. But once the radicals were contained, the *Mukhabarat* began to treat the movement like a Roman gladiator—permitting it just enough room to move in a closed arena where it could be hunted down.

This long and bitter experience must have been vividly present in the minds of the stranded prisoners in front of the deserted jail in the middle of nowhere. Many have endured long jail terms and suffered torture. For decades, they have learned to play the game according to the rules the *Mukhabarat* has laid down: they do not challenge the regime openly and they stoically accept the measured amounts of repression meted out.

During the preceding week, walking that tightrope had appeared particularly challenging. For at least a decade, especially under the outgoing leader 'General Guide' Mahdi 'Akif who stood down in 2010 (a first, and a great innovation for the movement to have a 'former' guide), the Ikhwan tried to push the boundaries. In 2004, it decided to join the umbrella Egyptian Movement for Change also known as *Kifaya* (Enough!), which agitated against Mubarak's re-election to the presidency and his crude attempts to line up his son Gamal for succession. That was regarded by the regime as crossing a red line, and the *Mukhabarat* came down heavily on the group.

A number of leading figures, including the Deputy Guide, were tried by military courts in 2007 on charges of money laundering and 'funding an illegal organisation'; heavy sentences of up to seven years in jail were handed down. Almost every week afterwards, scores of key activists were arrested without charge under emergency laws. The number of arrests rose sharply, with over 700 arrested during the 2005 parliamentary elections, and over a thousand in 2007 when the group decided to contest the upper house elections. By 2010, the number of detained *Ikhwan* cadres reached over 6,000. That was the year when the regime decided to conduct the most blatant election rigging yet. As it was the parliament which elected the president, Gamal Mubarak's succession in the 2011 presidential elections required a sanitised House. In preparation, a raft of draconian constitutional amendments was passed in the summer, the most important of which was to remove judicial oversight of elections. When the polls were held in December, not a single *Ikhwan* candidate managed to win a seat. Only a handful of opposition candidates from other parties were elected.

The Ikhwan *and the Protests*

In the context of controversy over the rigged elections and anger over the June 2010 murder of the blogger Khaled Said, the success of the uprising in neighbouring Tunisia (which forced Zine El Abidine Ben Ali to flee on 14 January) terrified the Egyptian regime. Still believing that only the Ikhwan could give momentum to the protests proposed for the following week, the *Mukhabarat* summoned Ikhwan leaders in the provinces and warned them of serious consequences should they take part. The following day the movement issued a communiqué deploring what it called 'threats and intimidation' and hinted that it would participate in demonstrations. The *Ikhwan* did offer partial support for the protests, even though one of its leaders, Al-Arian, was quoted by *The New York Times* on 22 January as suggesting non-participation (he later disavowed that quote). *Ikhwan* youth were already part of the coalition organising the protests, while former Ikhwan members of parliament were scheduled to take part in a token protest outside the High Court.

When they emerged from jail, the dazed Ikhwan prisoners were oblivious to the momentous change which had taken place. As far as they were concerned, the brutal *Mukhabarat* state which had terrorised them for over 60 years still existed. The day before, on the face of it, the *Mukhabarat* had in fact made a bid to take direct control of the state for the first time, when its chief, Omar Suleiman, was appointed Vice-President. The post had been vacant since its 1981 occupant, Mubarak himself, became president following Sadat's assassination. The reluctance to fill the post signalled Mubarak's wariness of any power sharing with an heir apparent, as well as his secret designs to keep power in the family.

Labouring under this misperception, the *Ikhwan* were on the verge of committing their most damaging blunder since backing the Nasser coup in 1952 and endorsing Nasser's decision to ban all political parties except theirs. When Suleiman asked to meet the opposition, including the *Ikhwan*, dangling the carrot of recognition coupled with a dark warning that 'this opportunity may not come again', the *Ikhwan* defied the near-unanimous rejection of the offer by the opposition and met Suleiman on 6 February. That was one of the regime's last desperate bids to avert collapse. Having sent the army to impose a curfew and restore order, appointing a Vice-President and a new cabinet, unleashing thugs and criminals on the protesters and the public at large, closing the Internet and mobile phone networks, all to no avail, the regime finally attempted to win the *Ikhwan* over in the hope of splitting the opposition. Had the *Ikhwan* gone along with this ruse, it would have been a disaster for them and for the revolution.

Luckily for everyone, they pulled back in time. Under pressure from the restless youth, the leadership was gradually forced to abandon its habitual caution and to give the protests its full support. The mobilisation on the Friday of Rage (28 January) was the first step. The second and most decisive moment was when the Ikhwan defended the beleaguered protesters in Tahrir Square, playing a significant role in defeating the regime's thugs. According to many observers, Ikhwan volunteers were pivotal in defending, organising and managing Tahrir Square, from manning the barricades to providing loudspeakers and clearing the garbage.

Most importantly, they worked seamlessly with everybody else and remained almost invisible. It was easy for Islamists to remain invisible in the midst of an Egyptian crowd, for Egypt had turned overwhelmingly Islamic during the Mubarak decades—a great irony given the regime's anti-Islamism. A recent study on Islamist organisations in Egypt lists 16 different groups spanning the spectrum from traditionalist and reformist to radical and modernist. Membership ranged from a few hundred to hundreds of thousands. The author of the study mentions established institutions such as Al-Azhar—which runs 10,000 mosques and 6,000 schools and colleges, producing tens of thousands of *ulama*—and the Sufi associations (whose members number millions), but does not count these among Islamist groups. He also neglects to mention organisations such as the Young Muslim Association, one of the oldest in Egypt, whose membership runs into the tens of thousands.

Prominent Egyptian intellectuals have made significant contributions to ensuring the hegemony of Islamic discourse. Foremost among these was Mustafa Mahmoud (1921–2009), a physician who was also a columnist in a popular (and very liberal) weekly magazine in the Nasserist era, and also an author and television presenter. Starting as a Marxist who wrote on modern philosophical theories and ideas (and some fiction as well), he experienced a very public conversion (explicitly narrated in his 1976 book *Rihlati min al-Shak ila al-Iman*), and became a fervent promoter of Islamic faith through his columns, books (eighty-nine of them) and his TV programmes (over 400). He had a huge following among the youth and many of those not habitually reached by traditional preachers or Islamists.

Another key contributor to the revival was the journalist Muhammad Jalal Kishk (1929–1993), who also had an interesting trajectory. Imprisoned as a young Communist activist, he broke with the Communists in 1958 due to differences over Arab unity. He was banned from writing for offending Moscow, and later became an independent Islamic writer. His most scathing attacks on the left and Arab nationalists came in the wake of the June 1967 Arab defeat by Israel, when he famously dubbed radical Arab rulers 'Socialist Mamluks'. At a time when Islamists were in jail or banned from writing, his best-selling series on the 'cultural invasion' did a mighty demolition job on the then prevailing nationalist ideologies using the weapons of ridicule and sarcasm. Working, like Mahmoud, from a quasi-secular, 'mainstream' perspective, the boost his work gave to the Islamist cause can hardly be overestimated.

The third major figure in this tide of revivalism was Sheikh Muhammad Mutwalli al-Sha'rawi (1911–1998), a traditional preacher who became a TV celebrity and bestselling author from the 1970s. Having graduated from Al-Azhar in 1943, he taught in Saudi and Algerian universities before returning to Egypt in the early 1970s, where he worked at Al-Azhar and the Islamic Endowments Ministry (*Awqaf*) before becoming Minister of *Awqaf* under Sadat in 1976. But he was best known for his radio and TV shows, where his reflections on the Qur'an and religious issues attracted millions of viewers in Egypt and all over the Arab world. He also reached a very broad audience well beyond traditionalists and Islamists, exerting immense influence.

In the wake of the Islamic Revolution in Iran, a veritable exodus of intellectuals took place from the left, liberal and nationalist camps towards Islamism. These intellectuals, already towering figures in their own right, mostly remained independent, but they made their contributions to the broader Islamist perspective, bringing in new insights and a new following. They pushed a line that was more open to other perspectives, in particular the liberal one. Due also to the great respect they enjoyed across the spectrum, they managed to bridge the gap between Islamists and the rest of society, and continued to play a prominent role in the political process. One of them, Tarek El-Bishri, a former senior judge, was selected to head the commission which proposed constitutional changes last March. Another, the late Abdel-Wahab Elmessiri (d. 2008), a professor of English literature, became the head of *Kifaya* in 2007.

More recently, the proliferation of religious-oriented satellite channels has produced conflicting trends. At one pole, Salafi and traditionalist trends gained considerable support. At another, 'modernist' preachers such as Amr Khalid are appealing to middle class and upwardly mobile youth, creating powerful networks of followers all over the Arab world. The Egyptian authorities banned Khalid from preaching precisely because of his success in appealing to the affluent young, but he circumscribed the ban by using Saudi-owned satellite television stations, reaching a much wider pan-Arab audience.

The Pan-Arab Scene

While politics in the Arab world remains largely country-specific, many 'pan-Arab' trends and inter-connections are clearly observable. The politics of pan-Arabism of the Nasserist era and its accompanying 'Arab Cold War' (between the radical pan-Arabists led by Egypt, and the conservative regimes led by Saudi Arabia) may now be a thing of the past, but the rise of pan-Arab media and the persistent appeal of the Palestinian cause continues to keep Arab politics interactive.

Islamism and its networks of solidarity are also a factor in this interconnection. The Egyptian *Ikhwan* had, since the 1940s, established branches in most Arab countries, and since the 1970s, these movements have joined a coordinating body presided over by the Egyptians. Not everyone agreed to join. The Sudanese and Iraqi movements insisted on maintaining their independence, while the Kuwaitis left after the Iraqi invasion of 1990, when the rest of the Brothers failed to back them. Some new movements such as the Algerian Front of Islamic Salvation (FIS), had emerged independently and were in fact in competition with local *Ikhwan* branches. And of course Shii Islamist parties were independent and often hostile to their Sunni rivals.

Not all Islamist movements suffered persecution. In Jordan, Kuwait, Bahrain and Yemen, the movements were able to operate legally and had a history of alliances with their respective regimes. In Yemen, the movement and its Islah party had a peculiar status, being a strongly Sunni group allied with the Saudis in a country dominated by Zaidism, a moderate Shii doctrine. Islah allied itself with the regime of Ali Abdallah Saleh, and its supporters played a decisive role in the 1994 civil war against Southern separatists. However, over the past few years, Islamists split from Saleh over his growing authoritarianism and joined their former enemies in the Yemen Socialist Party (former Communists) in the Joint Meeting of Parties (JMP) forum which has been pushing for reform since 2003.

As in Tunisia and Egypt, neither the Islamists on their own nor the JMP collectively played a leading role in instigating or sustaining the youth revolutions which began on 3 February. However, the JMP emerged as the main interlocutor with the regime when it came to negotiating change or signing agreements such as the one proposed by the Gulf Cooperation Council to ease the transition. The youth groups occupying the squares in Yemen consistently opposed the kind of compromises being negotiated and wanted President Saleh to leave without any conditions. But they did not disavow or condemn the JMP.

As a member of a broad opposition coalition and former partner in government the Islah party does not pose the same problem to democratisation that Islamist parties pose elsewhere. Yemen is a very conservative Muslim country in which the thousand-year Zaidi Imamate was only toppled in 1962. Islamisation is not an issue, and compromises between political forces have not been difficult to achieve. So in spite of appearances, the revolution in Yemen has followed a course similar to that of Egypt in the sense that the clear majority of people supported the revolution. Most tribal chiefs and many army commanders also joined the revolution, leaving Saleh very isolated. Even before Saleh's injury in a mysterious explosion on 3 June, support for him was ebbing fast.

In Libya, Colonel Muammar Gaddafi remained as isolated as Saleh. His attempts to stir up tribal and regional divisions largely failed, and there were no signs of any divisions in the liberated cities, or any genuine signs of support for Gaddafi beyond his militias. The Nato intervention has introduced an important complicating factor, but it has also failed to create any deep divisions among the population. Even Islamists supported the intervention.

Islamist parties were of course banned in Libya, like all other political parties, even though Gaddafi often tried to wear the Islamist mantle himself. The *Ikhwan* branch in Libya is weak, but the more radical jihadi *Gama'a Islamiyya* had been very active, even though it had renounced violence and was rewarded by the regime with a prisoner release. However, past treatment of Gama'a detainees played a crucial role in sparking the 17 February revolution. The arrest of a lawyer representing the families of 1,200 detainees massacred in a Benghazi prison in June 1996 was the spark for demonstrations in that eastern town on February 15, giving momentum to the demonstrations called by young activists for two days later. Many Islamists, including former jihadists, joined the revolution, but again this appeared to pose no problem to the democratic process (or for international support for the Libyan revolution).

Islamism is not an issue in Syria or Bahrain either, but sectarianism is. In Syria, the local *Ikhwan* branch is banned, and membership incurs an automatic death penalty according to Law 49 passed in 1980. In 1982, after *Ikhwan* fighters took over the city of Hama, the Syrian army and security and paramilitary forces shelled and then stormed the city, killing tens of thousands of civilians and militants (estimates vary from 10,000 to 40,000). In retrospect, Hama could be described as Benghazi without the Nato: a liberated city that was reclaimed by the dictator.

The Syrian regime is a curious beast. The bedrock of support on which it rests is the loyalty of the minority Alawite sect, and it is a *mukhabarat* state par excellence. However, over the years, the regime played clever, high stakes games, which broadened its international, if not domestic, support. It milked the Palestinian cause dry, posing as the main anti-Israeli power in the region. It buttressed this role by its close alliance with Iran, and remained a Soviet ally to the bitter end. It also supported (the more accurate term could be 'exploited') resistance movements in Palestine, Lebanon and Iraq. However, when the need arose, it could play its cards in such a way that would please the West. In Lebanon, it intervened with regional and international blessing to defend the Maronite Christians against the PLO and left-wing Lebanese forces. In 1990, it sent troops to fight side by side with the Americans against Iraq over Kuwait. It also frequently presented itself (citing its record in Hama) as a bulwark against Islamic extremism. Still, while it imposed the death penalty on its homegrown Islamists, the regime had no qualms about backing Hamas in Palestine, Hezbollah in Lebanon, and Salafi and pro-al-Qaeda radicals in Iraq.

In the current crisis, the regime appears to have overplayed its hand in its attempt to quash the peaceful protests that erupted in March with the tried and tested brutality used in Hama. After over 1,300 deaths and tens of thousands of injuries and arrests, it looks like things are getting worse for the regime rather than better. No one seems to believe its claims that the uprising is led by Islamist extremists, although as in other Arab revolutions the Islamists do play a part, and the populace at large is religious. Fridays remain the key days of mobilisation, precisely because of Friday prayers.

In Bahrain, the sectarian card was played as a trump. Bahrain is unique among Gulf countries in that it boasts a vibrant indigenous labour movement dating back to the 1930s. It also had a lively political culture which culminated in the establishment of a legislative assembly in 1973, two years after independence from Britain. However, the ruling Al Khalifa dynasty, which has ruled the island since 1783, decided to suspend the constitution and dissolve the assembly in 1975. This led to simmering resentment and protests against the ruling family, complicated by the fact that the majority of the population (around 70 per cent) are Shia while the rulers are Sunni. The Islamic revolution of 1979 exacerbated matters further, as Iran supported dissidents and renewed its claim over Bahrain. In 2001, King Hamad bin Isa Al Khalifa, who had succeeded his father in 1999, announced a series of reforms that included the promulgation of a new constitution and a partial restoration of electoral politics. A general amnesty of exiled dissidents followed, and Bahrain witnessed a brief 'spring' from 2002, in spite of reservations about the limited nature of the reforms and the refusal of the King to restore the old constitution. However, tensions began to rise again, and many political groups boycotted elections and some went back into exile, citing harassment, repressive measures and failure to institute meaningful reform.

Bahraini Islamists are influential in electoral politics. The moderate Shii Wefaq Society has regularly controlled eighteen of the forty seats in the lower chamber of parliament, while the Salafists and the Ikhwan usually had four seats each. However, given the sectarian divide, Islamist parties tend to cancel each other out, with the Sunni parties staunchly loyal to the royal family. When the uprising started last February, the Islamists were as stunned as everyone else. The demands put forth by the protesting youth echoed those of the exiled hardliners, calling for the resignation of the prime minster (the King's uncle and the most powerful man in the regime, having been in his post for forty years) and the restoration of the 1973 constitution. After an initial crackdown, the King bowed to Western pressure and withdrew troops from the streets. There was a brief spring as some exiles returned again. Wefaq and other Shii moderates tried to play catch up, but the Sunni Islamists resisted the reforms and organised pro-regime demonstrations.

Then in mid-March, the regime hardliners won the day. Citing intransigence from the protesters and overt sectarianism, the army, supported by Saudi crack troops, cleared the protesters and the security forces made mass arrests and a state of emergency was put in place. The end result was a silencing—temporarily at least—of all protest. It was not as bloody as in Syria or Libya, but that was mainly because the protesters were more restrained. However, the situation remains tense and potentially explosive, in spite of offers by the regime for dialogue and promises of reform.

It is to be recalled that the Arab Spring was triggered by events in Tunisia, now almost forgotten due to the torrent of events that followed. Ben Ali's Tunisia had been described as a success story in Western official circles precisely because of its apparent victory in containing Islamism and silencing most opposition. Its relative economic stability also received much praise. However, this was a gross misreading of events. The Islamist movement in Tunisia, represented mainly by Rachid Ghannouchi's Ennahda Party, was one of the most moderate and democracy-friendly Islamist parties. It did not have a programme other than democratisation, and the crack down on it was thus an attack on democracy rather than on Islamisation. The secular opposition parties and civil society groups realised this late in the day, and when they did, many began a rapprochement with Ennahda. This culminated in the 18 October Movement (in 2005) which, like *Kifaya* in Egypt, brought into existence a pro-democracy movement. Tensions between Islamists and their rivals have now returned, but the differences continue to be resolved democratically in spite of admission by secular groups that Islamists remain the most powerful party.

Islamism and the 'Post-Islamist' Revolution

Surveying the Egyptian scene in 2007, Asif Bayat, an Iranian sociologist who participated in the Iranian revolution before settling in Egypt during the 1980s and early 1990s, asked the question: Why did the Iran of the late 1970s, with its thriving economy, wealthy middle class, repressive political system, massive military might, and powerful international allies, experience an Islamic revolution, while the Egypt of the early 1980s, with similar international allies but a weaker economy, large impoverished middle class, and a more liberal political system, fell short of revolution and experienced only an Islamist movement?

In sum, why did Egypt have an Islamic movement without an Islamic revolution, while Iran appeared to have an Islamic revolution without an Islamic movement? Bayat's answer pinpoints what he sees as three fundamental differences between the two cases: 'the political status of the clergy; the way in which Islam was articulated; and the degree of political control over citizens'. In Iran, the clergy was institutionalised and hierarchically organised, making it potentially very influential, in spite of state efforts to weaken it. The absence in Iran of a powerful independent Islamic movement or of significant public expressions of religion also enhanced the role of the clergy. The strongly repressive regime was an additional factor in preventing the emergence of a strong Islamic movement and favoured the clergy as the representative and spokesperson for religion. In contrast, the clergy in Egypt remains marginalised, non-hierarchical, and deprived of a high status. Traditional religious institutions such as Al-Azhar had been 'nationalised' in accordance with the 1961 law which gave the president control over key appointments, having earlier asserted state control over religious endowments. In response, a strong bottom-up Islamic movement has emerged in Egypt, and has become a powerful and diverse social movement with deep and wide reach within society. This was helped by the relative openness of the Egyptian political system, in spite of continued attempts at repressing and containing Islamist movements.

As a consequence, the Shah's Iran remained highly polarised, with a strong repressive regime, a highly secularised society confronting an entrenched religious hierarchy, with no mediating forces, especially no modern Islamist movement to speak of. In contrast, the Islamist social movements played a stabilising role for the Egyptian system at several levels: by providing social services and emergency aid where the state was unable or unwilling to do so, and by providing for many 'both a way to express their discontent and a moral safety net'. This is why the confrontation in Iran had to explode into a revolution, while in Egypt it led to some form of accommodation/stalemate.

The absence of an Islamist movement in Iran was probably overstated by Bayat. The movement may have been politically weak, but the revolution could not have taken place without the mediation of a modern Islamist movement able to mobilise support beyond the narrow confines of the clergy and their traditionalist supporters. That is why the role of 'bridging' intellectuals such Ali Shari'ati was crucial. It might be equally an exaggeration to call Shari'ati the 'architect of the Islamic revolution', as scholars do. However, he was certainly, in Fischer's words, the 'hero of Iran's youth of the 1970s and one of the patron saints… of the 1977–79 revolution'. It is not plausible that an Islamic revolution could materialise out of no substantive antecedents. So it must be that the work done by intellectuals and activists like Shari'ati, Mehdi Bazargan, Ayatollahs Mutahari, Taliqani, etc, created some kind of 'movement', however diffuse and indeterminate, which paved the way for the great explosion that took place later. It is to be recalled that Bazargan and other Islamists formed the first government in revolutionary Iran.

Bayat contrasts Iran's trajectory to Egypt's 'passive revolution', which led to Islamisation without (in both senses) the state. But while Bayat argues that Egypt does not appear to have experienced a 'post-Islamist' turn similar to Iran in the early 1990s and the Khatami era (with many former revolutionary enthusiasts having second thoughts and advocating a more pluralistic and democratic approach to Islam and the state), this judgment is not entirely accurate. For the Islamist tide had produced its own excesses: wanton violence, bullying, unrealistic demands and gross errors of judgement. So while Egypt was becoming decidedly more Islamic, the understanding of what it means to be Islamic kept evolving.

Even Islamist movements such as the erstwhile violently jihadist Gama'a engaged in revisions and self-criticism. The radical groups were in the ascendancy from the mid-1970s, mainly among students and youth who espoused violent struggle as the appropriate method for the Islamisation of society. The violence ranged from attacks on individuals or groups deemed to have 'deviated' from Islamic norms, to burning shops, armed robbery and clashes with the state, and later with the world. While the majority of Egyptians, including the majority of Islamists, condemned these tendencies and distanced themselves from them, it took some time for the groups themselves to confront their problematic conduct and grasp its fundamental error. First the leadership of the Gama'a (in 1997) and then a faction of its rival, the Islamic Jihad, condemned the resort to violence and began a sophisticated ideological rethinking.

Other Islamists also began to learn from their mistakes, and started to build coalitions with allies and, less frequently, with rivals, as happened with *Kifaya* and the Egyptian Association for Change (EAC), which was set up in early 2010 as the *Ikhwan* had teamed up with former International Atomic Energy Agency chief and Nobel Peace laureate Mohamed El Baradei to create a vehicle for joint action. At the same time, an exodus of former secularist and left-wing intellectuals to Islamism, coupled with the emergence of new movements (or the shift in orientation of some, such the Labour Party), introduced a new dimension in Islamist thinking and action. For the *Ikhwan* to engage in such a coalition, with the explicit goal of restoring democracy, represents an important break with its past. The *Ikhwan*, it is to be recalled, emerged in 1928 as an anti-liberal rather than a pro-democracy movement. Its core concern was that the authorities, both state and religious, were not doing enough to stem the tide of westernisation and social liberalisation. It was critical of Al-Azhar and other traditional religious authorities for their lack of assertiveness in opposing the drift away from strict observance of religious teachings. In spite of Hassan al-Banna's own Sufi roots, the movement also inclined towards the habitual Salafi tendency associated with all modern reformist movements, opposing traditional Sufism as too obscurantist and un-enlightened. As a transformative movement critical of the majority of the population (either for being too liberal or too traditionalist) it could not advocate democracy, even though al-Banna endorsed constitutionalism and the parliamentary system.

However, having suffered for long enough under dictatorship, and with the disillusionment bred by the 'Islamist' experiments in Iran, Sudan and Afghanistan, the *Ikhwan*'s espousal of democracy became as attractive as it became unavoidable, even if its 'new language of democracy remained acutely uncertain and ambivalent, reflecting both experimentation and a growing generational struggle within the movement'. What mattered, however, was that this decisive alignment with the broader democratic mobilisation created the necessary conditions for the uprising. This shift to mass action had, in turn, been assisted by earlier campaigns, including those in support of the Palestinian *intifada* in 2000 or against the war on Iraq in 2003. The relative success of those campaigns in uniting diverse shades of opinion into joint action, and the increasingly repressive measures of the regime, which extended its heavy hand to liberals and nationalists as well, created an atmosphere in which mass action became possible. By 2005, a 'new Cairo spring' which 'reminded one of the Iran of the late 1990s', was already in the air. 'After years of political intimidation and fear, Egyptians began to express their grievances in the streets more daringly and loudly. Kifaya and then the Muslim Brotherhood broke the taboo of unlawful street marches by staging numerous demonstrations and rallies in urban squares. Protesters chanted slogans calling for and end to Emergency Law, the release of political prisoners, and no more torture, and they urged President Mubarak to step down'.

Rehearsals had begun for the big uprising, and they continued for the following five years, with a boost from 2008 provided by the 6 April Youth Movement and other Internet-based protest groups.

Rapprochement, Challenges

This convergence of positions between the main Islamist trends and the secular opposition prepared the ground for the democratic revolution, as the unity of opposition deprived the regime of its main divide-and-rule weapon. It took Tunisia to give the protests hope, determination and momentum. From that point on, comradeship in arms and shared suffering helped unite the opposition even more. However, even here, some cracks continued to show. The *Ikhwan*'s initial reluctance to participate fully in the revolution, which fitted into a pattern of caution that had irked partners in the past, and even more seriously, their agreement to enter into talks with the regime on 6 February in the face of boycott by all other major actors, threatened this solidarity. Yet part of the strength of the protest movement was its ability to show mutual tolerance for differences of opinion.

Such tolerance is not guaranteed in the post-revolutionary era, now that the competition for power is in full swing. Again, the *Ikhwan* appeared to be standing apart and regarded as a threat by others, precisely because they appeared to be the most popular and best organised force. The first rift appeared when the *Ikhwan* backed the Military Council which took over from Mubarak in its policy of making partial amendments to the constitution and having those endorsed by referendum in March 2011, while most other opposition groups, including the Coalition of the Youth of the Revolution (in which the *Ikhwan* are represented) wanted a completely new constitution. Many opposed the March referendum, and called for a boycott or a no vote. Christian leaders in particular urged a no vote and, interestingly, so did the radical Islamists of the Gama'a. In the end, in this first genuinely democratic poll in modern Egyptian history, 42 per cent of the electorate took part, of whom 77 per cent said yes to the amendments. The result was seen as another triumph for the *Ikhwan*, and also became a new source of worry for their rivals, who are now calling for a postponement of the parliamentary elections, initially scheduled for September 2011, for fear that the *Ikhwan* and other Islamists would win a majority.

The movement tried to reassure critics by taking steps in March 2011 to announce the setting up of a new party, the Freedom and Justice Party. It is headed by a former leading member of parliament, and has a Christian as vice-president. It also announced that it was not going to field a presidential candidate, and would only put forth candidates for 50 per cent of parliamentary seats. But the adversaries are still worried, and with some justification. For if this movement could be described, in Hamzawy and Brown's words, as 'the most successful social and political movement in modern Arab history', in spite of having 'lacked formal legal existence for six decades', then what will it do now it is free for the first time?

The temporary reassurances of the movement are genuine. It really does not want to take power in Egypt. And this has been its position for sometime. I recall asking the group's spokesman, the late Jabir Rizq, during a discussion in Cairo in 1985 about the movement's programmes if and when it came to power. His categorical answer was that the movement had no intention of taking power, 'even if it was handed over to us on a plate of gold'. The reason? 'The United States', he said, 'provides Egypt with $5bn in aid, and tourism brings in another $5bn. [His figures]. If we take over, the US will cut off aid, and our policies will all but stop tourism. How are we going to feed the people?'

Stunned, I had two questions. First: 'Why don't you tell this to Hosni Mubarak? He seems to be under the impression that you are keen on power, and that is why he is so hard on you'. And, second: 'Are you then waiting for Mubarak to improve the economy, make Egypt self-reliant, and then invite you to take over? Why not institute interim policies which would not put you in confrontation with the US or destroy tourism, and then work on gradual reform?' His angry reply was: 'How could you expect an Islamic movement to endorse the Camp David Accords and permit sales of alcohol?'

And this goes to the heart of the matter. By refraining from taking power, the movement in fact endorsed Camp David and the measures supporting tourism. It did so, furthermore, in a more explicit fashion since its members in parliament never tabled proposals to abrogate the agreements with Israel or called for a ban on alcohol sales or for 'modesty' requirements at beaches. However, it was not prepared to take a conscious decision to explicitly modify its policies to accommodate the realities it implicitly recognised. This stance is reinforced by the fact that the movement continues to enjoy rising popular support in spite of sticking to its rigid policies. It does not have the incentive to change.

In addition there is the fact that, in spite of its prominence, the Ikhwan is not the only Islamic movement on the scene. Other groups are vying for popularity and recognition. Of these, the Salafis have been the most assertive—and the ones giving most cause for alarm—in the post revolutionary period. The Salafis boast hundreds of thousands of supporters, but they do not have a unified leadership or a distinct organisation. Rather, they congregate around prominent individuals or local centres, and coordinate their activities loosely. Even though at least one Salafi group has announced its intention to form a political party, its leaders admitted that they had failed to win support from other Salafi groups, which means that more than one Salafi party will emerge.

The Salafi 'menace' plays a complex role; at one level, it helps make the *Ikhwan* look positively moderate; at another, it offers competition for the religious constituency. That role had been performed in the past by radicals such as the Gama'a and other former jihadi groups. Their cadres released from jail after the revolution, they are also trying to make their mark on the political scene. The Gama'a has been plagued by disputes over its stance against the protests (which was also the stance of the Salafis), but appeared to have resolved some of these problems and announced in May that it would form a political party to contest the coming elections.

The role of Islamism in general, and the *Ikhwan* in particular, has been central to the debate over change. The regimes and their western backers had continued to justify themselves by citing the 'Islamist threat'. The *Ikhwan's* depiction (by Rosefsky and Wickham) as 'the largest, most popular, and most effective opposition group in Egypt' is also true of Islamist opposition groups in Tunisia and Bahrain. The role of these movements has thus become crucial for leading (or obstructing) the democracy drive. Until January this year, most had failed to live up to this mission, which would have required more boldness in challenging the regimes and more inclination for compromise with rivals.

Up to now, the *Ikhwan's* strategy has been to give assurances through putting self-limits on their political role. Rachid Ghannouchi will not run for president in Tunisia, and the *Ikwhan's* new Freedom and Justice party would not seek a majority, and would not support a theocracy or a religious state, but would call for a 'civic state' (*dawla madaniyya*) with an 'Islamic basis' (*marji'iyya Islamiyya*). Similar assurances have also been given by Salafis and also Islamist parties elsewhere. But in putting self-limits on their role in terms of shying away from assuming full political responsibility, the movements make a public admission that their assumption of government would be disastrous for their countries. However, it would appear that the movements are not yet ready to *confront* that role by changing their vision and policies to make that role less toxic, as opposed to merely trying to mitigate its impact.

Ideally, Islamists should have tried to transform their movements along the lines seen in Turkey, Malaysia, Indonesia, Morocco, or even Tunisia, where movements worked to overhaul their programmes to enable them to realistically undertake governing responsibilities. But to just promise not to govern is not enough; for what happens if, as was the case of Hamas in Palestine, you find yourself suddenly saddled by the responsibility of governance 'by accident' or by default, in spite of your best intentions?

A 'Trans-Islamist' Era?

The Egyptian revolution (and to a lesser extent, its Tunisian precedent and the subsequent eruptions in other Arab countries) was the outcome of a convergence of trends, central to which was the evolution of a widening consensus among opposition forces, facilitated by the increased isolation and repressive nature of the regime. A combination of Islamist pragmatism and disillusionment among the secular opposition with the regimes that claimed to be their protectors facilitated the emergence of this consensus. The rise of new Internet-mediated youth movements and the intensification of their activism during the past few years also helped create a momentum for change.

Islam, and the political forces associated with agitation for its public role, did not disappear from the public arena. Only their role was transformed. The more radical and conservative Islamist forces were conspicuous by their absence during the protests, while the mainstream Islamists merged seamlessly into the broader democratic revolutionary trend. This was seen by some as a confirmation that Egypt (and the Arab world), was finally witnessing a 'post-Islamist turn', similar to that witnessed by Iran in the late 1990s, 'where pious sensibilities are able to incorporate a democratic ethos'. 'The growth of such 'post-Islamism' out of the anomalies of Islamist politics', writes Asef Bayat, 'represents an attempted fusion of elements hitherto often seen as mutually exclusive: religiosity and rights, faith and freedom, Islam and liberty. The daring logic is to turn the underlying principles of Islamism on their head by emphasising rights instead of duties, plurality in place of a singular authoritative voice, ambiguity instead of certainty, historicity rather than fixed scripture, and the future instead of the past'.

For the 'post-Islamist generation' which launched the revolution 'the great revolutionary movements of the 1970s and 1980s are history— something that mattered to their parents but not to them. This new generation is not interested in ideology'.

This may be an over-statement of the case. While the term 'post-Islamist' is useful in trying to capture a condition that cannot be adequately covered by other terms such as 'secular', or 'Islamic liberal', its application has been plagued by confusion and contradictions. While some of its proponents, including Bayat, who initially coined it, tried to critique and clarify some of those confusions the most problematic aspect of its use continues to be the implication that it denotes a form of 'anti-Islamist Islamism'. For the phenomenon on which the term was based, the 1990s reform movement in Iran, was spearheaded by reformist Islamists who continued to justify themselves in Islamic terms. However, proponents of the concept persist in using it as a synonym for 'anti-Islamist' or even anti-

Islamic, as Bayat himself did when he contrasted the durability of Islamist politics in Egypt to Iranian post-Islamism which, he argued, 'aspired to undo Islamism altogether'.

The significance of what happened in Egypt, and to some extent in Iran, Turkey, and elsewhere, is that the phenomenon in question did not coincide with a decline in religiosity; quite the reverse, in fact. The countries in question have become much more Islamic in countless ways. However, as Roy himself noted, 'the paradox' of this process of extensive and intensive Islamisation is that 'the very success of the Islamic revival has largely de-politicized Islam'. In this regard, it is not exactly the case that the revolutionaries of Arab squares have taken secularism as a given; they have, rather, taken Islam as a given.

For want of a better term, and since the term 'post-Islamism' has been so compromised and polluted, I prefer to call the current Arab revolutions 'trans-Islamic'. They have gone beyond the Islamist problem precisely because they now take for granted much of what Islamism has emerged to campaign for. One has just to observe Tahrir Square to note how almost everybody joined the prayers, while those who did not (mostly Christians) felt no awkwardness about it. For protesters from Tunisia through Egypt, and later Libya, Yemen, Bahrain and Syria, the big protests were organised on Fridays, with mosques as starting points. Islam was everywhere and nowhere. It was no longer an issue. Democracy, and how it could be achieved and sustained, became the main concern.

While Islamist themes and groups continue to be bones of contention, this is merely part of the political game. The disputes are raging as much within and between Islamist movements, as it is between them and their opponents. It is just politics as usual.

Conclusion

The 'miracle of Tahrir Square', as Slavoj Zizek aptly called it, was a miracle of the transformation of a whole people into a self-governing entity. It was a 'declaration of independence' by the people of Egypt. Not only did they defy the government and reject its authority over the people, but they managed to engage in self-defence (defeating and dispersing the police of the police state, and vanquishing the regime thugs), self-policing and self-organisation. The people discovered itself as a people, and defined its identity in terms of being Egyptian and being free. No symbol but the national flag ruled the spaces and myriad squares.

Egypt has been here before: in 1919, when it discovered itself and also decided who the enemy was, and what the common objective was: freedom. Then as now, Egyptians, Christian and Muslim, urban and rural, celebrated their shared identity and fought together. In this latter turn, the Islamists played a crucial role. They were there when the people needed them: to defend the squares, to fight off thugs, to organise the logistics of the protests, provide food and blankets, man the clinics and the barricades. And they kept invisible when their distinct appearance or slogans could have created problems.

In other revolutions, especially in 'tribal' societies such as Yemen and Libya, or in sectarian systems such as Bahrain and Syria, the transformation was even more remarkable. Even though the regimes unleashed massive violence and fomented divisions, the miracle of popular unity was surpassed only by the immense courage under fire of the peaceful protesters. They all knew what kind of regimes they were facing, but they did not flinch.

However, if democracy is to thrive, the approaches and techniques adopted to promote unity have to be perfected and employed in a sustainable fashion. The people need to perfect the art of living together, of accommodating difference, of ensuring a place in the Square for everyone. The burden should not only be on the Islamists, but Islamists do have to understand the insecurities of others who feel threatened by the apparently unstoppable Islamist ascendancy. As the people in the driving seat, they should learn to accommodate threatened minorities.

There are many lessons that could be learned from history, mainly about what not to do. In 1952, the Egyptian *Ikhwan* were also the most powerful group, and the only political group exempted from the dissolution of all political parties. This alienated other political forces and, when they overplayed their cards and suffered as a result, they did not find many supporters.

It is intriguing to recall that the choice of 25 January as the day to launch the protests was partly because it was a holiday, and also National Police Day—the protesters wanted to send a message about police brutality as well. But this day was chosen mainly because it was the anniversary of the day in 1952 when the police in the Suez Canal town of Ismailiyya defied an order from the chief of the British army garrison to surrender. In the ensuing battle, 80 police officers were killed and over 120 wounded. The day was remembered for the heroism of the police ever since.

That was not the whole story, however. On the following day, the whole of Cairo erupted in violent riots. The Great Cairo Fire was the result. Incensed by the refusal of the King to sever diplomatic relations with Britain, some protesters torched buildings, mainly those associated with western interests or the life styles of the westernised elite. The Opera House was the first to go, followed by foreign banks, posh hotels and shops, cinemas, bars, night clubs, and so on. It was the people's revenge on the hated symbols of westernisation and the luxury living of the elite.

The events of that day remain wrapped in mystery to this day. The leader of the ultra-nationalist Young Egypt Party was put on trial, and later the Nasser regime accused the *Ikhwan* of playing a role. The riots brought the army onto the streets and made it easy for Nasser and his Free Officers to organise their July coup. The events remain a salutary lesson about what could go wrong: not only the wanton self-destructiveness of uncontrolled rage, but the ease with which the prospect of chaos could be exploited by those who wanted to impose yet more tyranny.

DIGITAL GENERATION

Anne Alexander

—SMS— Sent: Feb 6, 2011 10:25 AM Subject: Jst entered
tahrir via… Jst entered tahrir via champollion. 3 or 4
barricades. Feels like 1848. But still festive. Families here. Thousands milling abt. Am outside kfc discussing ikhwan latest statement. Sent using BlackBerry®
from Orange

The text message above records the moment I crossed into Tahrir Square.
I sent it to a friend back in London while squatting on my heels on the
dusty pavement underneath Colonel Sanders' beaming face, listening to a
group of socialist activists planning their intervention in the day's protests.
My physical presence had, of course, been preceded by intensive virtual
surveillance: via Al-Jazeera's fixed camera overlooking the square, via
mobile phone footage on YouTube, via tweets, via emails, via blogs, via
Flickr, via video and reports from the Egyptian press, via Facebook
updates. I'd already spent hours studying the chants, the home-made placards and banners, the demands and statements of the organisations present
in the Square.

Thanks to a combination of ubiquitous social media and the designation
of the revolution as a global media event of epic proportions, I had been
able to construct for myself a digitally-enhanced view of the uprising,
turning myself temporarily into a kind of cyborg, with a panoptical vision
spliced together from multiple physical and political vantage points.

Yet despite this prior knowledge and preparation my mind was still
reeling from the impact of the things I hadn't seen or fully understood
with my digital eyes: the construction of the barricades, the organisation
of the checkpoints, the complex interactions between audiences and
speakers at the stages, and above all the emotions and moods of the crowd.
The crunch of stones beneath my feet all the way down Champollion

Street, a reminder that the liberation of the Square, only forty-eight hours before my arrival, had rested on the throwing arms of its defenders as they hurled rocks to fight off attacks by government thugs.

That gap between the revolution I had seen at a distance, despite the seductive quality of the detail offered over social media, and the revolution witnessed in person, is the starting point for this essay. Its purpose, however, is to open a wider discussion about the relationship between mediated representations of the Egyptian revolution and the actual process of self-liberation experienced by millions since the uprising began. Too much of the debate about this relationship has been trapped in a kind of technological determinism which attributes agency to strings of code and takes it away from human beings. However, the opposite perspective, denying that the mass use of social media by participants in the revolution had any impact at all, is no more helpful. A similarly unproductive binary divide exists between utopian and dystopian perspectives on the political potential of the Internet and social media.

In practice optimists and pessimists, utopians and dystopians, can all add weight to their arguments by reference to the Egyptian revolution. The Egyptian state proved it was willing and able to shut down both Internet access and mobile phone networks, as Evgeny Morozov had predicted in *The Net Delusion*. However, the revolution continued and expanded, with mobilising messages running through channels lying deep in the fabric of society: between neighbours, workmates and families, through mosques and churches, and between the swelling crowds in the streets and onlookers. Mubarak fell, removed by his own generals, who promptly set up their own page on Facebook (1.2 million 'likes' at the time of writing), and began sending mass text messages urging Egyptians to go back to work. Facebook use among Egyptians soared, with the site becoming an even larger domain for political activity than it had been before the revolution.

This essay discusses three phases in the unfolding revolution and the changing roles of different media in each. The first covers the early stages of the protests which began on 25 January 2011. At this stage, activists were able to deploy the full array of social media tools they had developed over the preceding years, and mobilise their connections to the global and regional media. The Mubarak regime too could count on its traditional media weapons—the state-run press and broadcasters were mobilised to flood Egyptian audiences with images of pro-government demonstrations.

Then around 27 January something shifted. Both the state and its challengers adopted new rules of engagement. Sensing a new level of threat in the unprecedented scale of the 25 and 26 January protests, the Egyptian government began to block selected social media sites, and then, a few hours before midnight on 27 January, ordered the main Egyptian Internet Service Providers to shut down, while similar pressure forced mobile phone networks to close. It was perhaps already too late to turn back the tide. In any case the threshold separating mass protest from popular insurrection would be decisively breached the following day in most of urban Egypt.

The key communication channels in this phase were the oldest and deepest Egyptians knew: from child to parent, neighbour to neighbour, workmate to workmate, using mosques and churches as rallying points. These channels were only minimally augmented by the new social media during the Internet and mobile phone blackout, but regional satellite broadcasters, in particular Al-Jazeera, did play an important role. Moreover, on 28 January and during the counter-attack by the regime's thugs on 2 and 3 February, the fate of the revolution hung on the battle for physical control of key urban spaces. That the people were able to defeat the state in pitched battle on the 'Day of Rage' protests of 28 January is all the more remarkable given the impact of the shutdown on activists' communications networks.

The failure of the regime's counterattack and the huge mobilisations which followed opened the door to a third phase. The mass movement of people in and out transformed Tahrir again from a besieged citadel of rebellion into a liberated space surrounded by breathing, porous membranes. New people came in. They brought their children and ate sandwiches on the grass, looking for all the world like the spring picnickers on Shem al-Nissim, Coptic Easter Monday. They went home and told their neighbours and family, who began to change their minds about what the government TV channels were telling them. Then in the dictator's last week the revolution reached the workplaces, with a wave of strikes which rippled through the country after 8 February.

The revolution's eruption into the familiar and everyday spaces of Egyptians' lives is crucial to understanding the reconfigured relationship between digital media and activism in the post-Mubarak era. The surge in Facebook sign-ups, the flowering of new online networks and organisations, the torrent of YouTube videos, are reflections of, rather than substitutes for, a ferment of new 'offline' political organisation, largely still driven by the immensity of the uprising, but renewing itself in new struggles over broader demands for social justice.

Revolution in the Panoptican

26 January. From my digital observatory I watched footage of the marches held on 25 January across Egypt. The thousands of small, blurry figures, shot on a mobile phone camera, chanting 'the people want the downfall of the regime' in their tinny voices as the march snaked its way through the back streets of Mansoura is the one I remember most. Links to other clips popped up in the window beside the screen on YouTube: Damietta, Ismailiyya, Alexandria, Assiyut, Nasr City and the other Cairo suburbs. I was dizzy with it. The #25 Jan hashtag was trending on Twitter as the hundreds of tweets coming out of Egypt were picked up and retweeted a thousandfold. Al-Jazeera was a little slow to respond at first, but by the 28th had mobilised its formidable network of correspondents across Egypt in saturation coverage of the protests, combined with its characteristic style of taking the temperature of the streets around the region, as its reporters stopped passers-by from Amman to Rabat and asked them if they supported the Egyptian uprising.

Getting the story of the protests out to the world was not simply a matter of relying on the inbuilt characteristics of social media and hoping that the message would find an audience. Networks of activists deployed tactics for reaching both the global media and sympathetic audiences abroad which had already been tested many times in the past. As blogger and activist Hossam el-Hamalawy explains:

'The first three days I was physically not in the streets ... I was posting and getting the news out, and even after the government banned Twitter I was logging-in via a proxy in order to disseminate the news about the protests to mainly people abroad. And that is part also of the division of labour, I mean we have allies abroad ... trade unionists, human rights activists, foreign journalists, all of these people we need to get the word out to'.

El-Hamalawy's contacts with the international media, his connections with activists abroad, his well-known personal profile in global social media platforms such as Twitter, and his fluency in English, were deployed as resources for the movement in co-ordination with networks of activists in the streets attempting to lead and shape the protests.

Noha Atef, an Egyptian journalist and anti-torture activist found herself studying in the UK as the protests unfolded. Like El-Hamalawy, she relayed messages from activists on the ground to a global audience, and acted as a bridge between the international media and protesters.

'People from Tahrir were tweeting, and there were some people, and I was one of them, I was retweeting them and translating them, so my tweet was in English and in Arabic ... you can imagine, I was spending the whole day, I was sleeping barely five or four hours, but I was all the day trying to find what's going on in Egypt, and in Cairo specifically ... because I'm a journalist, and I know some journalists around the world, in Latin America, Germany and the United States, specifically, and many of them and their friends were getting to Cairo to report on the revolution, so I was connecting them with people on the ground and I was giving them background information so I was fixing for a lot of people'.

Amr Gharbeia, also an Egyptian activist and blogger who was in Cairo throughout the uprising, found that Twitter was a particularly effective seedbed for initiating connections with foreign journalists.

'During the sit-in in Tahrir, people from the international media often looked for our hashtags, and got in touch with us through Twitter. This was how we got to speak on their shows. So some communication with the mainstream media internationally started on the social networks'.

Between 25 and late on 27 January, activists and their supporters manoeuvred constantly to break the regime's selective block on access to key social media platforms. El-Hamalawy was at first able to get round the government's Internet blockade using the proxy service Hidemyass.com, then by relaying information by phone call outside Egypt.

'When the Internet was down we had people calling us from America, mainly America, and from Saudi Arabia, like Egyptians in Saudi, friends of ours, who would call us up, and we will give them the updates, by phone, and they would post these updates on Twitter or Facebook'.

Activists took the block on key social media sites, such as Twitter and the live-streaming service Bambuser, which is particularly heavily used by Egyptian activists, as signs that the state was potentially preparing more drastic means of censorship, which would force them to rely on older means of communication. As El-Hamalawy recalls

'On the night of the 27 when the Internet was taken down, which some people have been anticipating ... news was coming out, rumours were coming out, that the government was going to take down the mobile network on the following day, so what we did was that we exchanged numbers, landline numbers, at least among the network of activists and journalists, so that we can stay in touch by landline'.

Lists of mosques and churches which would serve as rallying points for demonstrations on the planned 'Friday of Rage' protests were also already circulating.

From Protest to Insurrection

Deprived of their usual digital and mobile communication tools, activists quickly developed new ways of organising. The Front to Defend Egyptian Protesters, a coalition of human rights groups and lawyers, normally relies heavily on SMS messaging as a communication platform during demonstrations, receiving text messages on a special 'hotline' which is used to gather testimonies relating to arrests and police violence and put protesters in touch with legal support. Ramy Raoof, a digital activist and blogger who works with the Front, describes how he and colleagues adapted to the sudden reversion to a pre-mobile phone era.

'It was totally offline work, without any technical use, during these days we were just in the streets, moving with the people themselves, speaking with the people and gathering their testimonies. Sometime we agreed 'we will meet after six hours in the office', for example. Or 'we'll meet in a specific café tomorrow morning', for example... When the SMS was shut down we had to distribute ourselves geographically, in Cairo and Alexandria and Suez and Tanta. People travelled to different cities to gather information. I think we were successful in doing that. In some areas, for example in Suez, it was almost impossible to get any information in or out. Even on the ground it was very difficult to go to the city itself by car or train. Everything was shut down. There were police everywhere'.

El-Hamalawy left his laptop and went down into the streets on 28 January. Huge crowds were gathering in the Cairo suburb of Nasr City and moving towards Tahrir Square in the city centre. 'It was like an advancing army, you know, we were taking one square after the other, clashing with the police. It was like war, basically, to be in the streets', he recalls. Miles away to the south, Sayyed Abd-al-Rahman, a socialist activist from the suburb of Ma'adi, was fruitlessly attempting to convince the imam of his local mosque to make a clear call for a demonstration at the end of Friday prayers. When the worshippers dispersed without joining the march, he and a few friends went to the industrial centre of Helwan, where they found a crowd of thousands attacking the local police station. With other activists they won the leadership of the protest, and set off for the centre of Cairo, 50 kilometres distant. Meanwhile, Amr Gharbeia was stuck in Imbaba where knots of demonstrators had failed to reach the critical mass needed to break through police lines.

They were unable to connect directly with each other, largely cut off from information about protests beyond what they could see with their own eyes. Nevertheless the crowds moved with a remorseless common purpose towards Tahrir Square.

Throughout the battle, the state-run media continued to pump out propaganda against the protesters, labelling them paid agents of foreign powers, and lavishing attention on the small pro-Mubarak demonstrations organised by the regime's last supporters, such as the official trade union federation. The key alternative voice which could still reach a mass Egyptian audience was Al-Jazeera. Dispatches filed down crackling landlines by courageous correspondents such as Dina Samak, who reported from Suez, the scene of some of the fiercest battles with the security forces on 28 January, provided electrifying proof of the scale of the uprising.

Direct interaction between activists on the ground and the Al-Jazeera bureau played a crucial role in relaying protesters' messages back to a mass audience outside the liberated spaces in the streets, according to El-Hamalawy.

'You would go back home, and the only way that we know about what's going on in the rest of the country was to tune in to Al-Jazeera, basically, and if we wanted to get a message out that tomorrow there will be a one-million man protest, for example, how are you going to get this message to the rest of the country? It is actually by Al-Jazeera. So somebody would call up Al-Jazeera and say 'the people in Tahrir are having a one-million march tomorrow', so Al-Jazeera broadcasts this for everybody, and everybody knows that tomorrow there will be mass protests'.

Moreover, the activists had access to something the TV channels, both regional and global, desperately needed: videos of the protests. Thanks to the ubiquity of camera phones, the sea of protesters contained within it a citizen army of cameramen and women. Gharbeia and Raoof were among groups of activists who worked to break the Internet blockade by collecting videos and redistributing them to the media. As Gharbeia explains:

'The network I belong to includes a lot of bloggers, activists and journalists and we organised an operation to collect media throughout the blackout, when there was very little information coming out of Egypt. We collected it physically, and transmitted it physically or electronically so that the word can get out, and lots of videos were shown on BBC World and Al Jazeera internationally from this kind of work'.

Once Internet access was restored, Raoof and other activists began uploading material online once again, filling in the gaps in the digital record of the revolution.

'We built a media camp in Tahrir Square. It was two tents, and we were around five or six technical friends with their laptops, memory readers, hard disks, we had all physical means with us and we hanged a sign in Arabic and English on the tent itself saying "focal point to gather videos and pictures from people in the street". And we received huge amount of videos and pictures and then we go back online and keep posting them online. In the first few hours I gathered 75 gigabytes of pictures and videos from people in the streets'.

The emotional power of the raw, jerky footage filmed on mobile phone cameras was all the greater because its very capture was an act of defiance, a mass refusal to comply with the regime's command to disconnect and delete. The satellite networks relayed back to Egyptian audiences the acts of brutality committed by Interior Ministry forces under the cover of the communications blackout: the gunning down of an unarmed protester in the street in Alexandria was filmed from the balcony of a nearby house, the picture abruptly turning over as the camera's owner recoiled in physical shock at the murder.

The Media Ecology of Tahrir

I left the safety of my digital observatory and flew to Cairo early on 5 February. The descriptions which follow were mainly written on 5–7 February in the evenings after returning from the Square, and supplemented by notes from discussions with my Egyptian friends with whom I was staying. Looking back at my observations, three main themes stand out in relation to the role of digital and other media in the Square.

Firstly, the complexity of the interaction between different forms of media inside and outside the Square underlined to me the problems in abstracting digital and social media from the entire media ecology of the protests, despite the fact that Tahrir was one of the most self-consciously 'mediated' spaces I have ever entered. Everywhere you looked, there were people with mobile phone cameras recording video and pictures.

The symbolic resonance of the new social media platforms was clear in the hashtagged graffiti, the hand-made signs referencing Facebook and Twitter. I even passed a slogan in English and Arabic, picked out in stones left over from the battles of the previous week: 'We are the men of Facebook'. Moreover, the distinctions between the usual dichotomies of old/new and alternative/mainstream media became increasingly difficult to sustain. The synergy between text message and satellite TV through Al-Jazeera's 'ticker' of SMS messages running along the bottom of the live broadcast over Tahrir was one powerful example. Slogans scribbled on scraps of paper passed to speakers at the rickety, diesel-powered sound systems were echoed back by the crowd, tweeted from mobile phones and simultaneously filmed for TV then relayed back to the same protesters, their family and neighbours (not to mention the watching global audiences) on the evening news.

This leads on to the second crucial point, which is that although the penetration of the Square by various forms of media was important, as is indicated by the strenuous efforts made by the regime to control and regulate that process, this was far less important than the physical movement of masses of people in and out. The protests were in one sense the cumulative result of millions of conversations, all posing essentially the same questions: 'are you with us, or with Mubarak?', and 'if you're against Mubarak, will you join us?' Based on my own observations, I would argue that it was the hundreds of thousands who returned each night to their friends, families and workmates, and put those questions to bring reinforcements to the Square, who were the driving force behind the uprising.

The final point concerns the transforming impact of being there, as opposed to virtual observation from a distance. It is difficult to convey in words the intoxicating, beautiful collective madness of Tahrir. Madness, because the people in the Square, and elsewhere all over Egypt, dared to take on one of the oldest and cruellest states in the world, and armed with little more than their bare hands, tore a great hole in the miserable fabric of their everyday lives to create a kind of alternative reality. Beautiful, because it contained so many possibilities for a different society, without fear, without censorship and repression, without religious hatred, even without sexual harassment. From outside the Square, even once within Egypt, this bubble of potentialities looked small and besieged. Inside, my perspectives shifted to include an understanding of revolution as a process of self-transformation, inspiring millions of people to discover in their capacity to change the world. Ironically, the super-saturation of digital images of the protests did not diminish the status of the eye-witness, and perhaps even enhanced it.

—SMS— Sent: Feb 5, 2011 2:53 PM. Subject: Passed queue of hundreds waiting… Passed queue of hundreds waiting to enter sq. Bin bags piled up neatly by a burnt out car. We hv to move quickly area full of security police. my guides feel it too risky to enter sq now. conversation buzzes with tension, stories of attcks on human rights centres, friends arrested, journalists beaten. Fear, but also hope. He'll go, my guides say. for sure he'll go. Sent using BlackBerry® from Orange.

Saturday 5 February. We approached Tahrir Square from the North West. Blackened cars and police trucks were piled up along the side of the road. We turned along the river, with the burnt-out hulk of the NDP head-quarters looming over us. Graffiti covered the walls—the symbol of the cross and crescent and the words 'we are all against the regime'. The windows were twisted outwards from the heat of the fire which consumed the building from within.

—SMS— Sent: Feb 5, 2011 6:47 PM. Subject: Al jazeera re-porting army trying… Al jazeera reporting army trying to

```
clear tahrir sq. hv heard separately a snr army officer
tried to persuade them to leave and the crowd shouted
him down. Sent using BlackBerry® from Orange
```

At a friend's house later that evening, heated arguments broke out about next steps for the movement between those who have been to the Square and those still wavering, undecided about whether to join in. In the streets people were asking how long it will go on. 'What do the protestors want? They've achieved their demands now. The ones who are staying are the ones who don't have any jobs to go to'. That's what people outside are saying.

Sunday 6 February: We crossed the river on the 6 October bridge, passing tanks parked by the side of the road, soldiers leaning on the parapet, their rifles slumped by their sides. We cut down a side alley into Champollion Street. A few hundred yards down the street the first line of the square's defenders is stretched, arms linked, across the road. A single rank of men, mostly young. We showed IDs and passed the first checkpoint. Young women in hijab frisked the women and checked their bags, the men passed through another checkpoint. We weave our way between barricades built with the steel fence from a nearby building site.

Turning the corner from the end of Champollion Street, the Museum loomed up on our right on the other side of the square. Round again to where the pavement widens out in front of KFC. Smiles and hugs from comrades meeting here. Sitting in a circle on the floor were activists from the Revolutionary Socialists organising their intervention in the square. First topic of discussion: how to respond to the swirling rumours about committees being formed by the opposition parties to 'negotiate' with the regime. 'We need a short statement, putting the arguments against any negotiation before Mubarak goes. Agitational, just a paragraph. It needs to catch the mood of the people here—not a long-winded statement in the name of a party'. 'Who's going to write it?' A volunteer is quickly found and discussion moves on. 'Our intervention around the sound systems is really important. We need a list of comrades who can go up and lead the chants, talk to the crowd'. A list of names was compiled and agreed. 'There will be a funeral for a colleague from the journalist union who was killed. The demonstration will start at the union building—who's going to cover that?' Some nods, a quick discussion, a bite of warm sandwich, and the group dispersed into the crowd.

—SMS— Sent: Feb 6, 2011 10:57 AM. Subject: A christian song is blaring out… A christian song is blaring out ovr the square in preparation for sunday prayers. The crowd is chanting revolution thawra thawra. They r corecting a spkr who had said this is a demonstration. Sent using BlackBerry® from Orange

My friend went to join the group working round the sound systems. 'You go and look round the square, we'll meet later', and he disappeared into the thickening crowd. I wandered towards one of the stages. I chatted to an elderly woman holding a hand-written sign. 'My name is Zaynab', she said, tears starting in her eyes. 'We have waited so long for freedom'. 'How long have you been here?' I asked. 'Four days. We are sleeping in a mosque nearby, but our home is in Shubra'. Her son took our picture on his mobile phone.

I jumped onto the raised traffic island to talk to some men holding a blue banner. Two cog wheels around a red flame. 'Suez governorate. Around 5,000 came from Suez to defend the square. We came by public transport when we heard about the attacks'. Suez was still largely under popular control, they told me. 'The police have disappeared from the city, but the army is there and the popular committees. They cut communications, the Internet, phones, everything. We just organised ourselves, nobody had to tell us what to do. Everyone is fighting together against the system which oppresses us'.

—SMS— Sent: Feb 6, 2011 11:26 AM. Subject: Thousands here still, Thousands here still, prob tens of thousands. People milling abt chanting listening to speeches arguing debating. Real sense of a democracy of a new kind beginning to emerge. Demands and slogans are put to the crowds and adopted or rejected by acclaim. Sent using BlackBerry® from Orange

Tent cities had sprung on the grass in the traffic islands. Shelters cobbled together from advertising hoardings, rush mats and debris from the street. Everywhere was hung with placards and hand written signs. In the spaces between the crowd, people made their own art: slogans written out in the stones left over from the battles with the regime thugs, or demands spelt out with koshari tubs and plastic tea cups. A group surrounded a picture drawn on the ground in sand and ashes, ringed with black bin bags. 'Mubarak's face, ya gama'a. Spit on him, spit on him' shouted a man, gesturing proudly. Since this is Egypt, there was plenty of humour. A pile of rubbish in black bags was topped with a hand-written placard reading 'National Democratic Party HQ'. The blackened hulk of the real NDP headquarters loomed darkly in the distance, a few hundred metres across the square.

—SMS— Sent: Feb 6, 2011 11:43 AM. Subject: A boy who looks to be abt 8 or 9… A boy who looks to be abt 8 or 9 is declaiming poetry to a crowd of thousands. 'Brave lad, brave lad' shouts the man behind. We start talking. 'people in britain must know that we r united. Men and women together. When we hang mubarak from the lamppost it will b the women who go first. We've renamed this mar- tyrs of freedom sq. We will not leave it'. Sent using BlackBerry® from Orange

A man in a jacket began to speak as the chants died away. 'Who is he?' I asked. 'Someone from the church, a priest. We are all in this together. Muslims and Christians'. Other people listened and nodded. 'One hand, one hand', the crowd roared. This time they were not talking about the people and the army, but about Muslims and Christians: one hand. The sign of the crescent embracing the cross was everywhere: from the careful calligraphy of the handmade placards to scrawled graffiti on the burnt out NDP headquarters. I saw three elderly men, two of them Muslims clutch- ing gilded copies of the Qu'ran, their arms flung around a third who hugged an ornate cross to his chest.

—SMS— Sent: Feb 6, 2011 11:51 AM. Subject: A spker says we r muslims and… A spker says we r muslims and chris- tians tgthr. The crowd yells bk 'one fist' 'victory to the egyptian rev' and allahu akbar. Now everyone is sing- ing as a helicopter circles lazily overhead. 'i love you my country. Peace peace'.

Round the back of one of the stages I caught up with my friend. He was leading the chanting, arms spread as if to embrace the square. The sound system ran on a generator, since there was no electricity. This stage was organised by the Left, the one to the right belonged to the Ikhwan. 'But we go over and lead the chants for the Ikhwan too', said my friend with a smile. 'They aren't very good at chanting; we have more inventive slogans'. The stage buzzed with activity. A group of young men and women belted out a song of the 1919 revolution, accompanied by a guitar. 'Arise O Egypt, arise. Arise Egyptians: Muslims, Christians and Jews'. Statements, slogans, announcements scribbled on slips of paper were passed up and read out.

—SMS— Sent: Feb 6, 2011 3:36 PM. Subject: A friend says 'all the songs… A friend says 'all the songs changed their meaning, b4 we used to sing them on our own. They were communist, nationalist songs, but we sang them to ourselves. Now the crowd shouts them bk to us till the stones echo with them'. Sent using BlackBerry® from Orange

Dusk was starting to gather as I returned to the square. We moved back towards KFC. My friend grabs a pile of leaflets from a comrade—the statement against negotiations agreed at the meeting in the morning is being handed out among the crowd.

—SMS— Sent: Feb 6, 2011 3:35 PM. Subject: Fear. Fear. People the square are conscious of the gap opening up btwn the heart of the rev in the sq and the rest of the city. 'I am afraid we will not win' says a man in his twenties 'the americans are with the regime. In here we r strong but r the people outside with us still? I dont kno?'. Sent using BlackBerry® from Orange

Back at my friend's house late that evening it was clear that the revolutionary wave was beginning to fracture the pro-regime media. The privately-owned Egyptian satellite channels were now reporting openly and sympathetically on the uprising. The ebb and flow of the battle for the front pages of the print media was visible in the slew of newspapers scattered over the living room table. *Al-Ahram's* front page was covered with crowd scenes from Tahrir, but just visible underneath was a copy from a few days earlier, still vainly trumpeting pro-Mubarak demonstrations. The urgent beats of Mohamed Mounir's new song *Izzay*, an anthem for the revolution complete with YouTube style video, interrupted conversation. 'Fantastic', beamed my friend. 'My sister will come to Tahrir tomorrow for sure. She loves Mohamed Mounir'.

Facebook after Mubarak

The fall of Mubarak on 11 February did not bring an end to the revolution. The newly-awakened political energies of the millions who participated in the uprising were transferred to other domains, particularly their workplaces and local neighbourhoods. A deluge of strikes and protests washed through all sectors of the Egyptian economy after Mubarak's fall. Calls for *tathir* (the 'cleansing' of corrupt officials) intertwined with social demands for improved pay and conditions. In a vast number of workplaces, employees played out the drama of the uprising against their managers, often citing the role of State Security or Mubarak's National Democratic Party in senior appointments as justification.

The deepening of the revolutionary process through its eruption into Egyptians' everyday lives has, at the time of writing this article, produced contradictory results. On the one hand, the uprising has, for the time being, opened democratic spaces for mass political action which the generals ruling Egypt since the fall of Mubarak have found it difficult to suppress. And in some places, this ferment of organising from below has produced tangible results in reconfiguring relations of power in the workplace in radical ways. One example is the experience of the staff at Manshiyet al-Bakri General Hospital, who, through their newly-founded independent union, sacked the corrupt hospital director and ran a democratic election for his successor. On the other hand, by late May, Mubarak's generals in the Supreme Military Council had conceded few substantial political changes, and no significant social reforms, and were showing increasing willingness to use repression against protests and strikes.

These contradictions have left their traces in the digital media Egyptians use to communicate in their everyday lives. Facebook is awash with revolutionary initiatives, ranging from the black humour of mock-tribute pages to the dissolved State Security apparatus, through a bubbling mass of new parties and causes, to the local Committees to Defend the Revolution, the Doctors' Higher Strike Committee and the pages campaigning for the abolition of daylight saving time (one popular demand the Supreme Council of the Armed Forces has been happy to concede). YouTube buzzes with the traces of protests, marches, sit-ins, strikes and meetings. Some of these new political organisations still use digital platforms as tools to aggregate and visualise collective dissent, as testing grounds for new ideas, and as relatively protected spaces where it is possible to say the unsayable, just as they did before the revolution.

The *Officers For the Revolution* Facebook page is a striking example of the complex interaction between digital social media and offline protest. The page, created on 6 March 2011, claims to be the collective voice of a group of serving officers in the Egyptian army. According to the 'Description' in the 'Info' section the page owners:

'Swear by Almighty God that we are officers in the Egyptian Army, who join our voices and our demands to those of the Egyptian people, support-ing the principles of the revolution, and determined, God willing, to implement its demands in a peaceful manner. We do not have particular or sectional aims, nor will we carry any weapon, or release a single projectile to defend our peaceful and clear ideas. Our weapons are the truth and faith in God, may God be our witness'.

According the page's 'Info' section:

'The implementation of all the legitimate demands of the revolution is the aim of all honourable army officers. We fear for our country and pro-tect her and our people. We pledge that we will bring them to safety, God willing'.

These rather bland and open-ended statements have since been elabo-rated in a series of comments and statements articulating an increasingly radical critique of the Supreme Military Council and other military institu-tions. Communiqué No. 1 of the Officers for the Revolution, which was posted as a 'note' attached to the page at 19.05 on 6 March, listed a series of specific demands, including the immediate arrest of senior figures in the former ruling party such as Safwat Sharif and Fathi Surur, the transfer of Hosni, Suzanne, Gamal and Ala'a Mubarak and Omar Suleiman to house arrest in Cairo pending trial, a pardon for Major Ahmad Shuman, who shot to prominence during the uprising when he joined demonstrators in Tahrir in calling on Mubarak to resign, improvements in the conditions of officers and soldiers, and the replacement of senior figures in the Television and Broadcasting Authority associated with the old regime.

The page rapidly acquired a significant audience in Facebook terms. By 20 March it was 'liked' by over 1,200 people, and by 8 April that number had swelled to over 12,000, jumping a further 2,000 to over 14,000 by the end of the following week. At the end of May, the number of 'likes' stood at 16,571. The page's owners were increasingly active in posting to their wall towards the end of this period, contributing a mixture of reposted material from other campaigns, political organisations, social and mainstream media, with their own commentary and formal statements. These postings frequently attracted dozens of comments from a wide range of individual contributors.

The page's existence is extraordinary in itself, if it genuinely represents a public expression of dissent by serving army officers. And even if the page owners are not themselves officers, their criticism of Marshal Tantawi and the Supreme Military Council was far more radical than most organised political currents in Egypt were prepared to articulate in public, although the rapid growth in the page's popularity could be taken as evidence of the existence of a significant audience for these ideas.

Since its creation, the Officers for the Revolution page has been used for a variety of purposes by its owners. It has been used simultaneously as a means for communicating the page owners' ideas and a mechanism for building an audience for those ideas. They have also used the page to disseminate information and ideas from other sources. Sometimes this has taken the form of commentary on reposted material, at other times the straightforward re-dissemination of information about protests, campaigns and strikes. Unsurprisingly, many of these campaigns have a specific focus on the military, including a large amount of material about protests (both online and offline) in support of officers facing disciplinary action. The page owners frequently urge participation in offline events directly through comments and 'notes'. The page seems to have a further function for its owners as a space for discussion. It is not uncommon for the page owners to repost comments from visitors to the page wall thus giving them greater prominence and inviting further comments. The owners' comments themselves often include polemics against opinions they disagree with.

One of the important threads in the dialogue between the page's owners and their civilian audience has been a debate about the role of the military police. From the beginning, the page owners have been vocal in their criticism of the military police, and insistent on their role as a tool of repression within the armed forces. The first comment to mention the military police on 10 March at 18.45 asserts that the military police has been carrying out 'acts of illegal repression' against army officers, including arresting and detaining them for 'trivial reasons'. A longer comment, on 13 March at 17.54, elaborated further:

'The Military Police is a repressive military apparatus which has been used against the military over the past twenty years. Its presence was the most important reason for low morale of officers and rank-and-file soldiers in the armed forces'.

Another post later the same evening promised that the military police would be held accountable for acts of torture and repression.

'To the revolutionaries of Egypt's great people: record the names of those among the military police who torture you and who issue orders against you. Torture is not acceptable and those responsible will be held accountable with criminal charges of physical torture and psychological violence against the honourable citizens among this people'.

Reports in the media which failed to make the distinction between the military police and the wider armed forces earned critical comments from the page owners. On 2 April at 07.26, above a report reposted from the BBC Arabic website giving details of testimonies from activists who had been tortured, the page owners wrote:

'This is a disgrace ... They don't say the military police, they say it is "the army"'.

The importance of the page as a tool for aggregating and visualising collective dissent, and as a space for the discussion of topics which cross the 'red line' of political acceptability in the mainstream media is magnified in the current context in Egypt. Criticism of the army in general, and the Supreme Military Council in particular, was inhibited in the early days of the revolution by a number of factors. The army played little direct role in repression in the pre-revolutionary era, and thus when troops were mobilised on 28 January following the defeat of Interior Ministry forces and their withdrawal from the streets, the army's intervention was welcomed by the vast majority of protestors. The army's role in removing Mubarak from power was also viewed positively by the majority of Egyptians.

It is tempting to emphasise the similarities between the post-revolutionary and pre-revolutionary uses of Facebook, with *Officers for the Revolution* playing a similar role, albeit on a smaller scale, to the large Facebook groups and pages such as the *6 April Youth Movement* and *We are all Khaled Said* which first aggregated and made visible collective dissent online, then acted as forums for debate, and finally became tools for organising offline collective action. However, there is a fundamental difference between *Officers for the Revolution* and the pre-revolutionary Facebook pages, in that it was the mass protests of the popular uprising itself which created the crisis within the army and prompted the creation of the page and the political organisation behind it. Continuing demonstrations, many on a huge scale by pre-revolutionary standards, and interventions by the military leadership against protestors, form a new political context in which the page's owners and visitors must operate.

The continuing primacy of the dynamics of street protest was graphically confirmed by events on the night of 8–9 April. On 8 April Tahrir Square filled with protesters demanding the 'cleansing' of the country and the speeding up of prosecution of key figures from the old regime. It was also the first time that groups of army officers had openly joined the protests, addressing the crowds from the stage and leading chants. The *Officers for the Revolution* page announced at 18.22 that a group of officers was taking part in an attempt by a section of the crowd to hold the square overnight. One of the young officers read out a statement on behalf of 'the honourable officers', calling for the dissolution of the Supreme Military Council and its replacement by a civilian presidential council, the resignation of Marshal Tantawi, the minister of defence and military production, and prosecutions of those responsible for killing and injuring protesters during the uprising.

'We are not here for personal or sectional interests', explained Muhammad Mahmud Ahmad al-Hifni, a first lieutenant, to a video journalist from the daily paper al-Masry al-Yawm. 'I came to reassure people that I'm one of them. I was born in this country and I want to die here. I want to say to people that it is the army that protects the people, and the people who protect the army. I'm aware of the dangers. I want to say to every officer in the army, "You're not less than me, you are honourable too. Stand up. Enough of fear and silence. Say what you think."'

Tragically, however, the weight of numbers joining the protest camp proved too little to resist the attack launched by the military police and security forces in the early hours. After an intense battle in which hundreds were injured and an unconfirmed number killed, the Square was cleared of demonstrators. Although anyone reading the Facebook page could see the notice about the officers' intention to join the protest camp, it seemed that not enough of the crowd from earlier in the day was willing to stay with them, or were even aware of their presence.

On this occasion the protesters lost the battle for the streets, and the *Officers for the Revolution* retreated to cyberspace. Yet the brutal crackdown was itself another step towards the erosion of support for the Supreme Council of the Armed Forces. In late May a large scale mobilisation for a second 'Day of Rage' brought hundreds of thousands into the streets across Egypt, the ceaseless energy of the mass movement from below preventing Mubarak's old generals from turning the clock back to 24 January.

As Gil Scott-Heron once famously remarked, the fate of revolutions is not determined by the ways in which they are mediated. Revolutions are always 'live'.

FEMALE AND FIGHTING

Fadia Faqir

Arab women play a crucial role in the revolutions sweeping the region, but most men are not supportive of them and do not see the 'woman question' as crucial. Not one single slogan in all the uprisings is concerned with the inferior position of women or calls for parity between the sexes. Men still prioritise sovereignty and democracy over gender equality. There is a widespread belief in the Arab world, among most men and some women, that females are inferior. A number of intertwined historical, religious, political and social factors are behind this conviction. Many see women as lesser beings, weak and impressionable, who therefore cannot be trusted with the grave responsibilities of full citizenship and leadership.

Women's contribution to the popular protests that have swept the Arab world is energetic and inspiring and flies in the face of the above assumptions. Some of the bravest Arabs battling for a democratic future are women. They are doctors, lawyers, writers and human rights activists, among others.

The image of the silent and oppressed Arab woman was totally shattered when the twenty-year-old Bahraini poet Ayat Al-Qormezi read her poem in Tahrir Square. It was an amazing act of courage and defiance. She called for King Hamad Al-Khalifa's resignation and openly challenged his oppressive rule. 'Bahrain is not owned by Al Khalifa. It is my Bahrain', she said. As soon as she returned to Bahrain she went into hiding. The security forces coerced the Qormezi family into disclosing her whereabouts. On 31 March she was arrested and her family have heard no word from her since. Her mother, devastated, recorded a heart-rending plea for her release on YouTube, and it went viral. She also spoke to the international media begging for mercy for her daughter. She, like many other Arab mothers, was pushed into activism and visibility by her plight. When the family started searching for Ayat the police told them they had no information about her and tried to force them to sign a letter stating that their daughter had gone missing. In mid-April, an anonymous call was made to the Qormezi family informing them that Ayat was ill. Doctors confirmed that Ayat had gone into a coma after being raped several times. (Ayat has since been imprisoned for one year). Many other women, including doctors, university professors and students, have been kidnapped or arrested by the Bahraini security forces.

Libyan women work side by side with men to keep the revolution alive, society and economy functioning, and the uprising visible. They are fighting on the many fronts, organising popular committees, feeding families and nursing the sick. They also address the public and aid the international media herds. On 8 March, International Women's Day, thousands of women took to the streets in Benghazi to call for freedom, to clamour for peace, and to honour their dead. There is no doubt that women in Libya are the backbone of the revolutionary movement.

In Egypt, twenty-six-year-old Asmaa Mahfouz, a computer company employee and now a prominent member of Egypt's Coalition for the Youth Revolution, has been credited with having sparked the protests that began the 25 January uprising. In a video blog posted on Facebook on 18 January, she called on Egyptians to demand their human rights and to voice their disapproval of Hosni Mubarak's regime. She challenged Egyptians to take to the streets, saying, 'If you think yourself a man, come with me on 25 January. Whoever says women shouldn't go to protests because they will get beaten, let him have some honour and manhood and come with me on 25 January. Whoever says it is not worth it because there will only be a handful of people, I want to tell him, "You are the reason behind this, and you are a traitor, just like the president or any security policeman who beats us in the streets."' She appeared wearing the veil and her message was in harmony with her prescribed role as a Muslim woman.

The same tactic has been adopted by thirty-year-old Yemeni activist Tawakul Abdel Salam Karman. Karman is a journalist, a staunch defender of freedom of the press, an advocate for human rights, and a member of the Islamist party Islah. On 23 January, Yemeni officials detained Salam Karman for leading protests at the university in Sana'a in support of the Tunisian revolution and calling for the ousting of President Ali Abdallah Saleh, who has ruled the country with an iron fist for over thirty years. As a result of violent street protests that erupted against her arrest, the government soon released Salam Karman from detention.

Bringing to mind the Mothers of the Plaza de Mayo (of the 'disappeared') in Argentina, hundreds of Syrian women marched along the country's main coastal highway to demand the release of men seized from their home town of Baida, where the police beat and kicked handcuffed detainees on camera. This was one of many protests organised by Syrian women.

Many Arab women activists appear wearing a hijab. Although their messages are beamed through modern modes of communication and have a reformist agenda, they are clothed literally and metaphorically in traditional dress. Women's movements in the past were led by secular feminists. This tactic of exploiting and subverting 'traditional' images and roles of woman in the service of the revolution can be found in a number of women's movements in the region. It is a point of departure for Arab and Muslim women.

But no matter how much women conformed to their prescribed role or manoeuvred within what is expected and acceptable, many saw their presence in the public domain as a necessary and temporary evil. During the uprisings in Tunisia and Egypt most women were merely figureheads and some were used as mascots to mobilise men, but when the dust settled they were asked to go back to the kitchen. An Egyptian woman who took part in the uprising in Tahrir Square was worried. 'The men were keen for me to be here when we were demanding that Mubarak should go', she told Catherine Ashton in Cairo. 'But now he has gone, they want me to go home'.

After demonstrating on the streets women went home to archaic familial hierarchies. One of the most important institutions in the Arab world is the family, where patterns of oppression are normally produced and reproduced. Hisham Sharabi argues that the extended family is normally ruled by the father, who perceives his children as an extension of himself. The Arab child is oppressed by his father and is over-protected by his mother. 'Paternal domination can only be disabled by women emancipated through a complete restructuring of the nuclear family'. Drawing women into active participation in decision-making bodies starts by changing the family structure to make it more egalitarian. This will gradually be reflected in other institutions in society. As familial structures are revised, then other societal structures will follow.

Moreover, all citizens of the Arab world, whether male or female, have obligations towards the state, but do not enjoy many political, civil and social rights. Female citizens are less equal than their male counterparts. The majority of Arab women are second-class citizens, dependent and subordinate. As an illustration, some women in Jordan were energised and inspired by the uprisings and decided to divorce their abusive husbands, only to find that the whole system was tipped against them. Similar to many other Arab countries, women in Jordan cannot pass on their citizenship to their children or husbands; they are still discriminated against by the legal system and the judiciary; they need permission from their legal guardians to choose their place of residence or to join the labour market. Their right to divorce is still not included in the Personal Status Law, which is mostly based on selective interpretation of the Qur'an and the *hadith* (prophet Mohammad's sayings and deeds).

The recent remarks made by President Ali Abdullah Saleh condemning women's participation in public protests as being un-Islamic reflects the secondary status of Yemeni women. Gender discrimination in Yemen is practised and sanctioned by law. The Personal Status Law calls for 'wifely obedience', allows marital rape, reinforces stereotypes about women's roles as caretakers within the home and severely restricts women's freedom of movement. And most restrictions are imposed in the name of Islam, which some would argue is either patriarchal or has functioned under patriarchy for so long that it has been tarnished by it.

In every Arab country you find what Leila Ahmed dubbed 'Establishment Islam'. It is a technical and legalistic version of Islam that largely bypasses the ethical thrust of early Islam and its humane and egalitarian spirit. There are many manifestations of this narrow and selective interpretation of the Qur'an and hadith. For example, Saad al-Husseini, a member of the Egyptian Muslim Brotherhood's Guidance Bureau, its highest executive body, stated that while the Freedom and Justice party's new platform must still be approved by the Guidance Office and its Shura Consultative Council, it will adhere to the Muslim Brotherhood's long-held position on the presidency. They believe that women and non-Muslims cannot rule Muslim men. In other words neither a Coptic Christian nor a woman can be elected president of Egypt.

A large majority of Tunisia's High Commission, which is responsible for planning the 24 July elections, voted to ensure parity between men and women in the membership of the National Constituent Assembly. Electoral lists must have an equal number of male and female candidates to be accepted. However, Islamists, who are becoming more vocal in post-revolution Tunisia, pointed out that women should earn their political rights by merit and should not be granted automatic access to political positions by the application of positive discrimination. The debate is heated and the jury is out on this issue. Khadija Cherif, a feminist activist, said to America's National Public Radio that the return of Islamist parties to Tunisian politics could pose a threat, but women will remain vigilant. 'The force of the Tunisian feminist movement is that we've never separated it from the fight for democracy and a secular society. We will continue our combat, which is to make sure that religion remains completely separate from politics'. Even if the next elections bring in Islamic parties, their manifesto must be inclusive and egalitarian otherwise women's space in the emerging democracies will be defined and restricted by a narrow reading of religious canons. In other words, mosque and state must be separate.

Traditional forces, whether secular or religious, might curtail the role women could play in future democracies. If traditional forces triumph then women's rights will be last on the agenda and will perhaps be traded off in any future brokering for power. Moreover, fundamental issues related to women and their rights have yet to be addressed. Although the picture is grim the possibilities are endless in this period of transition. Equal rights for all citizens are a by-product of democracy, but the road to achieving that in the Arab world is long and winding. The future is unknown and unmapped.

Despite the challenges, women continue to be political within the neo-patriarchal and mostly authoritarian context. They are calling for a form of democracy in which they can play as great a role as men. However, there are worrying signs that this may be denied to them. Tackling women's rights is key to unleashing liberal and modernist forces in the Arab world, but old practices and prejudices prevail. The eradication of discrimination—whether on grounds of gender, race, religion or sexuality—is the only road to full citizenship rights. Participatory democracy requires not only the right to form political parties, freedom of expression, and fair elections, but the willingness to accept the other's point of view regardless of their gender.

The fact is that participatory democracy cannot be achieved without elevating women to the status of full citizenship. Democracy, women's liberation and equality are intimately connected and have in common a concern with freedom both personal and civic, human rights, integrity, dignity, autonomy, power-sharing, and pluralism. Women's emancipation leads to emancipation for other groups within the political polity. The 'women's question' is as important as sovereignty and democracy. No future state can be called democratic if personal and group freedoms are limited.

The Arab spring will not endure, the shoots planted will not grow, without liberating the 'last colony': Arab women.

PARTING THE WATERS

Jamal Mahjoub

Following the division of the country on 9 July 2011, the mood in the Sudanese capital Khartoum is one of dazed uncertainty. For years the North had taken comfort in the popular illusion that the South would never break away; that no matter how badly they were treated, the Nuer and smaller ethnic groups would prefer to take their chances in the North rather than fall under the domination of the larger ethnic groups in the South, most notably the Dinka who make up 40 per cent. But a resounding 98 per cent vote in favour of separation left the North in a stupor and put paid to that particular myth. It also provided some insight into the way the ruling National Congress Party (NCP) works, more by a process of knee-jerk reaction than any kind of strategy or vision. Apparently nobody saw separation coming. Just two months before January's referendum, Bashir's vice-president Ali Osman Taha reportedly stated that it would never happen.

It was Taha who negotiated the terms of the Comprehensive Peace Agreement (CPA) with John Garang, unity being the unquestioned goal towards which both sides were working. The clause stipulating the South's right to hold a referendum on its independence was included only at the last minute as a mere formality, a concession to the secessionists in the southern ranks with whom Garang had long been at odds. His twenty-one-year war against Khartoum had always been aimed at uniting the people of the country in a 'New Sudan', one in which all were equal regardless of race, tribe or creed. That dream died with him when his helicopter came down in July 2005 in the Zulia Mountains on the border with Uganda, just three weeks after being instated as vice-president of the interim Government of National Unity.

The uncertainty caused by the partition of the country may explain in part at least why we have not seen the kind of uprising witnessed by Sudan's northerly neighbours during the Arab Spring. There is endless speculation around the capital about the reasons for this absence of revolt. Sudan's current rulers, after all, have occupied the throne for twenty two years, only six years less than Egypt's despised and now deposed Mubarak, and Bashir's grip is a lot less firm than that of many other rulers who are currently being shaken by the unrest. It may be a matter of timing. Bashir remains surprisingly buoyant and popular. Many of those who admit to voting for him in last year's shambles of an election claim to have done so to avoid inviting further chaos. This is the same argument that has been used everywhere, including Egypt, to stifle change.

Khartoum, people will proudly tell you, has a tradition of civil uprisings; 1985 when then president Jaifar Nimeiri went, and before that October 1964—a popular revolution that has since achieved legendary status in the minds of Sudanese. But so far nothing has been seen on the streets of the capital to suggest a repeat is imminent. Supporters of the NCP are eager to point out that there is no need for a revolt, that unlike in Egypt and Tunisia, Islam has been the source of political ideology in Sudan since the coup of June 1989—indeed, it was arguably so before that. Nevertheless, in an attempt to defuse any possible tension, a spokesperson for Bashir made clear in February that the President would step down in 2015. Considering the problems facing the country, it is difficult to imagine anyone wanting to step into his shoes.

On the 9 July 30 heads of state and 160 dignitaries gathered in Juba to observe the raising of the new flag. What happens next is anyone's guess. The fear that war will break out again between North and South still lingers. The escalating violence in Abyei, where recently hundreds have been killed and thousands displaced, suggests that the potential for a full blown conflict is still there. It is not a course that Khartoum wants to take, and a withdrawal of army troops is currently underway. The world is watching and Bashir is not particularly interested in antagonising anyone, least of all Washington, until US trade sanctions are lifted. Efforts to improve relations with the United States have been continuing since the early post-9/11 days. On a personal level, Bashir has to play his cards carefully if he does not want to wind up on the ICC bench in the Hague.

Those concerned about a resurgence of North-South conflict include George Clooney, who has kindly stepped in to help set up the Satellite Sentinel Project to monitor the 2000 km borderline. 'We are the anti-genocide paparazzi', Clooney told Time magazine in December 2010. 'We want them to enjoy the level of celebrity attention that I usually get'. The signs are, however, that the new front line between North and South, 80 per cent of which is agreed in principle, is more likely to serve as a division of Sudan's eternal problems into two internally conflicted halves.

In the South a worrying series of clashes has begun to unfold. Long-standing distrust has been compounded by decades of war, the breakdown of civil society and the presence of large numbers of armed men facing redundancy with no skills other than their fighting abilities. The potential for lawlessness seems high. The role of Jonglei State Governor George Athor in instigating clashes between the SPLA and Nuer fighters in February calls into question the ability of the southern government to maintain stability. Three hundred soldiers were killed. Athor is rumoured to be supported by Khartoum in an effort to foment conflict—a charge he denies. These clashes between armed factions look set to continue and are lending weight to the possibility of the South dissolving into internecine ethnic conflict.

It was these old ethnic or tribal hatreds which John Garang sought to overcome with his notion of a New Sudan—a nation that would transcend racial, ethnic and religious differences. It was a bold aim and even those who were close to Garang question whether he would have been able to achieve it had he lived. It was the only ideology which addressed the true source of the country's conflicts. Without his presence, however, the SPLM has struggled to convince both North and South of the benefits of unity and has squandered much of the opportunity offered by the last six years of peace.

Dividing the country was never going to be easy and it is the sticky middle belt around South Kordofan and Blue Nile states which threatens to become a 'new' South Sudan within the North. In particular it is the disputed Abyei area which has seen most of the armed clashes in the last few years. Abyei's ambiguous status remains undecided and is further charged by the fact that it has been the centre of oil production for the last decade. A referendum due to be held in January 2011 to decide whether it would join the South or remain in the North was cancelled. Abyei is further complicated by population displacements that date back to 1905 under British rule. And there is more conflict in neighbouring South Kordofan, where an aggressive Islamisation policy carried out in the Nuba Mountains in the 1990s has left a bitter legacy. The tension is exacerbated by the presence of thousands of SPLA fighters under the command of Abd al Aziz Adam al-Hilu, a fierce opponent of Khartoum. Al-Hilu refused to recognise the results of May's dubious state elections for governor, which were won by the notorious Ahmed Haroun, who was indicted by the ICC along with Bashir for his part in war crimes in Darfur.

Secession really marks the end of the idyllic hiatus ushered in by the CPA in 2005. Ending four decades of civil war, the CPA offered an opportunity to address the underlying issues which had led to almost uninterrupted conflict in the country since independence in 1956. Tensions between the two parties in the interim government produced more bickering than effectiveness and few steps were taken to strengthen bonds between North and South. Oil revenue provided a welcome diversion and the lack of transparency encouraged corruption.

Partition for those Southerners who were born or have lived most or all of their lives in the North is a painful proposition, and the question of their status is only one of several unresolved issues in the terms of the split. The political inertia in the capital is also partly explained by the fact that the last six years created a sense of false stability and economic growth thanks to the wealth flowing from oil revenue. The former united Sudan currently produces some 475,000 barrels a day. High prices on the world oil market and direct foreign investment in the country meant that GDP growth continued to climb until 2007, when it peaked at 10 per cent. The boom years produced a new class of well-heeled Sudanese who profited from the money in circulation. They were able to afford a comfortable lifestyle as new cars, chic cafés and ridiculously expensive restaurants proliferated. The influx of a foreign labour force bringing much needed skills into the country only reinforced local perceptions of superiority.

Post partition, some 80 per cent of the oil lies south of the new border. And despite the fact that the South will remain dependent on the pipeline and refineries that deliver the oil to the Red Sea, the North is set to see a sharp drop in income over the coming years. There are rumours of other deposits in the North, but these remain untried as yet. North Sudan faces the prospect of falling into an economic trough, compounded by political isolation, particularly if there is a resurgence of war. Already, the rising star of the new state's capital in Juba has seen foreign missions, international agencies and organisations moving part or all of their operation to the South. Property prices around the North's capital have started to fall, further slowing the economy. The boom also served to obscure the almost complete absence of a long term government strategy. Over-reliance on oil money combined with a lack of initiative and lack of investment in institutions, education, healthcare, and infrastructure, has left the country in a vulnerable state. To overcome the inertia the North urgently needs political renewal, a strategy that will take advantage of the oil revenue while it lasts to invest in the country's future. Currently, 70 per cent of the budget is spent on defence, which is less a commitment to further conflict than a sad lack of imagination.

After twenty-two years of domination by Bashir, the political spectrum has narrowed. Opposition is limited largely to older, traditional parties bound to Islamic sects which have all tried and failed in the past to provide the kind of unity, vision and leadership the country desperately needs. There are no signs that the loss of the South has prompted any change of heart. On the contrary, there are rumours that hardliners in the ruling NCP wish to press for a more strictly Islamic state, and the signs are that it will continue to aggressively pursue the notion of Arab-Islamic identity for the whole country. The bombing of Jebel Marra in Darfur along with a stepping up of security forces on the ground would seem to confirm this. And attacks by Darfur rebels the JEM in Heglig suggest that Khartoum could be facing a far more complicated insurgency than it has anticipated.

The increasingly public splits within the ruling National Congress Party are also a concern, hinting that a coup d'état might be closer than many people think. Bashir has a close hold on the reins and over the years has removed power from the regular army and shifted it to an array of security forces. An attempt at a coup in the capital could potentially be disastrous if these factions turned on one another. Fighting in and around Abyei shortly before the July partition, killing hundreds and displacing tens of thousands, along with the air force bombing in South Kordofan, adds to the sensation that the North is heading back to war. This would be a mistake that could prove fatal for the regime. Discontent has grown in recent years within the regular army. And it was the military which pushed for peace in the years leading up to the CPA, after years of fighting a war they could not win.

Partition is not going to bring a solution to the problems, in either of the new halves. And while one might hope that it has brought home to Northerners the urgent necessity of coming to terms with their country's diversity, there is little evidence that this lesson, so long unheeded, will finally have its moment now. But as basic commodity prices continue to rise and discontent grows, time is clearly running out. If the North is not to descend into a maelstrom of warring factions, something is going to have to change. Anyone stepping into Bashir's shoes will have his work cut out. Even if there were a popular revolt tomorrow, it is difficult to see who would want to take on the immense task of turning the country around.

REBELLION IN SYRIA

Shadia Safwan

What is there to say about Syria—on the human level—that hasn't been said? The horror of the atrocities, the rising number of casualties, all of these can have a numbing effect. I remember thinking seven people killed in one day was an awful lot when the protests first started. One Friday in June 2011—it was reported that over sixty people were killed in Hama alone when security forces fired indiscriminately at a protest. One thousand, two thousand; at some point these people just become numbers. Our brains need a practical way to manage the information.

In February 2011 a small altercation with the police in a commercial area of Damascus quickly became a protest. Its slogan, 'The Syrian People will not be humiliated', quickly drew attention. The interior minister drove down to personally assure the protesters that the offending policemen would be punished. Then everybody went home. It seemed that Syria really wasn't going to be affected by the Arab Spring. The illusion faded a few weeks later when police arrested and brutalised a group of school children in Daraa who had been spray-painting popular revolutionary slogans onto the walls. One thing led to another, violence provoking more demonstrations which provoked more violence, and here we are today—it's the first week of June 2011 as I write.

Of all the countries that have been affected by the Arab Spring no country's situation is more complex, nor as confusing, as the one in Syria. At the centre of a nexus which connects Washington, London and Tel Aviv to Beirut and Tehran, Syria has survived in the region by making itself indispensible to any peace process with the Israelis and by capitalising on its 'special relationship' with the Iranian regime. The Syrian regime ensured tight control of its people with an ever watchful security service and apparently considered itself immune from the wave of revolution sweeping the Arab world. In a January interview with the *Wall Street Journal*, President Assad expressed the belief that his policy of 'resistance' against Israel and American hegemony made him sufficiently popular with his people. Two months later Syrians were taking to the streets in ever growing numbers.

At the time of writing, the situation in Syria remains unclear, hidden behind a cloud of misinformation. This is because Syria is the Arab dictatorship *par excellence*, one which has learnt lessons from each Arab regime that has collapsed before it. The first result is the regime's decision to spin a web of lies.

From the start, the Syrian regime was very careful to cultivate an atmosphere of organised chaos. One the one hand, it took careful steps to demonstrate its supposed openness and willingness to change. On the other, it cracked down brutally on any attempt to manifest dissatisfaction on the street. For example, as events in Tunisia, Egypt and Libya unfolded, the Syrian regime hastily announced social welfare programmes and opened access to Facebook and Youtube, previously blocked to Syrian Internet users. To a cross-section of the Syrian population, a narrative of steady and stable reform was cultivated. A number of factors underpinned this narrative, and it is these factors which help us in understanding the fear that many Syrians have of the change that might envelop Syria should the regime be forced from power.

The first fear is of sectarian war. We routinely hear state spokespeople referring to Iraq and Lebanon as examples of what would happen if the regime in Syria should ever fail. This regime, they proclaim, safeguards the rights and security of the minorities that constitute the mosaic of Syrian society.

Many members of the Shia-offshoot Alawi sect—from which the ruling family originates—have genuine fears of the Sunni majority's revenge should the regime collapse. They also remember an unpleasant history: before the growth of nationalism in the twentieth Century, the Alawis were oppressed and isolated. People of all sects fear the blood-spattered chaos which enveloped Iraq after the fall of its dictator.

All well and good, but what many commentators miss are the very different contexts in which the Lebanese and Iraqi wars unfolded. Both conflicts were provoked by outside interventions (Israeli, Palestinian and American) and then fanned quite deliberately by the Syrian regime in order to frustrate imperialist designs. During the successful attempt to force Syrian troops out of Lebanon in 2005, and the failed attempt to destroy Hezbollah in 2006, and the attempt to impose a neo-liberal 'New Middle East' in Iraq following the American invasion, it was clear that the Syrian regime had no qualms about provoking sectarian tensions in both countries in order to improve its hand. So who would provoke sectarian conflict in Syria if the regime no longer existed?

The second fear is that revolutionary Syria will be quickly transformed into an Islamic emirate. Some secularists and Christians, as well as Alawis, Druze and Ismailis, fear the rise of violent Islamists who may limit their personal freedoms or even seek to drive them out of the country. Here the regime builds on popular fears of the Syrian wing of the Muslim Brotherhood, which was guilty of terrorism and sectarian violence in the 1970s and 80s—until it was finally defeated by the even greater violence of the regime (at Hama in 1982, when perhaps 20,000 were killed). The Brotherhood has since regrouped abroad and, apparently, moderated. It has played a negligible part in the uprising, internally at least, yet is cast by state media in the starring role. Regime propaganda also confuses the Muslim Brotherhood with Salafist movements, and vastly overstates the influence of Salafism in Syria.

If the government's narrative is to be accepted at face value, then over an unspecified period of time—perhaps years—Syria has been invaded by Salafi groups that have formed armed networks right under the noses of the security services. As Syria is the most suffocating police state in the region, this is a ridiculous notion to entertain. Considering how impossible it was to express any kind of protest prior to 2011, a critical review of certain events which took place in Syria over the past decade provokes some surprising questions.

What should we make of the protests which targeted the US embassy, the British Council, or the Danish embassy? And what of the 'Salafist' terror attacks against the American embassy, or against the Syrian television station, or against a former UN building in Mezzeh which had been vacated long before the attack? Such quixotic operations go against the grain of typical Salafi attacks in other parts of the world, which usually aim for mass murder through well planned and focused assaults against symbols of power and control. And what were the true motives for the largely symbolic, and mostly irrelevant, law banning the niqab in Syrian educational establishments?

Such questions suggest that the regime has a perverse relationship with Salafism and sectarian conflict in the region.

The official media, albeit clumsily, has fought an intensive campaign to discredit the protestors and the mobile phone footage that is emerging from the besieged towns and streets of Syria. Most famously, the village of Beyda witnessed the abuse and humiliation of a group of young men in the middle of a distinctly recognisable market place. Regime media outlets dismissed the footage as having been filmed in Iraq, with one caller, supposedly a doctor from Baghdad, swearing on the life of his children and the Qur'an that the security forces in the film were Kurdish Peshmerga. Later a young man called Ahmed Baiasy was filmed showing his ID card in the same market, stating firmly that he was standing in the village of Beyda in Syria and that he was one of the young men who had been abused. Baiasy was later arrested. After rumours of his death had been circulated, the Syrian media shot themselves in the foot by interviewing him in person to prove he had not been killed. Simultaneously they confirmed that what they had earlier claimed was a complete fabrication—that the Beyda market incident had indeed taken place in Syria at the hands of regime thugs and the security services.

The most important element in the regime narrative is the lack of an alternative to the Assads. Syrians themselves, it is claimed, as much as the West, need the ruling clique firmly in control, otherwise the entire region risks being destabilised. But this regime discourse is split into domestic and international tracks, and when the two are placed beside each other they are found to be completely at odds.

Internationally, the regime presents itself as a potential partner for peace with Israel, as a secular administration which nevertheless has Iran's ear, and as a force which helps keep Islamist influence at bay. Domestically and on the popular Arab level, Syria portrays itself as a champion of the resistance through its support for Islamic groups such as Hamas and Hezbollah. But the contradiction between the two narratives has become visible only since the start of the uprising. Rami Makhlouf, the president's cousin, gave a controversial interview to *The New York Times* in which he declared that 'stability in Israel is linked to stability in Syria'. The interview was quickly dismissed by Syria's ambassador in Washington as unrepresentative of the official Syrian position, yet on the anniversary of the Nakba (the Catastrophe of the loss of Palestine) the regime unprecedentedly allowed a march of Palestinian refugees to reach the occupied Golan heights, where they proceeded to cross the barriers—one of them got as far as Tel Aviv. When one considers that it is impossible for a Syrian or Palestinian to reach this area without official government clearance, it becomes clear that the event was stage-managed by the regime to deflect attention from the dire domestic situation. It was also a reiteration of the statement made to *The New York Times*, and a message to the West warning it of the consequences should the regime fail.

The regime is assisted by the fact that Syria still does not have an opposition worthy of the name. A series of opposition conferences in Cairo, Antalya and Brussels have only highlighted the divisions plaguing any attempt to form a post-Assad vision for Syria. The Syrian Muslim Brotherhood only grudgingly accepted a statement proclaiming the secular nature of any future Syrian government. The exiled former vice president, Abdul Halim Khaddam, lambasted the Antalya conference for not allowing him to attend. The foreign opposition is a motley crew of exiled Islamists and neo-conservative-leaning liberals, and is largely irrelevant on the ground; every indication is that a domestic nucleus of opposition is emerging. Still, it remains unclear what a post-regime Syria will look like. In this regard, there are no guarantees.

In the byzantine relations that make up Middle East and inter-Arab politics, Syria has emerged as a key player. Naturally this has made it both powerful enemies and powerful friends, neither of whom would particularly like to see the regime go. Either out of pragmatism or due to fear of the unknown, both the Western/Israeli axis and the Iranian/Hezbollah camp would prefer to see Assad ride out this storm. But this does not mean that the regime will succeed in suppressing the protests, far from it.

Machiavellian politics work perfectly against external enemies and traditional challenges, but when social awareness transforms people's perspectives and causes them to rise up against a power structure from within, then Machiavelli is no longer the most effective model. In the face of a massive social uprising such as we are witnessing today, foreign alliances and domestic repression may not be sufficient to prevent the inevitable.

Turkey was until recently a strong ally. In the past decade the Turkish/Syrian relationship expanded into areas of trade and tourism and led to a waiving of visa requirements for Syrians and Turks visiting each others' countries. Turkish Prime Minister Erdogan, however, has been very outspoken concerning the regime's handling of the protests. Turkey did not close its border to refugees escaping feared reprisals by the Syrian army in the Jisr al Shughour area. Whilst the official Turkish position has been very popular with the protestors—some have waved Turkish flags and pro-Erdogan slogans—it has not gone down well with the Assad regime, which has directed its media to attack Turkey. The loss of such a considerable ally is a massive (self-inflicted) blow to the image of credibility and moderation that the regime had been trying to cultivate.

A dramatic split has also opened between Syria and Qatar—leading to the loss of almost $6 billion in Qatari investments—due to what the regime considers biased coverage by the Qatar-based Al-Jazeera news network. The loss of these two key allies, in spite of the staunch support of Iran and Hezbollah, will further isolate Syria. Faced with a domestic challenge it is unable to contain, the regime now faces a hostile international landscape. And as the Libyan example shows, the regime cannot forever count on the support of Russia and China in the UN Security Council.

The saying 'He who does not know history is destined to repeat it' rings especially true for the Syrian regime. Like the Eastern bloc regimes of the twentieth century, Syria is cursed by a heavily bureaucratic and all-pervasive state apparatus, a cult of personality based around the leader, and a dire economy controlled mainly by cronies of the dictator. Over the past forty years the once independent institutions of Syrian government and civil society, whether trade unions or the judiciary, have been completely absorbed into the state apparatus; their sole purpose has been to ensure the survival of the regime. The Syrian parliament, supposedly the supreme legislating body in the country, can do no more than rubber-stamp presidential decisions. Even MPs' traditional immunity from prosecution has been ignored, as in the case of MP Riad Seif, imprisoned for questioning the monopolisation of Syria's first mobile phone company by the Makhlouf family, cousins to the Assads.

Bashaar's belated reforms, touted as major concessions, had no real effect. The abolition of special military courts and the decades-long state of emergency meant nothing on the ground as protestors continued to be arrested and killed by security services. Over 11,000 people are reported to have been incarcerated (by June), some of them kept penned in football stadiums. Whilst the government triumphantly announces laws for new elections and the creation of political parties, large parts of the country remain besieged, without electricity, water or telephone and Internet accessed.

Real concessions would spell the beginning of the end of the regime. Its reform gestures are therefore theatrical, and are understood as such; dramatic announcements of sweeping changes or presidential pardons have failed to curb the protestors' anger. Ultimately, the internal contradictions the state machinery has papered over for decades will cause the state to fall, because it is a badly run state, one that impoverishes its people materially and spiritually. At some point, as with the Eastern-bloc countries in 1989, the house of cards must collapse.

No matter how prolific the propaganda machine, how brutal the state security services, or to what extent the regime diverts attention to the Golan Heights, it is simply not possible to maintain the current state of imbalance. The governorates of Idlib, Homs and Deir ez-Zor are burning. The economy has ground to a halt. The authorities appear to be experiencing confusion and panic. In spite of the ban on foreign media, news and videos of atrocities continue to trickle out. The regime makes the most ardent efforts to curb such information; recently Internet access went down over the entire country. But it cannot afford to apply such tactics indefinitely. The Syrian economy today, particularly the nascent banking sector, relies on connectivity with the world in order to function. It may be economic collapse which leads to the end game.

The Syrian people are protesting in cities and towns throughout the country. They are being killed and imprisoned on an unprecedented scale, and yet they are not slowing down. The Syrians have reached a point at which propaganda no longer pacifies and force no longer terrifies. For them change is not just inevitable, it has already happened.

BEING GREEN IN TEHRAN

Jasmin Ramsey

I have a confession to make. I did not want to write this article. Not on the Green Movement. Not on that elusive Iranian phenomenon that is as polarising a discussion topic now amongst Iranian communities as it was during its fiery inception. As an Iranian-born woman living in the West I was expected to join the movement along with my expatriate peers in 2009. But I only began to understand it while travelling through Iran this year. I understood, for example, that even though the Greens want to change the 1979-geared direction of the country, they are as much a product of the revolution as the ongoing power struggle in the regime. And despite their mutual antagonism, both the Greens and the Ahmadinejad-led nationalists are trying to challenge Iran's ruling elite in a way that has not been done before. But whereas in 2009 people were debating whether the Green Movement would bring about regime change, today many are wondering whether it even has the support, organisation and resilience necessary to stay alive.

Both my parents were members of the Communist Hezb-e Tudeh Iran (Tudeh party), and in the mid 70s my father was punished for his dissent by the Shah's regime. When, some years later, the Islamic Republic also deemed him an enemy of the state, this time the threat to his life was more serious. Iran was purging the country of leftist and nationalist groups and thousands were imprisoned or killed. So my family fled.

Before this, my parents, like many of their friends who suffered far worse consequences, welcomed the 1979 revolution, even if they were Communists and the revolution's leader was trying to implement the *Vilayat-e Faqih*, a controversial innovation in Shia Islam which elevated the clergy to a legislative authority. 'It was always the revolution we were supporting', says my father. 'The vast majority of Iranians wanted revolution. We didn't support the religious leadership; we wanted an anti-imperialist, democratic revolution'. The 1979 constitution, a strange mix of western democracy and Islamic theocracy, made it seem that my father's dreams would gradually be realised.

My parents were part of the same growing middle class that makes up the majority of the Green Movement today, and in the 70s they worked against their class interests. According to leading Iranian economist Djavad Salehi-Isfahani, Iran's poor have greatly benefited from the expanded education and health services that have penetrated rural areas since the revolution. Many have been upwardly mobile, resulting in a country in which 70% of the population now lives in urban areas. This has resulted in 'success in improving the standard of living and the quality of life for the poor' but 'failure in improving the overall distribution of income'. In light of these mixed results, Salehi-Isfahani concedes that the revolutionary goal of social justice is still unrealised.

Iran's government is now battling the unintended consequences of a better educated society which includes a large middle class. A large section of society, after exposure to outside models and influences found on the Internet and foreign television stations, is increasingly critical of regime authoritarianism. The government periodically sends teams to confiscate satellite dishes, particularly in Tehran where they are most abundant, and is constantly thinking up new ways to police the Internet. Education reforms are intended to root out Western ideas and 'perverted political movements'. Yet everywhere people chafe against the petty restrictions of state-directed daily life. Obvious examples of the chafing can be seen in the creative fashion styles of female Iranian students, who always find ways to push against the republic's dress codes by showing a little more (covered) leg beneath their overcoats, or a little more hair under their head scarves (when not wearing the forced hijab in school).

The educated middle class also sees Iran's financial support for the Palestinian and Lebanese resistance movements and opposition to American influence in the region as insincere when their own economic needs are not being met. Lack of government transparency also leads to accusations of corruption with regard to oil revenues. As one middle-aged Green supporter sympathetic to the Palestinian cause told me: 'It's like me going to help another family with their issues in a different city when my own family's home is being destroyed by rain pouring in from a unrepaired hole in the ceiling'.

Similarly, while Iran's foreign policy may be regionally popular, many Iranians now bemoan the lack of sophistication demonstrated by Iran's official and media responses to Arab revolutions—reading them falsely as Islamist uprisings, except in the case of its ally Syria, whose home-grown intifada is described as yet another foreign conspiracy. Such dishonesty signals the regime's weakness rather than its strength.

Rewind to June 2009, long before any talk of an 'Arab awakening'. The leading candidates in presidential elections were Mahmoud Ahmadinejad and Mir Hossein Mousavi. The race became very heated indeed. Iran hadn't seen this kind of voter enthusiasm since 1997 when reform leader Mohammed Khatami won the presidency in a landslide after an 80 per cent voter turnout. The 2009 election campaign had unfolded without surprises until Ahmadinejad, during the country's first ever televised presidential debates, questioned the validity of Mousavi's wife's academic qualifications. Mousavi kept his cool but the attack on his wife was likely an important boost for his campaign, galvanizing dormant potential voters into action. Ahmadinejad's attempts to align Mousavi with alleged corruption in the previous Khatami and Akbar Hashemi Rafsanjani administrations also likely energised his support base.

In Tehran, Iran's most populated city and one of the world's most over-populated, voters seemed overwhelmingly pro-Mousavi. Or at least that's how the Western media presented it, with almost all coverage featuring images of young, hip Iranians decked out in green.

Reporting from the capital for *The New York Times* on 10 June, Roger Cohen said: 'For several weeks, the campaign had been lifeless, but in the last two weeks it has sprung to life. And some informal polls are now showing Mousavi with a clear advantage over Ahmadinejad'. But according to the official results, Ahmadinejad beat Mousavi with a majority in the first round.

The election results were surprising. This we can agree on even if we believe that Ahmadinejad won legitimately. Running against Rafsanjani in 2005, on a 63 per cent turnout, he reportedly brought in about six million votes in the first round and 17 million in the second. This time he won almost 25 million on an 85 per cent voter turnout. Mousavi (the first candidate to announce he had won) reportedly received 34 per cent of the vote (just above 13 million), and Mehdi Karroubi received less than 1 per cent, beaten by conservative challenger Mohsen Rezai who received almost 2 per cent.

For those of us who had been gobbling up Western reports like Cohen's, this just didn't sound right. For two weeks we had been hearing how a 'green wave' was rolling through Tehran, enticing Iranians to admit they didn't want Ahmadinejad anymore. And 'who cares' about the perspective of the poor and the pious, wrote one Iranian to me before the results were announced, infuriated by my attempt to try draw attention to the other side.

But apart from the sensationalised media reports, Mousavi's announcement of his win after an alleged mysterious phone call, and a desire for all that beautiful green energy to be translated into victory, what did we have to suggest that Mousavi had actually won? Certainly not hard evidence. Of course, in a system as secretive and authoritarian as Iran's, hard evidence is not exactly easy to come by.

The Green wave turned into a movement when Ali Khamenei congratulated Ahmadinejad for his win less than 24 hours after voting stations closed. As almost all analysts noted at the time, this move by the *Rahbar* (leader) was especially curious because it came before the Guardian Council had certified the vote (one of their official tasks). Those who had been rooting for the Greens were momentarily stunned, and then Tehran came under a communication shut-down, with mobile phones, social networking tools and major foreign news sources blocked.

The surprise felt by Green supporters must have been felt among members of Iran's ruling elite too. In *The Ayatollah's Democracy: An Iranian Challenge* (2010), Hooman Majd notes that a right-wing newspaper run by one of Ahmadinejad's 'strongest supporters' reported that speaker of parliament Ali Larijani called Mousavi before the polls closed to congratulate him on his win. Majd points out that the unconfirmed claim was reported to implicate Larijani (an Ahmadinejad rival) in the election unrest, but inadvertently supported Mousavi's allegations against the incumbent by showing that Larijani had 'first-hand and classified information and news'.

In June 2009 Gary Sick suggested that the call 'perhaps served to temporarily lull them into complacency'. This was because the Mousavi camp had been reporting voting procedure complaints all day, including a shortage of ballot papers at stations across the country, even though, according to Majd, a surplus of six million had been printed. But if as Sick suggests, the desire to create temporary complacency was the real reason behind the call, wouldn't the government anticipate strong blowback from the expected announcement of a win by the Mousavi camp? Justified or not, blowback is certainly what followed.

Ironically, much of the analytical debate concerning the likelihood of an Ahmadinejad win took place after the results had been announced. What would become the most famous pre-election poll had been financed by the Rockefeller Brothers Foundation and carried out a consortium of US-based organisations by Terror Free Tomorrow (TFT), the Center for Public Opinion, the New America Foundation, and KA Europe SPRL. Aimed at informing US foreign policy decisions, the nationwide survey was conducted by telephone from 11–20 May and had a margin of error of +/-3.1 per cent.

Interestingly, 89 per cent of respondents said they intended to vote, with 27 per cent saying they were undecided, 34 per cent saying they would vote for Ahmadinejad, 14 per cent for Mousavi, 2 per cent for Mehdi Karroubi and 1 per cent for Mohsen Rezai. According to Just Foreign Policy's Robert Naiman, any reasoned variation of the poll's results would still produce an Ahmadinejad victory in the first round. Naiman was so unconvinced by arguments that the election had been stolen that less than two weeks after writing his first article on the topic he wrote another piece in the Huffington Post claiming he would give $10,000 to anyone who could prove the claims.

Citing the official tallied difference of votes between Ahmadinejad and Mousavi, Naiman writes: 'when I say your numbers have to add up, I mean your story of stolen votes has to overcome that 11 million vote gap'. To those who argue that the TFT poll was conducted three weeks before the election and that there was a surge of support for the opposition after that, Naiman responds: 'even if you allocate two-thirds of those not stating a preference to the opposition, you still get an election victory for Ahmadinejad in the first round'.

Yet expert opinion is bitterly divided. Citing a Chatham House study on the official results authored by Iranian historian Ali Ansari, US-based Mideast academic Juan Cole said there was proof of 'massive ballot fraud'. Not only were there more recorded voters than residents in some provinces, he claimed, but little could explain the vast swing to the Ahmadinejad camp. According to the study, 'In a third of all provinces, the official results would require that Ahmadinejad took not only all former conservative voters, and all former centrist voters, and all new voters, but also up to 44 per cent of former reformist voters, despite a decade of conflict between these two groups'. In turn, the Chatham House report received a lengthy response by Reza Esfandiari and Yousef Bozorgmehr, who concluded that it offered a 'superficial analysis' of the official results. These, they averred, were accurate, even if some fraud had occurred.

The debate about the election results has mostly simmered down with those who are convinced refusing to budge from their position and undecided journalists and analysts referring to the election as 'disputed'. Some have refused to consider the official results at all, arguing that the Iranian government either didn't count the votes fairly, or lied about them outright. This position is worth considering, given the general agreement on all sides about at least some ballot fraud taking place, the speed at which results were announced despite such a large voter turnout, and Khamenei's unprecedented show of bias for Ahmadinejad in June 2009 (and these are just a few of the points raised).

In 2009 Iranian chants on the ground of *ra-ye man koo?* (Where is My Vote?) were repeated in cyberspace on Facebook and Twitter. Twitter became so popular that the US State Department urged the company in June 2009 to delay a planned upgrade that would have otherwise cut day-time service to tweeting Iranians. While reporting that it had been blocked in Iran, YouTube blogged that it had become a 'citizen-fuelled news bureau of video reports filed straight from the streets of Tehran, unfiltered' and posted a collection of them.

But one year later talk of a 'Twitter revolution' was reduced to criticism of the idea. The *Guardian's* Matthew Weaver admitted that the emphasis on Twitter in aiding protestors was 'exaggerated' and more fuelled by 'western fantasies for new media than the reality in Iran'. Referencing an estimate by Global Voices, Hamid Tehrani Weaver writes, 'There were fewer than one thousand active Twitter users in Iran at the time of the election'. Writing about how many of the Iran-focused Twitter accounts of 2009 were based outside the country, Golnaz Esfandiari of Radio Free Europe/Radio Liberty noted, '[t]hrough it all, no one seemed to wonder why people trying to coordinate protests in Iran would be writing in any language other than Farsi'.

In Iran the use of social networking tools was certainly important, but even in 2011 I noticed that word of mouth is still the dominant mode of communication despite the fact that many more people have learned how to bypass government filters. People call lists of landlines, inform the receiver of a protest and urge them to attend, hanging up in under a minute. And Iran's many cab drivers (several of whom identified themselves as Greens) always seem to know about the protests beforehand, informing you why they're taking an alternate route by telling you it's going to get *shooloogh* (crowded) there.

The announcement of Ahmadinejad's win resulted in the worst unrest Iran had seen since 1979. While protests were also reported in Tabriz, Shiraz, Isfahan and Mashhad, the largest reported opposition demonstration to date happened in Tehran on 15 June, 2009 and was estimated at between one to three million, the higher number provided by conservative mayor of Tehran and Ahmadinejad rival, Mohammad Qalibaf.

Demonstrators were beaten, thousands were imprisoned and dozens were killed. Iranians refused to go home after an official announcement was made on 15 June 'that any kind of gathering ... without a license is forbidden', or after the horrifying murder of Neda Agha-Soltan on 20 June was publicised around the world. They continued protesting after reports of inhumane conditions and torture in Iranian prisons surfaced (though this was hardly anything new), the most famous cases occurring in Kahrizak and Evin prisons. Even after the government held a mass 'show trial' of over one hundred reformists, with many interpreting their 'confessions' as having been coerced through physical and psychological pressure, thousands of Iranians refused to go home.

But two years later, many Iranians have given up on protesting. The demonstrations today are much smaller and much less organised. The government's continued show of violent force against political dissent is proving successful as an intimidation tactic.

I witnessed a heavy security presence in Tehran before and after the protests which took place while I was there from February through to April 2011. Young men in riot gear armed with guns and batons lined up along popular streets ready to attack. Some *basijis* (paramilitary volunteers) also waited by their motorcycles (which they travel on in groups for their own protection).

Participants said that unlike in the years before, any group of two or more is immediately broken up, with those who aren't able to get away quickly enough arrested. When I asked one brave young woman why she didn't wear a chador so as to appear like an innocent bystander, she laughed and said, 'Are you kidding? No one accidentally wanders into these protests. Besides, you have to dress in clothes you can run in'.

After being searched, the captured protestors are interrogated and an assessment is made as to whether they're important enough to detain longer. If they're carrying a mobile it will be left on to see who contacts them for further leads. Those considered more politically active than the average protestor will endure further interrogation (which in Iran usually implies torture), court dates and imprisonment.

Unthreatening protestors are photographed, identified for the file that is made on them, and released after varying amounts of time. According to one protestor who was arrested twice but considered 'unimportant', the severity of your treatment often depends on who you're picked up by— one of the various security committees, the police or the *basij*.

Iran's powerful security apparatus cannot, however, be the only reason for the Green Movement's near dormancy today. Although many Iranians desire serious change, they have not yet been moved by a spark inspiring enough to keep them in the streets, refusing to go home until their demands are met—not even the house arrest of Green leaders Mousavi and Mehdi Karroubi, which continues to this day.

Over time Mousavi's statements have evolved from focusing on the election results to addressing methods of governance and issues pertaining to Iranian society as a whole. Now there is more of an emphasis on press freedom, respect for civil rights, the release of political prisoners, and the importance of holding government officials accountable for crimes committed during the election unrest. Karroubi, regarded by many as number two in the Green leadership, has made similar statements. Prominent Green supporters living outside the country have also contributed to the movement's goals, most notably with the 2010 Opposition Manifesto which was composed by exiled religious intellectuals who were prominent in the reform movement in the 1990s.

While Mousavi has pushed for the 'unconditional enactment of the constitution and the return of the Islamic Republic to its original ethical foundations', other prominent Greens seem to want more. The widely circulated Opposition Manifesto, which pledges 'full support' for Mousavi,

Karroubi and Khatami, also calls for an independent judiciary 'through the election [rather than appointment] of its head'. Most interesting is point number 10, which states: 'Elect all the officials who must become respond [sic] to criticisms and limit the number of terms that they can be elected'.

Mousavi has not used such direct language when referring to the power of Khamenei (the highest ranking authority in the Islamic Republic), but has stated that reforming Iran's constitution is not his only goal. In an interview posted on opposition website www.kaleme.org he states, 'I have said before that the constitution is not something that has been set in stone... Nevertheless, we must be aware that by itself, a good constitution is not the answer. We must move towards a [political] structure that imposes costly consequences on those who attempt to disobey or ignore the laws'.

This ambivalence between reform and a complete system overhaul raises questions about the direction and purpose of the Green Movement as a whole. If it is purely a civil rights movement as Iran scholar Hamid Dabashi called it in 2009, then its goal of 'bringing about change within the framework of the constitution' is understandable, even if that constitution is constantly being debated.

But constant discussion about Iran's governance amongst Greens makes theirs a political movement too. In this respect the leadership must also consider the many secular supporters inside (and outside) Iran who have rallied under what Mousavi refers to as the 'umbrella' of the Green Movement. In other words, at some point Mousavi will have to directly respond to those who continue to scream '*marg bar dictator*' (death to the dictator) in the streets because they have also been chanting '*Ya Hossein, Mir Hossein*'. That is, if he hasn't lost them already.

In his 2010 article 'What the Green Movement Needs Now', Iran analyst Karim Sadjadpour suggests the leadership must 'tread carefully' while trying to broaden its support base among Iranian youth and 'disaffected members of the traditional class'. Sadjadpour credits the Green leadership for eschewing hollow economic populism 'for more high-brow talk of democracy and human rights', but suggests they must also try to attract Iran's working class. Similarly, the movement must also tend to the desires of the Iranian middle class if it wants to keep the majority of its supporters, because despite its diversity, middle class Iranians certainly make up the Green base.

Two years after the unrest, most agree with Iran historian Ervand Abrahamian who noted at the time that the million-plus June 15 rally was attended by both the secular and religious. He described, '[l]ines of protesters nine kilometres long converged on the square from the northern, better-off districts as well as from the southern, working-class ones'. Iranians reiterated this, telling me that all of Tehran seemed to spill into the streets in June 2009. When I asked a war veteran and former *Basiji* turned Green supporter what he thought about the protestors' initial makeup, he gestured at his modest home and said, 'I run a takeout kitchen and live in this small home with my family ...Do you think I'm the only one?'

He lived in one of Tehran's crowded, working class districts, but just as the protests of 2009 weren't dominated by either the affluent or the poor, they weren't exactly working class either. Indeed, as Vali Nasr and others have pointed out, the protests of 2009 weren't only about the election results, they were also a place for Iranian youth and the middle class (large segments of the population) to air their grievances about the rising cost of living in a country that offers little to them in other measures of life quality, such as personal freedom. In fact, contrary to the human rights-centred discourse that dominates expatriate Iranian discussions about the Greens, the first complaint most Greens in the country voiced to me was the dire state of the Iranian economy, with its rising inflation and high unemployment.

At the time of the unrest, Iranian youth were estimated at 70 per cent of the population's total, with about 25 per cent under the voting age of 15. According to economist Djavad Salehi-Isfahani, Iran's middle class was estimated at 50 per cent of Iran's voting population in 2009. In a CNN article Dabashi tried to challenge the idea that the protests were a middle class movement by saying that they were dominated by fifteen to twenty-nine-year-olds who are mostly jobless and therefore not middle class because they don't have income. But these youth enjoy middle class living standards, since the vast majority live at home with their middle class parents who pay for their daily expenses. Indeed, according to Salehi-Isfahani, Iranians under the age of thirty account for about 70 per cent of the unemployed and more than 50 per cent of them live at home, with the lack of economic opportunities preventing them from marrying and moving out.

Interestingly, I observed youth from these social brackets attending the Tuesday protests which were held while I was there, even though they seemed apolitical. Living at home with his lower middle class parents and working a low-paying part-time job, one twenty-three-year-old man told me that he wasn't sure who had won the election, but sometimes joined the protests because they were on his way home from work.

Certainly many of the brave Iranian youth, still facing beatings and bullets, have more pressing reasons to join the protests. These correlate with the demands of the Green Movement Charter, greater civil and human rights.

Iran's leadership is independent, mostly isolated, and led by seasoned veterans of a revolution that not only defied Western exploitation but also shamed the subservient and corrupt governments around it. While Khamenei's line that the Arab Spring owes inspiration to Iran's Islamic revolution is blatantly propagandistic, it is still true that Iran was the first country in the region to overthrow a ruthless leader and force out American imperialism. It remains to be seen if revolutionary Egypt, Yemen and Tunisia will succeed in shaking off their status as Western clients and achieve full independence.

Iran may be an independent player, but its power structures remain rigidly unyielding, closing out dissent and vast swathes of public opinion. So long as the government has the backing of the powerful revolutionary guard, which is made up of ideologically driven and hardened veterans of the war, there is little that can move it. Accordingly, while the Green Movement was successful in bringing human and civil rights into focus in a country where they have usually been ignored, it has achieved little else. Indeed, two years after the Green challenge the government is concentrating most of its attention on conflicts within its own ruling elite.

Travelling through Iran this year I saw reminders of the revolution everywhere—the large faded murals with anti-American imagery or war martyrs painted on the sides of buildings, the street names changed to erase memories of the Shah's era, the framed pictures of Khomeini on the walls of businesses and other public places. But among the people, happiness was as hard to come by as true freedom has always been. Discontent was written on the faces of the rich and the poor, the young and the old.

A well-known saying was repeated several times while I was there: 'Iranians know what they don't want, but not what they want'. It is an expression of the exasperation felt by a generation that was once at the forefront of the revolutionary tide that is now sweeping through the rest of the region, a generation divided about the kind of country they want to live in. On the other hand, younger Iranians will tell you what they want willingly and with ease. Although their answers vary depending on their sex, social class and religious beliefs, their desires are not influenced by their parents' fight for the revolution or by Iran's sacrifice of more than 500,000 men during its eight-year war with Iraq. And while the 2009 election protests were diverse in social makeup, they were widely attended by middle class Iranian youth who make up the majority in the considerably smaller protests taking place today.

Since 1979, no movement has attracted as many young Iranians as the Green Movement, and this is one reason why it represents so much for so many. But will the Green leadership be able to preserve this support, and if so, will it be able to mobilise it effectively against the deeply entrenched ruling elite? In a country with a predominantly young population, the future of the Green Movement and Iran as a whole depends on what Iranian young people want and how hard they're willing to fight for it.

IBN KHALDUN AND
THE ARAB SPRING

Jerry Ravetz

Most Muslims know, or should know, that Ibn Khaldun was one of the greatest of social theorists, who lived at a time in the fifteenth century when the Islamic civilisation was perceptibly in decline. He pondered the causes of this sad state, and came up with a cyclical theory of degeneration. This relates to the general tendency of ruling elites to become effete and personally corrupted, so that they lose the ability to cope with crises and eventually even to govern. The story is well told in the Biblical narrative of Saul the warrior, David the king, Solomon the emperor, and finally his sons who fell into degeneracy and civil war. In industrial Lancashire, the same cycle was told as 'clogs to clogs in three generations', where the grandson of the ambitious worker ended his days wearing clogs back at the mill, having squandered the inheritance of his forbears.

There are two time-frames for this cycle. The first, most familiar, is that of civilisations, which take generations to work through. But in modern times we have seen a similar cycle in revolutions, where the route from liberation to renewed tyranny is traversed in decades or less. Since the 'Arab Spring' has significance at both levels, we can consider them both, the long-term cycle and the short.

The relevance of Ibn Khaldun's story is that in many ways the European empire seems to be in serious decline. For Muslims the natural hope is that as the West goes down, Islam, as a community and way of life, has at last a chance of a renaissance. But whether Islam does indeed rise again in triumph, or whether there will be an unstable or fluid period when all non-Western cultures struggle to regain strength and confidence, is really beyond the scope of this essay. I will simply explore some of the evidence for a decline, try out various explanations, some along Ibn Khaldun's lines, and finally indicate some grounds for hope that the future will not simply

136

repeat the mistakes of the past. I will focus on the 'Arab Spring' which we are just now celebrating.

I cannot resist citing one numerical coincidence that is telling even if not explanatory. It seems that the permanent expansion of Europe began with a Portuguese fortification on the North-West coast of Africa, sometime between 1413 and 1415. Exactly half a millennium later the Great War began, in which three European empires (German, Austrian, Russian), plus the remaining Islamic one (Ottoman), were destroyed, a large chunk of land was (temporarily) lost to the capitalist system (Russia), and colonial independence movements everywhere gained strength. Afterwards there was a very unstable generation of local booms and general bust, culminating in World War II, and then an apparent golden age of the Pax Americana lasting up to the end of the century. Few at the time realised how much this new empire was dependent on cheap oil, obtained by a mixture of aggression (as on Iran) or appeasement (as of Saudi Arabia), and the illusion persisted even through the rise of OPEC and the financial crises of late-century. Then just a century on came the Credit Crunch. The West will never be the same again.

What are the signs of a real, permanent decline of The West? The most obvious one is the collapse of the Western imperial financial system. This is euphemistically described in the West as 'the rise of emergent economies'. But it is also characterised by the parlous state of nearly all the Western economies, the exhaustion of the stocks of available capital in the West, and, most serious, by the loss of credibility of those who run and regulate the financial systems. Although there are some significant exceptions (mainly Germany) the Western nations in general have long since lost their lead in manufacturing; now they have ruined their reputation for competence and integrity in financial management. They all face permanent 'structural' mass unemployment of younger people of all classes, with political consequences that are only now beginning to appear. Even fighting a very small war, as in Libya, becomes onerous.

All this appeared to happen quite suddenly, as the financial classes of the West, abetted by their tame economists and mathematicians, went on a mega-binge of corrupt speculation, so that in 2008 they had to be bailed out immediately lest the whole banking system, the useful parts along with the useless, collapse and bring down the entire economy. When we see the arguments that Europeans must continue to run the IMF because only they know how to fix the mess they have made, we are reminded of the cartoon character that keeps on running beyond the edge of the cliff and realises only too late that there is no support under him. So in the present crisis there is a classic pattern of Ibn Khaldun's decline and fall through personal corruption, this time not within a palace but, worse, in the commanding heights of the economy. How can we usefully characterise this process?

I find it very useful to start with Quality. Leaving definitions aside, we can say that when things run well, there is Quality; otherwise, not. In their ordinary operation, the 'advanced' societies generally have high quality. Most goods in the shops are reliable, the lights nearly always go on, public servants do their jobs reasonably well, and so on. Of course there are lapses, causes of complaint, and corruption. But a comparison of their quality levels with those of the state-socialist societies, as long as they lasted, seemed a vindication of the free-enterprise system.

But underneath, things have been going systematically wrong. In the US, the manufacturing system was being steadily hollowed out, as firms produced for the closed market of the Pentagon. As early as 1981, one scholar, Seymour Melman, warned of the collapse of the 'machine tools' industry in the US; those are the tools that make tools, and without them a nation has lost its independence. Melman was of course ignored. Not long afterwards, a renegade (or reformed) Wall Street trader, Michael Lewis, exposed the total corruption of the market there. He had realised that the men who control vast fortunes and determine the fate of nations, are just a bunch of low-lifes. He published, and waited for the crash; it took nearly thirty years to arrive, but when it did it was real.

When we learned about the wonders of modern technology, we were rarely told about the quality-assurance systems that kept them working effectively and safely. For those systems do not depend so much on the equipment as on the skill and dedication of unknown people whose tasks of enforcing safety standards are frequently thankless. We all know of degrees of quality and safety among airlines, with those of some 'less developed' countries falling below the line for acceptability. We were less familiar, until recently, with the incompetence and corruption of the operators and regulators in the Japanese civil nuclear power industry. Only when the scale of the Fukushima catastrophe could no longer be hidden was the public allowed to learn of the scandals, going back for decades, of the abysmal quality of management and regulation in Japan. At this point we, or rather those of us who read the blogs or the quality press, learned that regulation in the US is not much better, as the spent fuel rods sit in their many cooling ponds waiting for some external event to cut the power supply that stops them going critical. Quality assurance is finally being recognised as crucial to the well-being and even survival of high-technology civilisation.

This issue of quality relates directly to the 'Arab Spring', since one of the main manifestations of social pathology in the autocracies is that for those without privilege, no system works. Those who are formally entrusted with certain social tasks perform them with indifference, incompetence or contempt. They are not necessarily bad people, but they have learned that it is pointless to try to do otherwise. They might even get into trouble for showing up the others. And the reason for their indiscipline is that those higher up, right to the top, are as bad or worse. It was this sort of top-down corruption that triggered the initial revolutions of Tunisia and Egypt.

So poorness of quality, as one leading form of corruption, is not mainly a matter of bad or weak people. It is a systemic pathology of a social order, of the sort that Ibn Khaldun identified in the conditions of his own time. Lower-level abuses and high-level cover-ups are integral complementary elements of the system. This was shown by the recent scandals in the Roman Catholic Church. Only a small proportion of priests succumbed to the illness of sexual abuse, but absolutely all the bishops acted (rationally) to protect the paedophiles and further victimise the victims, as they were constrained to obey orders in the interest of the good name of the Universal Church. One could hardly find a better example of the evils of obedience and of the suppression of criticism, and also how, sooner or later, reality catches up and destroys the corrupted institution.

Looking around the world, at all its institutions, we might say that a few islands of high quality float in a sea of squalor and corruption. This is very different from the picture conveyed by Western academia concerning society and its institutions, but it will seem natural to those from beyond the academy's borders. Perhaps the most pertinent question is: How does high quality survive at all when pursuing it can be onerous, even risky? The obvious answer is that quality is enforced on individuals by their peer-group. But that only leads to a further question: Why should the peer-group bother in some cases but not in others?

I first pondered these questions when considering the issue of quality in science, which is generally taken for granted by everyone outside science ('scientists discover facts that are true') but by few inside ('scientists solve problems, with higher or lower quality'). Based on my experience of scientific fields where research is weak, I came to the conclusion that the achievement of objective knowledge depends on a moral commitment of the whole community, which in turn is critically dependent on the quality of its leadership. In the absence of such a commitment, there is a degeneration of quality, down to outright pseudo-science. It is not easy to document such cases, for obvious reasons. But one recent example is suggestive: the amount of money spent on the research that was intended to prove Carbon-based Anthropogenic Global Warming is estimated at thirty billion dollars. Given the scarcity of conclusive results, this research campaign might be considered to have achieved an all-time low in research effectiveness, or in the quality of research strategy and performance.

My argument so far has shown that quality, like other positive social commitments (such as integrity or compassion) can be protected or enhanced by particular social mechanisms, but in the last resort it depends on the commitment of a community to good or moral behaviour. It requires both leadership and dialogue, lest (as Ibn Khaldun descried) the normal tendencies produce a slide and degeneration.

Where are the roots of these sustaining forces? People must believe in something that makes their sacrifices worthwhile, something that makes their meritorious acts become real 'sacrifices' or holy deeds. This belief need not be an explicit religious doctrine; experience shows that the religious seem just as vulnerable to corruption as the irreligious. But it must exist.

Here is the argument: quality of performance depends on quality assurance, and quality assurance depends on some sort of ideology. Where does that ideology come from, and how is its quality maintained? To answer the first question, it doesn't seem to matter: the ideology may arise from conscience, fear of guilt or shame, or loyalty to a leader or to an affinity group, or to an ideal or idea, as religion or patriotism. All of these sometimes work and sometimes fail.

So what determines if they work or fail? Here is where Ibn Khaldun's cycle of degeneration comes into play. In his vision, the ideology that enabled a conquest becomes progressively less relevant as the conquerors settle down. The conqueror's quality, the warrior's life in the saddle, becomes irrelevant for his son the king, and finally seems ridiculous to his grandsons raised in the palace. That was the pattern in pre-modern times; now, even if there is an explicit benevolent ideal that led to the initial seizure of power, it suffers the same sort of fate when new generations want no more than a peaceful and prosperous life, or new leaders want the privileges of the old. That has been the sad fate of nearly all twentieth-century revolutions. George Orwell summed it up in *Animal Farm*.

Under modern conditions, the processes of degeneration work partly in such traditional ways, but also through institutions. I can offer my own short-term cycle of degeneration, derived from observing failed modern imperialist wars in Vietnam and Iraq-Afghanistan. In these cases the defining ideology is a fantasy, easily recognised as such by all those who are not caught up in it. In the former case it was 'anti-communism', in the latter, a 'war on terror'. Since the fantasy has so very little relation to what is happening on the ground, to maintain it requires a heavy dose of mendacity. In Vietnam this was exposed by the 'Pentagon Papers', while for Iraq the various pathetic WMD ruses promoted by Bush & Blair served only to make the war even less popular outside the US. When an activity is ruled by mendacity, extreme corruption is inevitable, since there can be no reality-testing of quality of performance. All sides are caught up in this corruption, the invading armies along with their client governments. From corruption follows incompetence, which does not prevent violent action but which makes it very brutal and counterproductive (see Fallujah in Iraq and the drone attacks on wedding parties in Afghanistan). And eventually there is failure.

Unfortunately, not only the malevolent and powerful are prone to this type of quality-collapse. Movements for idealistic radical reform are even more prone to start with fantasy, since the enemy they face is usually all-powerful, and no 'reasonable' solution has any hope of success. Only now are Christians coming to admit that 'Crusade' is not a term of approbation, since the original crusades (intended to rescue the Holy Land for Catholic followers of Jesus) were large-scale acts of criminal folly (some more criminal, some more folly). The French Revolution started with the fall of the Bastille in 1789, proceeded through the execution of the king and queen, endured a Terror and then a counter-Terror, and wound up with Napoleon crowning himself Holy Roman Emperor in 1808. The American war of independence started with the noble sentiments of Thomas Jefferson, that 'all men are created equal', but owing to practical considerations some remained less equal than others, being slaves. That particular contradiction festered for seventy years, until the civil war. I could continue. Readers from the Muslim world will have their own examples of idealistic 'modernising' movements which have led only to disappointment.

All this may seem discouraging to those brave and good people in the Arab world who are leading revolutions against autocratic regimes and against those who would either restore them or replace them with something worse. What grounds for hope are there just now? Are Arab calls for reform just another fantasy?

First, we should remember the good news from the history of campaigns for reform. The anti-slavery struggle was long and confused, but through the nineteenth century it gained moral and, eventually, political ascendancy. The last half-century has seen a real revolution in attitudes to all the creatures who are not upper-class white Protestant males. No-one in the advanced nations now dares to argue publicly for discrimination on the basis of gender, age, ethnicity or religion, and even the stigma of minority sexual preference is slowly and painfully being overcome. Young people may find it difficult to imagine how attitudes that are now seen as unacceptably prejudiced were until quite recently considered common sense, established by the authority of Scripture or Science, depending on your preference. Furthermore, today we not only appreciate our kinship to other mammals, but show increasing concern about cruelty even to species that have no obvious means of emotional expression. Needless to say, all these enlightened attitudes are patchy in their acceptance, adopted with a fair dose of inconsistency and hypocrisy, and occasionally even become counterproductive. But the progress is real.

How did it all happen? Ideologically, in modern Europe such principles are the fruit of the Enlightenment, when the good of mankind was established as the basic guiding principle. American schoolchildren are fortunate in learning the totally utopian manifesto of the Declaration of Independence: 'We hold these truths to be self-evident, that all men are created equal'. Of course there were fatal compromises, notably over slavery, and many betrayals of these fine principles as the United States grew by conquest and genocide. But as ideals they were powerful, and they gave hope to oppressed masses all over the world.

The nineteenth and twentieth centuries saw the extension of democracy into ever more spheres of life in ever more countries. It wasn't easy; there were terrible errors and failures. With the Great War, when nationalism triumphed over idealism, and then with Hitler, when absolute evil nearly won, the march of progress seemed to stumble. But then with the long period of postwar prosperity in the West, eventually spreading (in however distorted a way) elsewhere, the world became a less horrible place in principle, although not always in practice. Again, this didn't happen automatically; the struggles for democracy in the Victorian age were echoed by the struggles for justice and dignity of the later twentieth century.

The distinguished theorist of non-violent action Brian Martin uses the illuminating term 'backfire' to describe a regime's performance of an act so loathsome that its victims are filled with a rage that overcomes their fear. It happened in the movements for colonial freedom when the rulers perpetrated massacres. And most recently it has been the catalyst for revolutionary zeal in Tunisia, Egypt, Libya, Syria and Bahrain. Of course, not every atrocity produces blowback; the spark requires a tinder ready to burst into flame.

The moral element in political struggles, not merely expressed in fine rhetoric but worked out in practical politics and sacrifice, is the great defining difference between this age and all previous ones. Non-violence has emerged as the great guiding principle of the new politics of protest. In one way it is elementary prudence: the ruling elites can always deploy more violence than the protestors. And when that fails, as when the troops refuse to shoot at protestors in city squares, the cause is usually political and moral rather than military. But there is more: merely following orders is radically insufficient for nonviolence; it requires a deep personal commitment which, once achieved, can never be forgotten. This is why 'Tahrir' has become such a potent symbol of hope in the world, of a better way of bringing about change.

There are several reasons to hope that the moral ideology of non-violence will protect the 'Arab spring' from going through the usual cycle of degeneration. Non-violence is something much bigger and deeper than a simple abstention from violence. For it to really work, it requires activists who have thought through the issues and have been trained to control their emotions and responses. Such activists will never just 'follow orders'; nor will they fall into aggressive sectarian dogmatism in conducting arguments with those of a different point of view.

In the practice of revolution, non-violence means a natural assumption of equality and comradeship across all differences, including gender, religion and class. In particular, women are liberated and a 'green' philosophy is taken for granted. Spontaneous local actions, such as for neighbourhood protection, are fostered.

Activists with a prior personal commitment to a religion take their inspiration from the humane insights of the prophetic founders rather than from the doctrines of contemporary priestly castes, and they then argue within their own communities for the new approach.

Of course there will be many confusions and setbacks; yet the process is irreversible, and partly because of the technology that has enabled this particular wave of revolution to take its special form. The interaction of information technology with politics is not a new thing. In Europe it started with the Reformation, when the invention of cheap printing enabled every man to 'be his own priest' (in Martin Luther's empowering phrase), and also to read or even write a pamphlet about his views. The hegemony of The Church was shattered forever. Then in the nineteenth century, cheaper printing, the telegraph and railroads enabled the exploited urban working classes to organise, demonstrate and go on strike, gradually forcing the upper orders into a retreat that has never been fully reversed. Now, even if Twitter and Facebook are not the cure-alls for revolt, and (of course) are being combatted and co-opted by rulers, still they give an empowering ease and immediacy to communication.

These new technologies, following on from television, have created a new and potentially radical class: world citizens. Although everyone has their own language, gender, ethnicity and religion, still none are as sealed in their culture by walls of separation and ignorance as their parents were. Many millions have now shared in the ideal of a global culture. Yesterday's strangers are seen as really like us, and increasingly we all share the same ideals, of broadening compassion extending to all humanity and beyond.

In spite of all its fantasies and hypocrisies, the post-war period in the West did give a glimpse of something better: a world where the productive process did not require the brutalisation of labour. One great prophet of technology, Norbert Wiener, said it all in the title of his book, *The Human Use of Human Beings*. The sort of toil that ruins bodies and numbs minds is no longer necessary; there are increasingly intelligent machines to do it for us. Of course, machines are introduced in order to serve profit rather than welfare, and for many people a dirty job is better than none at all. But the vision of work as a pleasure, even a form of worship, is now realistic. Under our new material conditions, those of good fortune do not need to justify their oppression of an underclass by dehumanising them.

I know that liberal Westerners are rather surprised, and pleased, to see how protestors from Over There can be so articulate and enlightened when interviewed for television. The revolutionary spokespeople are not only graduates; some are very ordinary and obviously poor people. But their ideas are the same as ours, centred on freedom and dignity. Truly, this is a glimpse of One World. As the tent-cities of the youth and 'structurally unemployed' in Europe are now starting to show, we may be at the dawn of a new sort of radical politics, one where non-violence is at the core of consciousness, and takeovers by demagogues and dictators are less likely. Adherents of older political philosophies may find it difficult to comprehend how non-violence can be such a powerful political force. If they fail to account for it, they will most certainly be consigned to history.

It is much too early to say anything in any detail about the prospect for these revolutions. Certainly there is no guarantee that Ibn Khaldun's gloomy cycles, long-term and short-term, will not operate again, in a new form. But we have reason to hope that this time it will be different.

READING THE QUR'AN
ZIAUDDIN SARDAR

'This lucid, scholarly and exciting book could not be more timely; it takes the reader on a spiritual and intellectual journey that is essential for Muslim and non-Muslim alike and addresses some of the most pressing needs of our time.' — Karen Armstrong, author of *A History of God and Muhammad: A Biography of the Prophet*

'If one could pick just one book to connect the Muslim past with its complex present and future potential, *Reading the Qur'an* would be that book. To use a metaphor from the eleventh-century exemplar of rational mysticism, Imam Ghazzali, both Muslims and non-Muslims must "sail into the endless ocean of its meanings", with Ziauddin Sardar the nimble captain on that voyage of hope and discovery.' — Professor Bruce Lawrence, Duke University

'Ziauddin Sardar's *Reading the Qur'an*, is the most exciting book on the Qur'an in recent years; it is a poignant and intimate work on Islam's central text. ... Sardar approaches the Qur'an as both a lay believer, like the majority of Muslims, and an astute scholar of Islam. By providing a personal account of the relationship that he has with the Qur'an, Sardar echoes the cherished position which the Qur'an has for many Muslims. ... This is a wonderfully intelligent reading of a complex text within a contemporary context. ... By providing the Qur'an with a dynamic and empathetic voice on issues such as domestic violence, suicide, evolution, sex and sexuality, art, politics and power, Sardar ensures the Qur'an remains a warm, relevant and vibrant force within contemporary Muslim discourse. — Farid Esack, University of Johannesberg

9781849041072 / June 2011 / £20.00 hardback / 416pp / 225 x 145mm

HURST PUBLISHERS

41 GREAT RUSSELL ST, LONDON, WC1B 3PL
WWW.HURSTPUB.CO.UK
WWW.FBOOK.ME/HURST
020 7255 2201

ART AND LETTERS

Crescent Films is an award-winning independent production company with a record of producing high quality, original and entertaining television programmes for, amongst others, the BBC and Channel 4.

Based in London, Crescent films specialises in documentaries on South Asia and the Muslim World. Our recent productions include 'The Life of Muhammad' a three part documentary series for the BBC, 'Seven Wonders of the Muslim World', 'Muslim and looking for Love' and 'Women only Jihad' for Channel 4.

www.crescentfilms.co.uk
crescentfilms@btinternet.com

SPRING POEMS

Poetry in the Arab world, like ballet in Russia and football in England, is public property. Poetry retains mass popularity and an immediate political significance. It isn't surprising, therefore, that poems have played an important role on the streets during the revolutions.

First, some background. The context of military, social and economic failure, and of spiritual stagnation, which stretched from 1967 to 2011 is perhaps most effectively evoked by Syrian poet Nizar Qabbani's 'Footnotes to the Book of the Setback'. Qabbani was better known for his love poetry until the Arab defeat (or Setback) of 1967 prompted him to address his people's political malaise head on. The poem became an instant classic despite being instantly banned. It rails against Arab dictatorship and backwardness, and calls for a new generation of Arabs to break their chains and overcome defeat.

Footnotes to the Book of the Setback by Nizar Qabbani

1
Friends,
The old word is dead.
The old books are dead.
Our speech with holes like worn-out shoes is dead.
Dead is the mind that led to defeat.

2
Our poetry has gone sour.
Women's hair, nights, curtains and sofas
Have gone sour.
Everything has gone sour.

3
My grieved country,
In a flash
You changed me from a poet who wrote love poems
To a poet who writes with a knife.

4
What we feel is beyond words:
We should be ashamed of our poems.

5
Stirred by Oriental bombast,
By boastful swaggering that never killed a fly,
By the fiddle and the drum,
We went to war
And lost.

6
Our shouting is louder than our actions,
Our swords are taller than us,
This is our tragedy.

7
In short
We wear the cape of civilisation
But our souls live in the stone age.

8
You don't win a war
With a reed and a flute.

9
Our impatience
Cost us fifty thousand new tents.

10
Don't curse heaven
If it abandons you,
Don't curse circumstances.
God gives victory to whom He wishes.
God is not a blacksmith to beat swords.

11
It's painful to listen to the news in the morning.
It's painful to listen to the barking of dogs.

12
Our enemies did not cross the border
They crept through our weakness like ants.

13

Five thousand years
Growing beards
In our caves.
Our currency is unknown,
Our eyes are a haven for flies.
Friends,
Smash the doors,
Wash your brains,
Wash your clothes.
Friends,
Read a book,
Write a book,
Grow words, pomegranates and grapes,
Sail to the country of fog and snow.
Nobody knows you exist in caves.
People take you for a breed of mongrels.

14

We are thick-skinned people
With empty souls.
We spend our days practising witchcraft,
Playing chess and sleeping.
And we the 'Nation by which God blessed mankind'?

15

Our desert oil could have become
Daggers of flame and fire.
We're a disgrace to our noble ancestors:
We let our oil flow through the toes of whores.

16

We run wildly through streets
Dragging people with ropes,
Smashing windows and locks.
We praise like frogs,
Swear like frogs,
Turn midgets into heroes,

And heroes into scum:
We never stop and think.
In mosques
We crouch idly,
Write poems,
Proverbs
And beg God for victory
Over our enemy.

17
If I knew I'd come to no harm,
And could see the Sultan,
I'd tell him:
'Sultan,
Your wild dogs have torn my clothes
Your spies hound me
Their eyes hound me
Their noses hound me
Their feet hound me
They hound me like Fate
Interrogate my wife
And take down the names of my friends,
Sultan,
When I came close to your walls
And talked about my pains,
Your soldiers beat me with their boots,
Forced me to eat my shoes.
Sultan,
You lost two wars.
Sultan,
Half of our people are without tongues,
What's the use of people without tongues?
Half of our people
Are trapped like ants and rats
Between walls'.
If I knew I'd come to no harm
I'd tell him:

'You lost two wars
You lost touch with children'

18

If we hadn't buried our unity
If we hadn't ripped its young body with bayonets
If it had stayed in our eyes
The dogs wouldn't have savaged our flesh.

19

We want an angry generation
To plough the sky
To blow up history
To blow up our thoughts.
We want a new generation
That does not forgive mistakes
That does not bend.
We want a generation of giants.

20

Arab children,
Corn ears of the future,
You will break our chains.
Kill the opium in our heads,
Kill the illusions.
Arab children,
Don't read about our windowless generation,
We are a hopeless case.
We are as worthless as watermelon rind.
Don't read about us,
Don't ape us,
Don't accept us,
Don't accept our ideas,
We are a nation of crooks and jugglers.
Arab children,
Spring rain,
Corn ears of the future,

You are a generation
That will overcome defeat.

Translation by Abdullah al-Udhari

More than four decades later the spring rain fell, and it fell to the sound of
poetry. When crowds in Tunisia marched against the despotism of Zine El
Abidine Ben Ali, they chanted a short poem by the Tunisian poet Abu al-
Qasim al-Shabi. A few months later the poem was being sung from Manama
to Morocco, and appeared on t-shirts sold in Cairo's Tahrir Square.

If a People Desires to Live by Abu al-Qasim al-Shabi

If, one day, a people desires to live, then fate will answer their call.
And their night will then begin to fade, and their chains break and
fall.
For he who is not embraced by a passion for life will dissipate into
thin air,
At least that is what all creation has told me, and what its hidden
spirits declare.

Translation by Elliott Colla

The revolutions gave a new lease of life to an enormously popular poem
by Palestinian-Israeli poet and activist Tawfiq Zayyad. 'I Call on You' had
previously been set to music by the Lebanese musician Marcel Khalifeh.
Now a new generation of Arabs addressed the poem to the masses in the
streets.

I Call on You by Tawfiq Zayyad

I call on you
I clasp your hands
I kiss the ground under your feet
And I say: I offer my life for yours
I give you the light of my eyes
as a present
and the warmth of my heart
The tragedy I live

is but my share of your tragedies
I call on you
I clasp your hands
I was not humiliated in my homeland
Nor was I diminished
I stood up to my oppressors
orphaned, nude, and barefoot
I carried my blood in my palm
I never lowered my flags
I guarded the green grass
over my ancestor's graves
I call on you
I clasp your hands

When it becomes a protest, poetry has a price. Ayat al-Qormezi, a twenty-year-old Bahraini woman, galvanised the crowd at Manama's Pearl Round-about by reciting an imagined dialogue between King Hamad Aal Khalifa and Satan. Shortly afterwards security forces stormed the protest camp and, with the aid of Saudi troops, began a campaign of repression. Ayat was arrested, allegedly tortured, and sentenced to a year in prison. The charges were 'insulting the king, taking part in banned gatherings, and spreading false information'.

Hamad and Satan (abridged) by Ayat al-Qormezi

We don't want to live in a palace, nor do we desire the presidency
We are a people who slays humiliation and assassinates misery
We are a people who demolishes injustice at its base
We are a people who doesn't want to continue this catastrophe.

On a table laid with people's pains Satan and Hamad sit and talk:

Satan: 'Oh, Hamad, fear God. My heart is breaking over them.
Although I am Satan I'm tempted to put my hand in theirs,
To rebel against you, to bow down right now to their prophet,
To repent to my God, for I am astounded by their struggle'.

Hamad: 'You, my ally, are the one who taught me how to deny them
How to humiliate them and hurt them and inflict woes upon them
Yet now you come asking for mercy towards them?

It seems you have been shaken by their new state of awareness'.

Satan: 'Yes, Hamad, your people have shaken me.
Haven't you heard them?
Haven't you seen the crowds and heard their shouts?
Haven't you heard their complaints and their sober reasoning?
Hamad, these people cannot be bought'.
Hamad: 'O, Satan, my belly hasn't yet brimmed with their blood
I haven't yet tortured every man with a turban
I haven't yet tortured each child and each youth
I haven't yet crushed each man in his prime
I haven't yet opened a million doors to humiliation
I haven't yet forced each one to cry mercy'.

Satan: 'Listen, my student whose cunning has exceeded his master's,
Your people have defeated me. Those proud revolutionaries have bewil-
dered me.
Sunna or Shia'a, there's no difference between them!
God protect all of them; they've sacrificed seven martyrs for the land,
Yet your heart remains stony. Do you want my advice?
Pack your rubbish and leave; you cannot meet the high standards of your
people'.

Translation by Rana Zaitoon

Finally a perspective on the Arab revolutions from the West. British poet
Naomi Foyle contrasts there with here, daring to hope that the spirit of
Tahrir Square will travel the distance between them.

Departure Day by Naomi Foyle

For Egypt

Everywhere, the revolution
nods off in the wings, misses its cue
and the long-scripted farce bangs another door
in the face of the people

Here, the people resist
each other, the television flattens

and expands against the wall
until it is the wall

and its cold grey plasma
seeps like damp into our lungs.

There, it is blood that rises
in the back of the throat
spills on the pavement

with the little girl's mango juice
and as she cries, the revolution
jerks awake, not too late

to bring the house down.

'AFFIRMATIVE ACTION'

Taus Makhacheva

Taus Makhacheva lives and works in Moscow and Makhachkala, a simultaneous existence that has shaped her perception of the Other, inspiring the social dimension of her work to resonate with personal history. Belonging to a Dagestani family, her experience of cultural heterogeneity and the perception of self was enriched by a period spent in the UK. Understanding the difficulty in overcoming cultural differences continues to form the essence of her artistic practice.

Makhacheva studied at Goldsmiths College, London, where she obtained a BA in Fine Art in 2007. Upon moving back to Russia, she studied at the Institute of Contemporary Arts, Moscow, graduating in 2009. She has participated in a number of national and international exhibitions including: *Practice for Everyday Life—Young Artists from Russia*, Calvert 22, London, 2011; *Zones of Estrangement*, Land of Tomorrow, Lexington, USA, 2010; *History of Russian Video Art, Volume 3*, Moscow Museum of Modern Art, Moscow, 2010; and *Really?*, II Moscow International Biennale of Contemporary Art, parallel programme, 2009. Her solo exhibition *Affirmative Actions* opened at Impronte Contemporary Art, Milan in March 2011 and was curated by Marco Scotini. Her works are in the collections of The Moscow Museum of Modern Art and The Dagestan Museum of Visual Arts.

Makhacheva describes her art as utilising irony and sarcasm as a way of challenging the notion of 'normality' within social life and revealing the hidden controversies and fiction of public politics towards cultural minorities. She illustrates ways in which outward adherence to social norms of behaviour, with respect to people of other cultures, does not imply acceptance of the inconsistencies, problems and conflicts that are hidden and out of view but very much in existence. She emphasises that it is not enough to offer the 'Other' an opportunity to speak, in fact it takes an entirely unique approach to hear and recognise an individual's subjective and symbolic status.

Bullet

Video documentation of performance / 4.39 min., colour,
sound / Dagestan, 2010

'When I flew home to Makhachkala from Moscow to shoot this video I found out that on the corner of my street right by the school three policeman had been shot dead that same day.

What can this work be about, when shot in such a context? I shoot into the sand with a 'Makarov', a service gun used by the local police. As soon as I take the gun I feel the power of this instrument. I ask my cameraman to move away, afraid that the bullet might ricochet. I shoot, blow-back, sound, crater in the sand. As I start digging I realise that the crater was only on the surface so it is impossible to distinguish a trajectory of a bullet and I need to dig at random. By the time I find a bullet I have fired almost the whole magazine of bullets. I leave a big hole behind. All the other bullets I shot into the sand but couldn't find stayed somewhere in the beach near the city of Makhachkala, Dagestan. A gunshot into the sand. The hole that is left behind from my digging, retrieving only one of the many bullets fired, acts as an imaginary, fictitious form of violence that belongs to the discourse of media and public politics'.

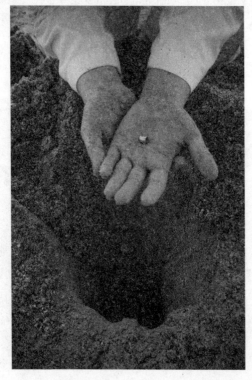

Delinking, 2011

'The term "delinking", emerged from the decolonial project developed by W Mignolo and M Tlostanova, is a way to break from the theo- and ego-logical epistemic tyranny of the modern world and its epistemological and cultural consequences: the coloniality of knowledge and of being.

Mehndi is a ceremonial art form, an application of henna as a temporary form of skin decoration, it is usually applied at the pre-wedding rituals or festivities, on hands and legs, but never on the face. For this performance the artist's face is painted with the designs of three traditional Mehndi schools: African, Indian and Middle Eastern. As soon as the face is completely covered with leafy and symmetrical patterns the destruction starts: all the blanks where the skin is still visible are filled with henna, so by the end of the painting process no designs can be distinguished, the whole face is covered with dark green paste. After a few hours, when the paste dries and is washed off, the artist is left with a new facial orange/brown colour, a new mask that will last for about a week.

One of the key aspects of this work is continuity, the continuity that goes beyond exhibition opening or festival. The fact is that the perfor-

mance doesn't end on the evening of the event, but continues for one week, continues in the artist's everyday interactions, in the change and in the anxiety that this change can trigger'.

Endeavour
Video / 9.00 min., colour, sound / Tsada mountain village,
Dagestan, 2010

'Frozen pictorialism is not characteristic of video art. The statics of mountain scenery is animated by one small, barely noticeable human figure. The massive rock seems unstable, but there is little chance to change anything. What is this about? About the comparable immensity of the human condition? About standing still and movement? About futility and necessity of ones endeavours? About the role of the artist in society that is ready for change?'

RehIen (translated from the Avar language means flock)
Video / 7.21 min., colour, silent / Dagestan, 2009

'The work is shot in terrain that lies between the Caucasus mountain villages of Tsada and Ahalchi in the Republic of Dagestan. It has a simple narrative. A young man is wearing a traditional sheepskin coat called a Timug. This was worn by shepherds who would then attempt to scramble as close as possible to the flock of sheep. A literal interpretation of this work may concern itself with local nature or traditional cultural symbols. The viewer is compelled to ask 'What is the goal behind the performer's actions?' RehIen deals with the complexities of social relations that demand an adherence to certain rules and regulations for social and cultural integration to be successful. This work asks what we are prepared to do in order to become part of a community. What choices do we need to make to achieve integration? Are we willing to wear clothes that are heavy and highly uncomfortable, from the perspective of modern man, and force ourselves down onto all fours?'

CAFÉ LA VIE

Rachel Holmes

Café La Vie, Ramallah. Chat, chink of glasses and beer bottles. Sweet apple smoke narghila and the tang of lemon and almond trees shading the café garden and the periphery of the adjacent refugee camp. Real Madrid v Barcelona on an outdoor screen. The match is projected from the laptop of café proprietor Saleh Totah. He moves genially amongst the tables of his varied clientele of all ages and classes; many locals, a few foreigners. Spirited groups of students, builders, musicians, white-collar professionals, poets, activists, NGO workers, academics, cracking nuts, munching cucumber slices, sipping wine, beer, hot chocolate, or fresh mint lemonade. Elsewhere, individual punters in the lonely company of a glass of arak or whiskey. They look either deeply contemplative or vacant, bewildered—lost. Each has a story: ejected from their ancestral village; injured; family members killed or dead from broken hearts; home destroyed; jobless; refused entry into Jerusalem; separated from wife and children in Jordanian camps; or—further afield—the US, by whom they've been refused re-entry to rejoin their families after 9/11.

Broken and whole, all life is at Café La Vie.

It's 27 April 2011 and I've just finished a long interview de-brief with the first graduates of the Palestine Writing Workshop (PWW). We've reviewed our journey of the last eighteen months together and their experience of this new creative writing programme, the first in Palestine. PWW works to foster a community of emerging writers in Palestine through an array of programmes in both Arabic and English. We've reflected on the Palestinian education system of the past 18 years since the Palestinian Ministry of Education and Higher Education came into existence in August 1994 following the transfer of authority agreement between the PLO and Israel, a result of the Oslo Accords. Coming up to date, students have explained to me the impact of the recent Egyptian revolution on Palestinian curriculum reform. This group of students are the new generation inheriting the failed spring and bankrupt promises of the Oslo Accords of 1993–4—born on the cusp of the 90s, their ages ranging between 18 and 24. They now look to Egypt and the Middle Eastern civil uprisings for a revivification of Palestinian politics.

Lingering over the last heavenly crumbs of shared cakes, we praise the confectioner genie in Saleh's kitchen. These are the generous and insistent treats of Adila Habib, just promoted after a few months in her first job at the Ministry of Education and Culture. Her promotion rests on her reading, writing and critical skills. She edits and redrafts better than anyone else in the ministerial office. Tia Issa and I have just confirmed the next title for the Cloudwalkers Book Club. Tia runs the group, and oversees the circulation of books to the burgeoning spin-off book clubs; all share the same precious set of books. Tia clasps my hands gently—'*Ahleen!* Thanks PalFest for making it possible for us to meet and work together'. We celebrate Egyptian writer and activist Ahdaf Soueif, founder and chair of the Palestine Literature Festival, and forcefield of intellectual brilliance, integrity and beauty.

It's because of Ahdaf and PalFest that we are all here now.

Suad Amiry arrives. We have a dinner date. She has the charismatic presence of a great movie star. I introduce Tia, Adila', Lubna, Kanza, Abra and Safa as 6 of the 12 first graduates of the Palestine Writing Workshop. Suad knows of PWW through her involvement in PalFest. The students are thrilled to meet one of Palestine's leading writers and architects—already a legend in her lifetime. Suad reciprocates their pleasure and inquisitiveness—quizzing each of them, a flash of the curiosity and compassionate empathy that define her luminous writing talent.

I contemplate this intergenerational powerhouse of emerging and established writers and activists congregated under Saleh's lemon trees. Fittingly named, Café La Vie is Saleh's family home. He was born and grew up here. 'You are a crazy donkey', his friends said when he opened for business in 2009. 'A café restaurant in an oasis wedged between a risky refugee camp and a manic bus station? It'll never, ever work. People won't come. Don't worry, we'll feed you when you're bankrupt'. This evening, as every other, La Vie is a heartthrob of Ramallah. The football, the flirting, the discussions about the line-up of the next PWW Poetry of Palestine open mike event now a regular happening in the city, the eating of fragrant lamb chops, rosemary infused prawns, haute-cuisine salads, the shoe-shopping comparisons, the arguing over whether Egypt will now open the Gaza border.

Since my induction through PalFest, I've visited Palestine regularly. One cultural enterprise, a travelling literature festival—an annual caravan of worldwide writers—has led to many others. PalFest launched in 2008, bringing world class cultural events to Palestinian communities that would otherwise have no access to them; supporting Palestinian cultural life; and creating active, nurturing cultural links between Palestine and the UK. The festival has renewed media interest in the human situation in Palestine. For a week each year, PalFest puts on at least twenty free public events in various locations in the West Bank; including East Jerusalem, Ramallah, Bethlehem, Nablus, Al-Khalil/Hebron, and Jenin. Palestinian Israelis are served by events in Nazareth. Readings, poetry, spoken word performances, music and debate are accompanied by an intense daily schedule of workshops in refugee camps, universities, cultural and community centres. Video-conferences take place with students, teachers and activists in Gaza. Every year the organisers have tried to take the festival into Gaza: and every year the applications for permits have been rejected by the Israeli military authorities. Instead, PalFest runs blockade-busting e-workshops and debates online between Gaza and the West Bank; as does PWW.

Over the past three years PalFest has initiated and inspired a number of innovative and promising educational and artistic activities, PWW amongst them. I'm here to conclude my current research into education and civil society in Palestine for Writers' Bloc, an independent, international writer-run collective of which I am a founder member with Zadie Smith, Kamila Shamsie, Nick Laird and Hari Kunzru. Writers' Bloc is funded by Open Society Foundation. I want to see for myself what impact reading, writing and literary culture have in the context of resistance and redress to cultural occupation. And possibly the overthrow of cultural colonisation. Israel has declared war on Palestinian culture. It systematically appropriates, steals, undermines, represses or trashes it. How has Palestinian leadership at home and in the diaspora responded to this assault? How does the structure and delivery of Palestinian education teach and encourage the skills needed for the arts of writing, articulacy, creativity and critical think-ing—skills required by the students to challenge the Israeli cultural ambush they have been born into. And can an extra-curricular literary festival of eclectic, insubordinate international writers contribute to crea-tive education and civil society development in Palestine? What, in short, are the roles and responsibilities of writers—if any—in solidarity with or just curious about Palestinian politics and society?

I've read the documentation on the Five-Year Education Development Plan (2001–2005), the subsequent Education Development Strategic Plan (2008–2012), the review process of the pre-tertiary education sub sector, the World Bank funded sector study of higher education, and the in-depth analysis of the Technical and Vocational Education sub-sector. They have lots and lots of tables and graphs. I've sat and listened attentively with courtesy and feigned patience through discussions with charming men in inter-changeable suits with interchangeable nameplates on their interchangeable doors and desks—Dean of … Vice-Principal of … President of … and so on. Mostly, I've come away from these meetings delivered of hospitable coffee and an on-message executive summary restatement of the executive summary statement of Palestinian Authority endorsed review processes and policies. For which please see list above. But what I want to know is how these education policies respond to the emergency of illegal occupa-tion and colonisation of the mind and body? What does all of it mean in practice, for Palestinians of all ages in the education system? What kind of students do these educational policies seek to produce? How does this system nurture artists, political thinkers and comedians? What can young Palestinians expect from their existing education system?

There's a warm breeze and fragrance of thyme and roses in the garden of Café La Vie. Suad and I are joined by Sophie De Witt, Director of PWW. Sophie and I tell Suad the story of the windflower bush and the big yellow watering can we took to Birzeit Village today for Safa Zabib to plant in the garden of the newly donated premises of the Palestine Writing Workshop, Beit Nimeh—Nimeh's building. Safa, a graduate of the first PWW cohort, is developing the gardens of the programme's first designated home. Beit Nimeh is named in honour of Nimeh Nasir, brilliant feminist pioneer of Palestinian education and cultural development in the 1920s. The building is shared collaboratively with PalFest, and in time will house partner cul-tural and community projects.

Sophie and I show Suad our lopsided photos snapped at arms length on our mobile cameras in front of the freshly painted bookshelves in the Reading Room. Framing our big smiles, the multicoloured spines of Shehadeh's *Palestinian Walks*, Shamsie's *Kartography*, Amiry's *Sharon and My Mother-in-law*, Calil's *Bad Faith*, Abulhawa's *Mornings in Jenin*, Aboulelah's *Lyrics Alley*, Bidisha's *Venetian Masters*, Yassin-Kassab's *Road From Damascus*, Kricorian's *Dreams of Bread and Fire*, Younge's *Who are We and Should it Matter in the 21ˢᵗ Century?* Blockbusters by Kate Mosse and Henning Mankell. Poetry collections by Nathalie Handal, Suheir Hamad and Najwan Darwish. Biographies, histories, philosophy and politics. Every copy has either been brought into Palestine by the author themselves, or sent via a circuitous route supported by angels who spirit them away from confiscation by the Israeli customs and postal services. Books don't arrive if they are sent by post. Even from the mighty Amazon.

The PWW Reading Room creates a vital new space for readers and writers. Universities in Palestine close at 4pm. Libraries are shut, student unions are closed. There are a few late classes until 5.30pm; security then escorts the students off campus. Public transport to and from the university stops running. Part of the experience of the Palestine Writing Workshop for students has been a different structure and exploratory freedom of movement. Early evening workshops in central city locations. Hikes in the hills of Ramallah.

Shortly, more workshops for students and residencies for local and international writers will be announced. Sophie and I banter about our tree-planting, competing for the worst puns about the deep-rooted need for this garden as a hotbed of flowering creative space in which students of all ages can sow the seeds of their talent, cultivate the diverse branches of their abilities, harvest the skills to challenge, persuade and speak truth to power. Can the yellow watering can quench the fire of a country burst into flames?

'How did you two meet?' Suad asks.

May, 2009. I'm steering a course through Salah Eddin Street, edging around an artillery manned tank in the elegant Talbiyeh neighbourhood that divides East and West Jerusalem. I'm in an unpunctuated line of writers, poets, novelists, publishers, and journalists being led determinedly by Ahdaf Soueif and Omar Hamilton towards the French Cultural Institute.

We're hedged and trailed by IDF armoured jeeps—flashing lights, ear-blasting sirens—progress is slow. It's the opening night of the second Pal-Fest and armed Israeli soldiers have just boorishly ejected us from the Palestinian National Theatre. As the gala event of poetry and prose readings began, they stormed the venue waving a closure order (written in very bad Arabic) on the theatre, ejecting us from the site and blocking the streets around it. Unhesitatingly, the French Cultural Attaché offered the diplo-matically immunised garden of his nation's Cultural Institute as an alterna-tive venue.

Festival volunteers pick up the platters of food and drink carefully pre-pared and laid out for the planned reception in the theatre lobby, carrying them through the streets to the new venue. After a six and a half hour wait at the King Hussein/Allenby Bridge border check point earlier in the day, I'm hungry. A tall, poised woman with a long luscious Rapunzel plait down her back is walking in front of me, holding aloft a tinfoil platter piled with a tempting rainbow of cucumbers, tomatoes, peppers, celery and carrots. As she pauses to negotiate a military jeep blocking the road, I stick my hand up, grab a fistful of tomatoes, and grin at her. After eight years of living in Palestine, she's mistrustful of people who grab other people's food without asking. She glares at me, challenging, *Who* are you?

That's how Sophie DeWitt and I met.

A few days later, I run a workshop at Birzeit University. Handed the title, 'Advocating for Human Rights in Fiction', I offend an earnest tutor by immediately changing the theme to 'Advocating Nothing: Writing about Human Rights, Wrongs and Ambivalence in Fiction'. The students clamour to discuss the ethics and representation of human rights in political dis-course and the media—in their view constantly promised but perpetually denied them in global media rhetoric. And, some of the Christian students ask, why is so much of the western media so ignorant about Muslim and Christian Arab cultures? Time bends me back 20 years to 1991, South Africa, teaching semiotics and critical theory—feminism, Freud, Fou-cault—to youth activist struggle students at the University of the Western Cape; the 'People's University', with its massive and inspiring ceiling-to-floor library banner EDUCATION FOR LIBERATION. Truth be told, those students, the first university intake after the 1991 political unban-nings, taught me a great deal more than they ever learned from me. Like these Palestinians, those South African students were a multi-culti post-ethnic mixture of Muslims, Christians, secularists and atheists. The difference was, there were also Jews amongst them. I share with the Palestinian students how those young South Africans—the generation of '76—grew up with a fascist, racist, totalitarian apartheid that seemed utterly intractable, but proved to be solvable. Many of them are now political, cultural, business and civil society leaders of post-apartheid South Africa.

The Birzeit students are passionate, perceptive, absorbant—evidently sucking in information and inspiration from wherever they can garner it. Their brains are also, I realise immediately, starving from lack of access to good books, struggling to construct coherent argument and unable to project their minds beyond the conditions of their immediate lived existence. Pretty much like university undergraduates the world over, then? Not quite. Unlike students in, for example, Western Europe or America, they can't get regular, affordable access to recently published books to read, or easily plug in to robust, counter-cultural media. And by recent, I mean books published in the last forty odd years, since—not un-coincidentally—the Arab-Israeli War of 1967. It's not a question of cost or class; the books are simply unreachable. Their course materials are all photocopies.

Sophie, who liaised the PalFest workshops at Birzeit University, observed my seminar. She told me she wanted to start a creative writing workshop. 'In my humble opinion, we need a creative economy here. There's a particular value placed on poetry and the poet, but not on youngsters learning poetry or engaging in a wider literary culture. From a life and career perspective, there's this attitude: why would you want to write poetry, fiction, history or political thoughts? The whole culture is desperately reliant on aid, NGO and foreign-agency employment. You can get a job in a heartbeat if you can write a funding proposal. Why write to challenge, or to persuade, or to imagine? And if you do, where do Palestinians get published? There's barely any publishing industry in Palestine; Palestinians are published mostly from outside of the country. And if you do, who will listen?'

So during the week of the literature festival—at Birzeit and workshops at other universities, I learn about the hunger for new books and the urgent need for transferable creative skills in Palestine. Storytelling. Analysis. Editing. Public Speaking. Satire. Comedy. The weapons needed to fight cultural occupation of the mind and soul. Studies for action. Looking at the lunatic Separation Wall in all its complete absence of metaphor, I begin to think of these tools as springboard skills—Olympic pole-vaulting for the imagination; to jump the multiple barriers, blocks and obstacles of the military occupation; the walls inside heads. For there is no more natural justice, truth, logic or rationality in this evil situation than there was in the deformed inventions of apartheid. To challenge fiction or manipulated facts you have to know how they are constructed. Wafa Darwish at Al-Quds university explains, 'War on culture is more dangerous and important to resist than physical war, because it is more discrete and intricate. In addition to its actual physical war of ethnic cleansing against Palestinians, Israel more quietly and more dangerously conquers our culture. PalFest solidifies and reinforces Palestinian literature and culture thus helping the Palestinian people resist Israeli conquest of Palestinian literary and cultural identity'.

In a Jerusalem restaurant on the last night of the festival, Sophie unclasps from her neck the silver olive tree pendant with a Palestinian flag embedded in its branches and refastens it around mine. 'Would you come back to teach a pilot creative writing course?'

I returned later that year, in November 2009, to teach a 20-hour, week-long pilot course called The Writer's Tool Box, followed up by a Continuation Course in May 2010. The continuation course supported the students by creating practical opportunities to further develop their skills and engagement in global culture with practical experience of further training and voluntary work in the cultural and artistic sectors.

Following the inaugural workshop, Palestinian-American spoken word poet and activist Remi Kanazi taught the second course in February 2010, Jeremy Harding followed in July, and Robin Yassin-Kassab conducted the first workshop to take place in Nablus last September. So far, all programmes have been organised and run on a voluntary basis. As yet, there is no funding. A nominal registration fee—that started at ILS125 (£22.50) and is now ILS200 (£35)—secures commitment to a place on the course and contributes to the pot to cover the student's subsistence for the week.

Lubna Taha, who recently won a journalism prize for a published article on the PWW, describes the PWW creative writing workshop as 'my sesame gate': 'This experience never ends. I've learned that you can write if you possess a feeling for the language, for meaning and words, as well as a willingness to liberate the mind from imprisoned language and thought. One of the most distinguishing characteristics about this workshop was the fact that it was taught through a creative methodology, unlike in our schools and universities where teaching and lecturing is based on old and didactic teaching methods. These methods imprison our ability to challenge, ask difficult questions, criticise and fantasise'. As a further result of her participation in PWW, Lubna also recently translated an article written by Hussam Ghosheh from Arabic to English for the UK *Guardian*.

PalFest participant writers, invited to Palestine as guests of the festival, reciprocate the hospitality by returning to teach on PWW on a purely voluntary basis. All of them have jobs, families to support, and homes to run. Their teaching time has been taken from annual holiday, and the routes into Palestine are complex and potentially emotionally and physically taxing. I ask Sophie what has mostly characterised the writers who have taught on the course so far. 'Apart from flexibility, cultural sensitivity, a proven ability for creative teaching? A sense of adventure and a sense of humour are essential'.

A prerequisite for teaching on the Palestine Writing Workshop is that foreign writers must have previous experience in Palestine. If not, PalFest provides a crucial orientation for them. This measure provides a broader collective selection process, peer review under pressure, and ensures that tutors have been inducted into the terrain of contemporary Palestine before teaching on PWW. PalFest made the Palestine Writing Workshop possible, combining the energy and resources of an international literature festival grounded in grass-roots work with local civil society.

Most of us writers like to think that we are somewhat well-informed about the world. Fairly media savvy. It should, after all, go with an artistic vocation based on human empathy and independent mindedness. Shouldn't it? Novelist William Sutcliffe speaks for many of us who were brought to the realisation of our worldly complaisance through PalFest,

'My trip to the West Bank with the Palestine Festival of Literature was truly life-changing. Despite thinking I was reasonably well-informed about the region, this week of intense travelling, talking, listening, teaching and learning demonstrated to me that nothing you can read will ever give you a real sense of what it means to live under military occupation ... seeing the wall, talking to people who live in its shadow, and going through the checkpoints was a visceral and unforgettable experience. To feel the shock of undergoing these daily realities of Palestinian life is to make the simplest yet most profound connection between politics and human emotion, and therefore to understand the situation in a way that no-one who has never visited could. As a human being and as a writer, this was a revelatory experience ...though I have never witnessed more brutal oppression in twenty years of travelling on every continent of the globe, my encounters with the writers, students and residents of the West Bank, and also with the inspiring group of fellow participants from around the world, left me uplifted and inspired'.

Like the generalised models of colonisation, there are very broadly speaking three kinds of international literary festivals: assimilationist, integrationist and those that function by indirect rule. In the latter cohort are those festivals that have tended to parachute in international writers who skim superficially through the host country giving readings, public performance and shaking a few official bureaucratic palms at gala dinners with very little notion of the national politics or engagement in the local culture beyond probably anachronistic 'traditional' dancing or music tagged onto evening events and perhaps a trip to visit kids at a local school or writers' union. Of the other assimilationist, integrationist sorts are those festivals that bed-in, requiring more engagement from their writers and audiences as co-participants, leading them into exploration, dialogue and cultural exchange. PalFest is of the latter sort. As well as increasingly providing a platform for local talent, it crucially enables diasporic Palestinian writers the brief remission of returning home. Palestinian-American Remi Kanazi, who lives in New York, describes how, 'As a poet and teacher, PalFest provided me with an invaluable opportunity to connect with Palestinian youth, educators and local communities in a way I hadn't before'. PalFest is providing a significant channel for exiled writers back into border-locked Palestine. The now regular Poetry of Palestine open mic nights are the result of Remi's PWW spoken word workshop.

Literature festivals have been one of the biggest cultural growth industries of the past decade. Festival brands have gone international, with Hay Festivals the market leader, and now developing its own publishing projects. Until recently, with the notable and persistent exception of the British Council, not much serious thought, programming or investment has gone into the role and impact of literature festivals in local civil society, into meaningful cultural collision, cultural tourism and dialogue—where the audience are as much active participants as the performers.

PalFest is a counter-cultural move against the Israeli cultural blockade on the West Bank and Gaza. It is also an active assertion against the cultural clichés about kuffiyeh/hijab-wearing-gun-toting/bomb-throwing-Islamist-Hamas-supporting Palestinians that still, wearily, ballast Zionist imperialism in appeasing Western nations. Like PalFest audiences, the PWW student groups and Saleh Totah's café customers in downtown Ramallah, modern Palestine is characterised by a prevailing impetus towards secular governance, multi-faith religious tolerance, and a liberal—sometimes libertarian—mix-up of cultures, faiths and traditions that sometimes makes even the old Ottoman empire look a bit suburban. PalFest busts open the myths of militant Palestine; or, as Booker Prize nominated novelist and poet Adam Foulds puts it, removes the ideological 'barrier of fear': 'The festival is a recognition of the independent life of the Palestinian people. Coming through the invisible barrier of fear has actually filled me with hope. I have found deep humanity on the other side'. Foulds told me that his experience of the festival was like 'seeing for the first time from the other side of the mirror'. On his return, he wrote an article for the Jewish Chronicle, entitled 'Correcting my Vision in Palestine', eloquently describing this experience.

Back in the garden of Café La Vie, we debated the Palestinian education system. But surely everything can't be blamed on the Israelis and the occupation?

The biggest complaint of the students is the narrowness of the curriculum. 'In Palestine', says Kanza Said, 'it's treated as more of a fundamental text than the Qu'ran or the Bible. Like a religious book. We are made to stick to every word at school and at university. The teachers don't create new techniques'. I ask why new techniques are needed. 'Because the educational system is based on didactic rote learning. Educational institutions are concerned about quantity not quality. The teachers are poor, because they're a product of these schools and universities and have limited resources. At the end of each semester of drilling in the syllabus, all students go through a national exam. They don't teach you how to think, they teach you how they think'.

Adila' Habib confirms the didactic structure of the curriculum: 'Take for example Arabic and English language teaching. I always hated these classes because you had to sit down and copy what the teacher wrote. It was all the same. The same olive trees. The same transition of winter into the same spring. The perfect composition is by a student who can transcribe and follow the technique on the prescribed subject. There's no creativity'. Abra Awad concurs. 'I think education in Palestine is a weak system. We learn ABC and 123, but they don't also give us enough space for our imaginations to get wider. We are made to concentrate on memorising rather than being creative. School and university are totally closed fields; we need activities to widen the borders of our minds'.

This passionate and urgent desire for the broadening of their imaginative and critical reach is something I hear repeatedly. 'One of our main problems is the total separation between education and society. There's no integration. Why don't teachers at school and university talk about what's going on here? Why are they so scared? Do they think they can protect us from this reality? The political conditions we live in are part of all of our lives'. There's a consensus amongst these students that they have been discouraged by the educational system from learning how to use language to reflect and critique. And there's an overwhelming craving to express themselves and tell their own stories.

Adila' believes teachers should try to develop the critical thinking skills and imagination of their students. 'I don't believe the Palestinian Authority want to encourage people who will criticise the society. They are closed-minded. At university you are presented with limited options from which you are expected to print your personality—you will be Fatah, Hamas, or al-Jabhah (the Front). But actually what happens is that you are exposed to insight into who really works, who doesn't, and what people do rather than what they symbolise. We'd like better courses in philosophy and cultural science with instructors to open and extend our minds to different things'.

Why the diffidence and weakness of a Palestinian state education system that started with hard work and the best intentions?

The Palestinian Curriculum Centre operates under the Palestine Ministry of Education. The national Palestinian Reform and Development Plan (PRDP) of 2007, maintains the position that education is a basic human right, but all state-run education suffers from two factors that have determined the shape of contemporary school and higher education in Palestine: rushed development and political timidity.

It's the occupation, stupid.

The years 2001–2005 were dominated by emergencies caused by the second intifada. The West Bank and Gaza were bombarded by relentless Israeli military incursions, border closures, multiplying checkpoints, draconian restrictions on movement and travel and an array of other obstacles to normal life imposed by Israel. The Separation Wall constructed by Israel in the West Bank led to the isolation of communities and, in a growing number of cases, increasing as the construction of the wall spreads, the separation of children from the schools closest to them. In these adverse conditions, the Ministry of Education tried to maintain a long-term strategic view and hold onto its cooperation with donors and other development partners. The Palestinian Legislative Council elections in January 2006 and the rise of Hamas to power in the Palestinian Government led to a formal withdrawal of most donors and development partners with the Ministry of Education, jeopardising the completion of the second five-year plan—the Education Strategic Plan 2008–2012. A return to donor investment in late 2007 in tandem with renewed interest in the peace process brought the Palestinian Reform and Development Plan back on track. Education is central to this impetus. It positions education as a basic human right, a vital tool for socio-economic development, and for instilling moral values and civic responsibility. The plan tries to guarantee equitable access to a comprehensive education system consisting of pre-school, basic and secondary education; formal and non-formal education; technical and vocational education; and higher education. The strategic plan summary stresses, 'The focus is on the modernisation of the education system and better preparing Palestinian citizens, particularly the youth, for the future. This will include modernisation of the curriculum in line with the PNA's vision of a future Palestinian state—a state with a knowledge-based economy, connected to the global community that embraces humanistic values and is tolerant'. The report goes on to make all the right noises about training, capacity building, sustainability, better coordination with the United Nations Relief and Works Agency for Palestinian Refugees (UNRWA), NGOs and the private sector.

The national development context is fraught with complex challenges, yet the plan is committed 'to restore good governance and the rule of law to the West Bank, which the Palestinian National Authority aspires to replicate in Gaza'. The Vocational Training Initiative Program, central to the thrust of the plan, focuses on the provision of vocational and technical training at the secondary and tertiary levels, to better prepare young Palestinians for the job market. I put all this to the PWW students. The effort, the work, the determination of the Ministry of Education to deliver an education system and project into the future, against seemingly impossible odds. I goad them—'Aren't you being unfair? This is a determined attempt to deliver a universal access, multi-faith and secular, rights-based, tolerant education programme under extraordinarily complex and challenging circumstances. Cut the Ministry of Education and Culture and your university tutors some slack, guys'.

Tia sips her marshmallow hot chocolate thoughtfully and sighs. 'They are really trying what they think is their best. But there is a lot of fear, and they pass on that anxiety and fear. The big problem is that the system was developed far too fast. And it's stuffed with *stuff*; we call them 'stuffed subjects'. In primary school I took 10 subjects instead of just learning language, basic science and civil education. My head was so *stuffed with stuff* I lost concentration. It was all memorisation. No thinking. Then high school. *More* stuffed subjects. Get good grades. Go to university. Then graduate. Get married. Get a job. Whatever limited choice of job the occupation allows you'. Tia's comments represent the prevailing view of these students that they are uncomfortable with the way their education system is trying to inculcate a sense of normalisation into what they know is a wholly abnormal situation.

When I suggest they are being too hard on the education authorities, and their parents and community elders, all of them respond that they want a politicisation of the school and university system, and an upgrading to make it more contemporary and relevant—connections with other civil society and cultural organisations, focus groups with students, workshops and further trainings for teachers to improve their skills and, concomitantly, the environment of the schools and universities.

'The Ministry of Education want people to be static—they don't want people to revolt. There's a fear of the unknown; and a great fear of resistance because of vested interests', Kanza explains. Recently, a process of changing the curriculum has been implemented in direct response to the Egyptian revolution. 'I think this is one of the main successes of the Egyptian revolution', she says, 'because when Egyptian children and students have a curriculum that doesn't have Hosni Mubarak's image on every page, a new space of mental freedom is created. Our minds are colonised by the logo of the Ministry of Education on every page of our text books, and tired old repetitive nationalist stories that do not inflame children's imaginations'.

Inflaming imaginations is one of the objectives of the Palestine Writing Workshop.

There were twelve graduates of the pilot Writer's Tool Box course. So far, six of this initial cohort have gone onto further placements. All are now volunteers on the programme, in PalFest or other related literary and cultural initiatives. Almas Bayt and Safa Zabib were selected for internships at the Southbank Centre Poetry International 2010 festival that focused on poetry from the Arab world. They described their week of shadowing programmers, interviewing writers, blogging, visiting publishers, and inhaling the cultural life of London as, simply, 'life-changing', as did their host families. Incidentally, Almas and Safa were penalised—not rewarded—for their internships on Poetry International by being summarily issued with unexcused absences for all their missed classes by the administration of their university English Department, notwithstanding advance application for study leave to the department, and interventions to provide secure, compliant alternatives for them to complete their missed coursework. Both were sanguine about the bureaucratic punishment. Almas shrugged, 'It was worth it'. This episode rather seems to confirm the students' claims about the narrowness of the curriculum and timidity of their tutors.

Four other students were nominated and selected for the Bloomsbury Qatar Foundation Summer Writing Institute. As well as enjoying the fiction workshop taught by Greg Mosse, they were fascinated by their experiences visiting a Gulf city. This week-long course focused on training to develop their skills as teachers, equipping them to go home and teach workshops in Arabic. Lubna Taha, who went to Qatar, takes up the story, 'When we came back to Palestine after the Bloomsbury-Qatar workshop we started directly preparing for the 10 weeks summer training. A lot of students registered. The training was conducted one day each week. This experience was different because now we were the teachers. We felt the responsibility of transforming and sharing our experience with other emerging writers. I learned that knowledge should not be monopolised because if we do not share it, it will die like a poet who refuses to write metaphor. After each workshop, the PWW family grew more and more. We now have a great number of volunteers and we are expanding our activities to reach more people who dream, like I did, of writing and being heard'. In under two years, the graduates of PWW have taken ownership of the project, and partially solved the problem of access being open only to those who have English. The collective possessive nouns in Lubna's article say it all. The problem of getting contemporary Arab writers and poets as Writers in Residence and to conduct workshops remains. Israel won't let them in.

There are now just over 100 graduates of PWW workshops. All the writers who have taught on the programme who are not Palestinian or of Palestinian heritage are alumni of PalFest. At Beit Nimeh this summer these students are organising and tutoring teacher training and creative writing workshops in Arabic. Safa, who as a child used to go with her grandmother every year to harvest olives from the family orchard in the hills of Ramallah, is supervising the development of the garden and shady arbours for the students to read, think, reflect and debate in a peaceful, safe space. And, I hope, showing them how to make good use of the big yellow watering can to cultivate the windflower bushes.

At Café La Vie, the conversation continues.

NAJAF

CAPITAL OF ISLAMIC CULTURE

Rose Aslan

Most people do not consider taking their next vacation to Iraq. The residents of the city of Najaf hope to change that. One of the holiest cities in Islam, Najaf is home to the tomb of Imam Ali ibn Abi Talib, cousin and son-in-law of the Prophet Muhammad. It also contains the biggest cemetery in the world, Wadi al-Salam (the Valley of Peace), famous in recent years as the site of deadly battles between Iraqi insurgents and coalition forces. Muslims, in particular Shiis from Iran, Pakistan, India, Lebanon and Afghanistan, flock to Najaf, as well as the other important shrine cities of Karbala, Samarra, and Kadhimiya in Baghdad, to visit the tombs of the family of the Prophet Muhammad, considered to be infallible in Shii theology.

The city developed around the Tomb of Imam Ali, which was first constructed by the Abbasid Caliph Harun al-Rashid in the late eighth century. It later became the centre of Shii Islamic learning when Sheikh al-Tusi, escaping to the safety of Najaf during widespread persecution of Shiis in Baghdad, founded the first madrasa, or school of higher Islamic education, in the eleventh century. The ancient city of Kufa, right next to Najaf, has pre-Islamic origins and is a must-visit for any history buff. It is home to the seventh-century Kufa Mosque and other important religious sites from early Islamic history. Babylon is only an hour's drive away, another attraction for those interested in Iraq's pre-Islamic civilisations.

Despite Najaf's violent recent past and its reputation for being the headquarters of Muqtada al-Sadr and his supporters, people from all walks of life are trying to change their city's negative image on the global stage. Najaf may soon make its way onto the tourism radar beyond its status among the devout as a pilgrimage destination.

Early last May, I found myself disembarking from an Air Arabia plane at the recently-built Najaf Airport along with a large group of Indian pilgrims who had transited through Sharjah. Greeted by my host Sami Rasouli, director of the Muslim Peacemaker Teams, I entered Iraq with some apprehension, but excited nevertheless to begin my new adventure. Packed into an SUV, we made our way out of the airport to my host's home in Kufa.

It was my first time in Iraq. I held onto the door handle for dear life, imagining that militants lay in wait to attack the car or that IEDs lined the road from the airport. Bombarded with propaganda about the dangers of Iraq since my childhood, I thought I was entering a country in a constant state of violence, with shootings and bombings occurring on a daily basis in every city and town. Little did I know that several weeks later I would be navigating the city on my own, depending on public transport to move around the city. I never travelled in a convoy or even thought of obtaining a flak vest or other protection. I was living with and among Iraqis and was determined to avoid sticking out. Dressed in a black abaya (similiar to the Iranian chador) from head to toe, I was able to blend in and walk around the city unhindered (women, beware: while wearing the abaya is not required in the shrine cities, outside of the old city, you won't see a single woman without one). In the past few years the city has become a safe refuge for Iraq's Shiis, and Shiis from Baghdad and other more volatile regions have been moving to both Najaf as well as Karbala, where they are able to live in relative safety.

I quickly learned how to navigate the religious, social and political geography of the city with the help of my hosts and others who generously took time to orient me to the Najafi way of life. I was there to learn about the situation in Iraq, to hear first-hand stories about Iraqis' lives, as well as to conduct research for my PhD dissertation on the history of pilgrimage to the shrine of Imam Ali. During the month I was there, I met with intellectuals, academics, religious leaders, peacemakers, doctors, engineers, students, housewives and other hard-working Iraqis. I also discovered that the city was involved in intense preparations as it had been chosen to be the 2012 Capital of Islamic Culture for the Arab region by the Islamic Educational, Scientific and Cultural Organization (ISESCO), a global Islamic organisation based in Morocco that works to promote education, culture and science in concordance with Islamic values among Muslim societies. Each year the organisation chooses three cities, in the African,

Arab, and Asian regions of the Muslim-majority world, to be capitals of Islamic culture. In 2011, the cities of Tlemcen in Morocco, Jakarta in Indonesia, and Conakry in Guinea celebrated their religious heritage. For 2012, ISESCO's designated capitals are Niamey in Niger, Dhaka in Bangladesh, and Najaf.

The main idea of ISESCO's Capitals of Islamic Culture Program is to bring cities that have played an important role in Islamic history into the spotlight and to celebrate their religious, cultural, scientific and intellectual contribution to the world. The programme not only attracts positive media coverage to the chosen cities, but also plays a role in revitalising them, especially those that have suffered from the effects of war, such as Najaf or Ghazni in Afghanistan (chosen for 2013). UNESCO's Iraq office is also offering assistance to the organisers of Najaf 2012, as Najaf is the first Iraqi city to be chosen as a capital of Islamic culture. Organisers hope to highlight Iraq's importance as the cradle of civilisation and an important cultural centre rather than its image as victim of America's 'war on terror'.

Officials have decided to use the opportunity to comprehensively rehaul the city by surfacing previously unsurfaced roads, building highway overpasses, and constructing a conference hall, a 'cultural palace', the city's first museum and its first five-star hotel. Added to infrastructural problems, the intellectual and religious heritage of the city was neglected or actively destroyed by Saddam Hussain's regime. In response, officials are working to conserve and catalogue important historical buildings as well as valuable books, manuscripts, and documents. Academics at the University of Kufa and religious scholars from the traditional madrasas are planning conferences and cultural events covering everything related to Najaf, from Orientalist writings on the city to research on historical Najafi personalities and aspects of Najaf's art and architecture.

The officials here must overcome a number of obstacles to ensure the success of the upcoming events. Construction of the cultural palace and other buildings only started in earnest at the end of 2010 and might not be completed according to schedule. It is possible that Najaf will not have a single five-star hotel and not enough four-star hotels to house all of its VIP guests in time for the opening. The city continues to suffer from constant electricity shortages, limited Internet connectivity, an old and quickly deteriorating infrastructure and a corrupt bureaucracy. Yet the organisers have high aspirations, with plans to plant more than a million trees, open up job opportunities for unemployed youth, and to revive Najaf's reputation as a centre of Islamic learning and scholarship. While they may not be able to meet their goals before the end of the year, the project is certainly giving the city the push it needs to overcome the effects of the previous decades of oppression and violence.

Located down the street from the office of Najaf's governor, the headquarters of the 2012 Cultural Capital project is buzzing with activity. Although these are the official headquarters, the project's various committees are spread throughout the city. The office is run by Mundhir al-Hatami, the liaison for the committees as well as a student of Islamic law, who greeted me at the centre and gave me a tour of the grounds.

One of the bigger and most productive committees connected to the project is responsible for publishing works produced by scholars with links to Najaf. I discovered the Office for Writing and Publishing near the end of my stay while speaking with Sheikh Muhammad al-Kerbasi, the head of the Historical Document Section of Kashif al-Gheita Library. Al-Kerbasi is a turban-and-robe-wearing graduate of Najaf's madrasa system, an alternative to the modern university system that continues to function in Iraq. He told me how a number of religious scholars, frustrated by the slow stream of funds, got together to ensure that the religious heritage of the city was given enough emphasis.

Paying from their own personal funds, they took over a madrasa near the tomb of Imam Ali to use as their headquarters. I visited the office during the two hours in the evening when they were open, after they had finished their work outside and when electricity was guaranteed (the electricity would cut out at 8.30 every evening without fail). Sitting by myself on a couch across the room from a group of religious scholars, I was allotted only a short time to speak to Sheikh Ali Mirza, general director of Najaf 2012 and, again, a turban-wearing religious scholar.

The lower floor of the madrasa was now a storehouse for every book and document ever written about Najaf; the upper floor was full of offices where young men typed away on their laptops (due to the electricity problem in Iraq, you hardly see a desktop computer).

This project is just one step in raising awareness about a multi-dimensional Iraq that exists beyond the headlines, beyond the violence and corruption, an Iraq with thousands of years of history and culture and a rich Islamic heritage.

BLACKBOARDS

Bilal Tanweer

When I abuse I do not know I am abusing. This first happened when I was at school. I have protruding teeth and because of this, everyone called me parrot, parrot. One day I beat up this one boy who called me parrot, parrot even though I did not say anything to him. He had short brown hair. I caught him by his hair and then I beat him. But I did not know I abused him and his father and his sister. This happens when I am angry. One of the other boys later told me I used the sister-word to abuse that boy-with-brown-hair, his father and his sister. He said that I said *Bhenchod* to him . It is not a word I will say. Not to his father. But everyone says that I said this word. Everyone cannot lie.

My teacher called Baba to school. Baba did not believe that I knew the words my teacher said I used when abusing her and the boy. She said I abused her when she was trying to pull me away from the boy. I had pulled him down with his hair and climbed on his chest and slapped his face many times. In return, he scratched my face with his nails. I remember all this but not the swearing.

At first, Baba doubted the teacher, but then when other people also told him that they heard me abusing, he was angry and stopped talking to me. I said sorry, sorry to him so many times but he would not say anything or even look at me. Then I became angry and started to cry. And I shouted at him as well. My sister and mother were very scared when I was shouting at Baba. My mother was eating when I was shouting; she stopped chewing her food and her eyes grew big. I saw her looking at me. But I only knew I was angry and I was crying. I did not know what I was saying. Amma beat me with the big steel spoon for getting angry at Baba. She had bought this spoon from the bazaar two days back and it was dipped in the curry bowl.

187

When Amma hit me, it was hot and I could smell the curry on my hand all night. But I was already crying so her beating did not do anything to me. There were red marks on my arms later. But I am strong. After that everyone became quiet. I was sitting alone on the sofa. My mother took my sister in a corner and told her to make me eat food because I had not eaten. They thought I did not know what they talked about in the corner. But I know. My sister came with the food. She fed me food with her hands, and she told me that I should say sorry to Baba.

I apologised but nothing really happened. He kept quiet. He said to Amma, 'I do not know where he learned this language. He is so small'.

Very few people at school fight. But that is because no one calls them parrot, parrot. Soon I left that school. Not only because of fights but because Amma said it had a bad environment. She found a tutor for me. He was tall and his nose was curved. I liked him. He was nice to me. I did all the work he gave me. At school I had problems learning spellings and tables. My tutor taught me about the blackboard we have in our minds, and we can use it to draw in our heads with coloured chalks. I used to close my eyes and draw on the blackboard. And whenever I wanted to remember spellings, I copied them from the blackboard. After that I did not find it difficult to remember things. I even drew things on the blackboard when I went to sleep at night.

I taught Baba to draw on the blackboard also. When he came back from office, I took off his glasses, sat on his stomach (Baba was fat and his stomach jiggled), and then we closed our eyes. Initially, Baba drew only sceneries: one house and one sun and six hills. But then I explained to him that we had a big board, and we could draw anything, with any colour . So then we drew Pakistan's flag. I drew small flags, I liked them. Baba said his flags were large. While drawing, I would sometimes forget what I was drawing and listen to the chalk's sounds—tak-takka-tak-tak and sss-hisssss. But I did not tell Baba this. I knew he would not understand. I just told him to make things: fish, grass, stars (they were the easiest), a big-sized sun. I would always make three suns: one sun for the morning, one for the evening and one for the night. Whatever scenery I made, I had a sun there. I liked the sun. Sun contains light in it. I liked the bulb as well. Bulbs are suns. Small suns. But I like the big sun that no one can turn off. Sometimes, I would just tell Baba to fill his blackboard with light. We did this with yellow chalk. Then one day, just like that, Baba and I started drawing cars and big houses, with big terraces. We chose different colours for rooms and cars. And then, when we finished drawing, we would tell each other how our cars looked like, what the shape of the windows was, what all we could see outside, what colour the floors in the house were.

I always told Baba about my drawing first because if he told me his I would forget mine.

I also left school because we had become poor. Baba lost his job. And the new job was not good. The old uncle Baba worked for was shot while walking out of a bank. Two people on a motorcycle tried to snatch his money. When he refused, they shot him. After that, uncle's brother, the new uncle, took over the business. But he did not like Baba because Baba always spoke the truth. One day the new uncle told him to leave the job.

But much before that, when the new uncle took the place of the old (nice) uncle, Baba was saying to Amma 'I don't think they are happy with me. I had a fight today as well. No, they did not say anything. I just don't like to fight the family I have worked for all my life. His brother and his family have been our guardians for the past fifteen years. But if they want to change their ways, I don't know how I will get along'. Amma was quiet. Everyone was sleeping. They were talking in the dark in low voices. My sister was sleeping, but I was awake. Baba and Amma talked every night like this. Baba said little and then Amma said little. And then they would turn quiet. And then they would say little, little things again and again. And then everyone would go to sleep.

On the day I shouted at Baba, he was completely quiet that night. Amma said, 'He is so small. He will learn'. Then she went silent for some time. I thought they were asleep. She spoke again, 'Someone must have taught him at school'. I heard her hand rubbing Baba's chest. 'You must not worry so much about him. He is so small'. Usually they laughed lightly when they talked about me. They would just laugh lightly. But that day Baba was not saying anything to Amma. Just like he was not saying anything to me. I heard him breathe. He said, 'I think we will have to take him out of school. I don't think I will have this job for too long'.

I felt Baba was drawing a night on his blackboard; a night with a lot of rain and the wet lights of cars, but no sun.

Before we were poor, we used to go out to some nice place to eat every week. I liked that place along the sea where I had spicy barbeque chicken.

My chicken piece was so spicy that I used to get tears. But then we became poor. But Amma tells me I should not say we are poor. After all, we have enough to eat and drink, and have a place to sleep and we are better than millions. So one day when I started crying, Baba told me, 'Don't cry, don't cry. Let us go to the sea on the bus'. I had not been on the bus before, so I was happy and wanted to go with Baba. Baba says that it is one and the same sea everywhere around the world, but he also says there are only very few cities have the sea. Karachi has a sea.

Amma dressed me in dress-pants and put a lot of powder on me so that I would not get skin rash from the heat.

The bus is not like a car. It does not stop. It moves and we have to sit in it while it moves. Baba lifted me on the bus, the conductor pulled me in, and then running, Baba also got onto the bus. The conductor was the last one to get in. It was dangerous. My heartbeat grew fast. At such times I do not feel good. Doctors have told me not to play too hard, and not to fight. Because then I become ill for long. And because old uncle is not here, Baba will have to pay the doctor's fee. Old uncle always used to pay our doctor's bill.

Baba paid the conductor, who had all the money in his hands. I asked Baba, 'Why doesn't the conductor keep the money in his pockets?' Baba said because there is too much of it and someone might steal it from his pocket. But why don't people steal from his hands? Baba said because he is always watching his hands. When you don't want your things to be stolen, you must always watch them. We were sitting at the back of the bus, and Baba was looking out of the window. The bus seats were red and looked dirty. I did not touch them but I was sitting on them. There were designs on the roof with glitter on them. I closed my eyes, opened my blackboard and made those same designs in one of the rooms in my house. The big eagle, white horse with wings, lots of green hills, a big light-pink rose in the middle of the green hills, and shining gold, red, ruby red colours surrounding them. It is difficult to make shiny things on blackboards, but I had a trick. I threw water on the chalk to make it shiny. The floor of the bus was dirty. It had grease-like things all over it. You should not draw dirty things on the blackboard.

The man sitting next to us leaned out of the open door (yes, yes... the bus-door was always open) and spit out every few minutes. I looked away. Baba was not even noticing them.

The bus was going very fast and the wind that came in from the windows was very hot. So I hid myself behind Baba. It was like being in a shadow. Shadows are empty places in things. The colour of shadows is also black, which is the colour of empty things. Blackboard is also black when it is empty. No one can draw shadows on blackboards because shadows keep on changing. You cannot draw changing things. But this happens, you know; you draw and you look and it has changed. Blackboards are quiet places.

Then a fat man without a leg got on the bus. He was even fatter than Baba. He was smiling. He got on the bus and made a joke, 'Aray bhayya! Slow down! If I fall out of the bus, my wife will not wash my clothes!' Everyone smiled. The conductor also smiled. He paid the conductor in coins. The conductor gave him a discount.

The fat man without a leg made me think of my toffee-uncle. Even he does not have a leg. He lost it in a bomb blast. He was going shopping. He does not remember what happened. He only remembers a loud explosion and then he was holding his legs and there were dead bodies all around him.

The fat man without a leg was a nice man. My toffee-uncle is also nice. He was even nicer when he had both legs. He was tall and everyone in the family liked him. He brought me toffees; many kinds of toffees, and biscuits. He brings me toffees even now, after he lost his leg, but now I run away from him. His skin under his eye is burnt. He sometimes holds me for so long that I don't want to come near him because he would hold me for so long again. He does not say his prayers. He says there is no Allah. Many people say he lost his leg because of that. He shouts at them who tell him to pray. He was not like this before. He used to smile when they told him to pray. He is a Marxist. This is the name of people who do not pray.

The fat man asked me my name, my school and what I would become when I grew up. I told him I will be a pilot and fly fighter planes and fight with India. He told me that fighting is not good, and told me to fly planes to carry people from one place to another. I said but those planes do not fly fast. He said they are very fast. I said but I do not like the way they looked, like eggs. I told him I did not like egg-planes. He started laughing. His stomach moved even more than Baba's when he laughed. His teeth were very dirty. He gave me the cow-toffee. Baba said I should thank him. Then Baba told the fat man about me. He said this boy is very naughty and loves to fight and beats his classmates. I said that is because they call me parrot, parrot.

Then I went to sleep. Baba put his arm around me and I was in the shadow and the hot wind coming in through the door did not touch my face and I went to sleep. I woke up when someone was shouting. Three thief-men had come in the bus. One of them sat next to the backdoor, on Baba's side. The other was at the front door. And the third one stood in the middle with his gun. They all had shiny guns and their faces were covered with cloth, which kept falling away. (We all saw their faces. One of them had a thin moustache. The other had a thick, short beard; he was chewing the hair of his lower lip.) The one standing in the middle of the bus was shouting loudly. We were all scared. He said, 'Close the windows!' One window would not close. It was stuck. The thief was shouting at the man sitting next to that window asking him to shut it. I was so scared. I thought the beard-thief would shoot this man for not shutting the window. But then he told him to leave it. He also told the conductor to close the doors.

The bearded thief-man shouted at us, 'Whatever, whatever you have, drop it on the floor in front of you. If I find anything near anyone, I swear to God, I will fire a bullet through his head without a thought'.

The thief-man sitting next to us stood up and started taking everyone's money. He took it first from Baba. I wanted to fight him. But I was scared. No one stood up to fight him.

The thief-man who was at the front sitting with the driver said to the ladies in the front compartment: 'Do not fear. You are like our mothers and sisters. We will not bother you. We do not need your money'. When he said this, the fat man said, 'Please let us go. Aren't we like your brothers and fathers?' The thief thought that the fat man was trying to make fun of him. He looked at him straight in his eyes, 'What did you say? *Haan?*' and then slapped him. It made a loud sound. He put the gun on his head, 'You find this very funny, *haan? Funny*, haan?' And he slapped him again. Everyone turned to see the man being slapped. It was like in the class. When the teacher slapped one boy, no one spoke again.

The thieves took all the money but kept riding the bus with us. They took the money from the conductor. The conductor was watching his notes when the thief took it from him. One of the thieves took the money and put it in his bag. Everyone was looking at them doing this.

Then at one place suddenly the bus slowed down. The thief-man who was sitting with the driver said, 'Don't move anyone, keep sitting, keep sitting...' And then we saw from the one window that was open that a group of people were running after the bus, banging it to stop. They had big sticks in their hands. There were fires burning inside cars and tires on the road. The bearded thief-man opened one window and took his hand out of it and shot the gun in the air three, four times. Everyone who was chasing us with sticks started running away and then the driver drove really very, very fast.

One thief was telling the driver where to go and how to drive, when to slow down, when to drive fast. He also hit the driver once on his head; it did not make any sound. The slaps on the fat man's face were louder. The thieves took the bus very far and after driving for a long time they told the driver to stop. Their motorcycles were parked there. Two thieves quickly ran out and started the motorcycles, the third thief shouted at the bus driver to get away. The bus driver drove so fast and everyone was so quiet.

The bus driver stopped the bus at the sea, and said it would not go any further. 'Get other buses if you want to go anywhere'. Everyone suddenly became angry. They started to fight with him because thieves had taken their money.

Baba and I got off at the sea. The fat man without a leg was also going to the sea. He was not smiling now. His face was red. Baba had a secret pocket in his shalwar where he always hid some money. He gave a few notes to the fat man. Then he took me to the sea.

We sat on the shore. Baba said we will have to stay there until evening. 'There are riots in the city'. I asked Baba what is a riot and he said it is when people fight each other and burn things like cars and tires and shops.

We sat there for a long time watching the waves that came so slowly. There were so few people there and the wind was cool. I wanted to go on a camel ride, but I knew that Baba did not have the money for that. Baba was quiet. I felt he was drawing the night without a sun on his blackboard again. So I snuggled under his arm and said, 'Baba, let us draw even bigger camels than there are here'. I was so afraid to close my eyes because it was getting darker and I was afraid that new thieves might come. But I think it made Baba happy. When I drew the camels, Baba said, 'Let us sit on these camels as well!' So I sat on my very, very big camel. I rode on it. And when Baba asked me, 'How does it feel riding such a big camel?' I said, 'It is like riding on waves. Hard-type of waves'.

Evening came. Baba and I sat on a bench and had roasted peanuts. Baba asked me if I was afraid of the thieves. I told him I was not. I wanted to fight them. He smiled. He told me never to fight thieves and if something like this ever happens, 'give them everything without saying anything'.

When we were returning home, we took the bus again. This time I ran and got on the bus myself without the conductor's help. On our way, we passed that place where we used to have barbeque and where my chicken was the spiciest. I put my head on Baba's arm and he put it around me and I was in the shadow again. As I slept, I imagined my blackboard as big as the sea on which I drew a ship—a big ship moving on waves like a camel. And then I saw the cloth with which the thief covered his face, which kept on slipping and revealing his face. I wanted to draw a sun in the sea because it was dark and I wanted to give light to the ship, but then I fell asleep. But I remember the ship looked like an empty place, like a shadow, and the cloth was fluttering in the wind like its flag.

REVIEWS

THE TURKISH MODEL

S. Parvez Manzoor

Secularism has become the hallmark not only of our political order but also of the rationality, tolerance and humanity of modern man. Today it stands for all that distinguishes reason from fanaticism, enlightened governance from theocratic terror, civilisation from barbarity. Those not bemused by the ideological hype of our times, however, are apt to conceive of secularism as the cult of Mammon, the regime of the global market that kneels before neither God nor Caesar. We need not forget that the initial sign of the secularist will-to-power was its fervour 'to rob God to pay Caesar', to confiscate church property and transfer it to the crown. Later, this project required the rejection of all forms of authority, whether institutional and material or metaphysical and mental, that would confine politics to the realm of instrumentality and legitimise, or merely tolerate, the state because of its pursuit of ultimate goals. The political regime, or the state, secularists now insisted, must be sovereign, and statecraft regulated only by the constraints of power and history. Ironically, all visions of historical order informed by the God-Caesar imagery and the institutional set-up that formalised it appear dated and defunct today. For, despite the centrality of the 'war on terror' for *Pax Americana*, the cunning of history has rendered both God and Caesar redundant for the constitution of the globalised *raj* that we all are subjects of. Though the church was defeated and the state did enjoy a short period of hegemony, today the church has no vision of politics and the state does not exercise self-rule: its sovereignty has been drastically curtailed by the forces of global capitalism. Both God and Caesar, to continue our metaphor, have been outflanked by Mammon.

Turkey alone among all the Muslim countries has tried to define its national identity in terms of modernity. She has tenaciously pursued a political path that does not alienate her from the broad currents of history, even if the cost has been cultural alienation and an ever present sense of loss (*huzun*). She has constituted herself as a secular state but remains a palpably vibrant Muslim nation—a paradox to some, an anomaly to others—which is not only an ontological datum but also defines the terms of her ongoing dialogue with history, past and future. Furthermore, Turkish society's commitment to the *ethos* of modernity is genuine and steadfast: neither the philosophical naiveté of the official ideology of *laicism* nor the draconian statutes of the Republic's legal order, not even the imperial disdain of her military for democratic rule, seems to weaken that resolve. For all the pride she feels in her past, the Turkish nation, unlike many other Muslim peoples, looks forward towards history and will not suffer to be held hostage to a bygone age. Not surprisingly, Turkey has come to be regarded as 'the only country in the Middle East actually pointing to the future'. (Paul Salem, Director of Carnegie Middle East Centre).

Books mentioned in this review

Turkey, Islam, Nationalism, and Modernity. Carter Vaughn Findley. Yale University Press, New Haven and London, 2010. pp. 527.

Passive Revolution: Absorbing the Islamic Challenge to Capitalism. Cihan Tugal. Stanford University Press, 2009. pp. 320.

Globalization and Islamism: Beyond Fundamentalism. Nevzat Soguk. Rowman & Littlefield Publishers, 2010. pp. 246.

Secularism and State Policies toward Religion: The United States, France, and Turkey. Ahmet T. Kuru. Cambridge University Press, 2009. pp. 334.

The New Cultural Climate in Turkey: Living in a Shop Window. Nurdan Gurbilek. Zed Books London, 2011. pp 128.

The Long Divergence: How Islamic Law Held Back the Middle East. Timur Kuran. Princeton University Press, 2010. pp. 424. IS.

With her economy booming and self-confidence on the rise, Turkey is continually reforming its political culture and moving towards a freer, more democratic and more liberal society. The path entails demolishing some of the bugbears of Islamophobic laicism, but also resolutely dismissing all Islamist fantasies about the revival of a theocratic state. A state-centred vision of Islam has no place in modern Turkey, not even under the present, putatively 'Islamist', regime. Like the majority of Muslims everywhere, Turks have not failed to notice the abject intellectual, moral and spiritual poverty of the nihilistic Islamist ideologies and the misery of their theocratic solutions. To remain faithful to the secular constitution of the Republic and still find a public expression—spiritual, moral, cultural—of their faith is the main challenge before the Muslim Turks today. All the evidence suggests that they are facing the challenge with courage and wisdom, worldliness and piety, renouncing neither authenticity nor modernity. No wonder that Turkey is poised to become not only a role model for other states in the region, but also destined to play a significant role on the world stage. Given the recent developments in the Middle East, the advent of the 'Arab Spring', a Muslim focus on Turkey's bid to be part of the global 'we' and to rediscover its historic mission is apt and timely. The works discussed here deal with different aspects of Turkish politics and history but all of them provide insights and accounts that are worthy of note.

For a synoptic view of Turkey's modern history, Carter Vaughn Findley's most recent volume, *Turkey, Islam, Nationalism, and Modernity: A History, 1789–2007*, is indispensable. It is a scholarly effort that is truly a labour of love and a veritable tribute to the historian's craft. Monumental in format, encyclopaedic in scope, panoramic in vision, it also manages to be sugges-tive and thoughtful, stimulating and gratifying, acute and perspicacious. Findley, Professor of History at Ohio State University, has already given us a broad historical account of the Turkic peoples, *The Turks in World History* (Oxford, 2005). In the present volume, he shifts his gaze from *Turkic* to *Turkish* history, restricting his focus to the late Ottoman Empire and Republican Turkey. He is candid enough to admit that his ambition was to produce a work of synthesis that would supplant earlier scholarly studies, written mainly during the 1960s, which all suffer, according to him, from the distinctive biases and prejudices of the modernisation theory that was current in those times. Or, more plainly, he feels the 'greatest flaw' of these studies was 'their teleological vision of an upward march from Islamic empire to secular republic'.

The evolutionary model was not merely an academic trend; it reaf-firmed the supreme meta-narrative of modernity and the legitimacy of its project. It validated the ideological claim that the march of 'universal his-tory' is visibly reflected in the transition of political structures from multinational empires to nation-states. The trajectory of Turkish history, an 'Islamic' empire transforming itself into a secular republic, was perfectly congruent with the modernist paradigm and hence was adduced as a proof of its universality. However, the affinity between western secular teleology and the republican ideology of Turkey was far more intimate and direct: indeed it was symbiotic. Or, as Findley observes, 'As it turns out, Turkey's conformity to (secular) theory was no accident; several of the scholars most active in developing the 1960s modernisation theory were experts on Turkey and theorised with Turkey in mind'. One may just as well contend that Turkey acted as a political laboratory for secularist theory where its theses were tested and refined. In fact, this intimate relationship continues to this day, as the hype and fanfare of the annually held *Istanbul Seminars*, where the most prestigious philosophical proponents of the secularist theory propound on its civilising mission and contribute to the national and regional debate, amply testifies.

According to Findley, however, 'the inadequacies of the teleological secularisation visions' and 'the circular relationship between the Turkish case and modernisation theory' became apparent with the advent of the so-called 'Islamic resurgence' and its questioning of the Eurocentric meta-narratives. With the politicisation of culture in Turkey, historiography became a contested field, with the consequence that 'many scholars wrote to promote partisan positions'. Equally problematic for him is 'the old practice of leaving the Ottoman Empire to historians and the Turkish republic to social scientists' (read, modernist ideologues), because the synchronic vision of the latter 'no longer suffices for the study of the republican experience'. Or, in plainer words, republican Turkey is not a clean slate upon which modern social imaginaries may write whatever they wish, for her relationship with the past still provides meaning to her political existence. This may also account for the structure and format of Findley's own study which brings both the late Ottoman Empire and Republican Turkey under a single review. Despite all the fascination theories of postmodernity hold for the West, Findley is convinced that the Turks, like many others in 'the developing world', are 'still preoccupied with modernity itself', and that both sides of the Turkish ideological divide, 'the advocates of rapid change and religious and cultural conservatives', share this preoccupation. Modernity, in other words, has neither been rejected by Islamic forces nor

fully endorsed by the secularists—a fairly obvious and reasonable conclusion that attests to the ambivalence of the Turkish response to the historic
forces that have ushered us into the modern era.

Findley came to the conclusion that 'scholarly literature would not support synthesis on some topics and that 'the quality-of-life side of social
history and cultural history' would require original research. It is this
realisation of 'the imaginative realm as the primary site for the construction of new images of modernity' and the consequent integration of literary texts in this historiographic account that make his book, as he himself
confesses, 'move beyond synthesising others' works to present original
findings'. Certainly, the present volume is distinctive in its focus on the
creative writings of the Turks. This considerably extends the scholarly significance of the historical inquiry and the insights the book offers. Each
chapter, structured around a chronological scheme that makes eminent
sense, ends with a short essay that explores the chosen author's world,
'reflecting not only on cultural production but also on political, social and
economic issues' of the period under discussion. Needless to say, through
this gratifying enhancement of the discursive by the intuitive (as it were),
the reader acquires a more palpable feeling for the life-world of the society
and of the *Zeitgeist* informing it. This, however, is not the only, or the chief,
merit of Findley's richly rewarding volume.

Findley's work further distinguishes itself by its 'aspiration to overcome
the secular biases of the foundational studies on Ottoman and Turkish
modernity'. Nor is it a history without a perspective, an empiricism run
amok, that drowns in its own ocean of discovered facts and texts. Quite the
contrary, it presents a thesis, a theoretical insight that gives it both structure and meaning. The title, for which, Findley admits, he had to search
long, encapsulates the three principal forces of Turkish history—Islam,
nationalism and modernity—each of which had to find its own accord with
the other two. Reiterating Zia Gökalp's claim that 'both the ethno-linguis-
tic and religious identity shaped the Turk's engagement with modernity',
Findley sums up his own take on the march of Turkish history as: 'The
challenges of triangulating among these three reference points led to the
development of two alternative approaches to the choice they represented:
a comparatively radical, secularising current and a more conservative,
Islamically committed current'. Rejecting the facile binarism of secular

theory, Findley is thus led to conclude that like all large sociocultural formations, the Turkish currents also included divergent tendencies and inner contradictions. Many Ottomans and Turks, furthermore, 'identified with both currents and resisted choosing between them'. However, what is distinctive about the Turkish encounter with modernity, Findley opines, is that at some critical moments the choice embodied by the two currents became unavoidable, thus polarising Turkish society into religious-conservative and secular-radical constellations. The rest of the Muslim world, we may hasten to add, has not made such painful choices, mainly because its resolve to become part of the modern civilisation, or—to express it more candidly—to reclaim its historic destiny, has not been as firm and unwavering as that of Turkey.

Notwithstanding the author's commendable modesty and his disclaimer that 'scholarly literature would not support synthesis', his is a work of superb synthesis; a formidable achievement by any standards, academic or cultural. It is lucidly written and logically structured, moderate in tone but not reticent, full of facts but never without theoretical insights, critical and discerning without being censorious or dismissive. Findley's history of the late Ottomans and modern Turks is sure to become a standard academic text and required reading for neophytes. But more than that, it treats the reader to a rich selection of photographs, some quite old and rare, as well to a comprehensive and functional bibliography. Even in terms of ideas and theory, it is often quite original and suggestive, particularly in the discussion of the role of 'print capitalism' in the spread of Islamic discourses and political activism. Specialists may quibble about some of the details, but I cannot see how anyone interested in the history of modern Turkey will be able to do without Findley's book.

We have seen that, in the Turkish case, secular theory and praxis, academic discourse and everyday politics, had a symbiotic relationship. Everybody, however, accepted the religion-politics dichotomy as paradigmatic of modern statehood. In fact, political science as an academic discipline could not articulate anything about modern politics without some explicit or implicit avowal of the legitimacy of the secularist ideology and worldview. Hence 'religion' was banished from this academic discipline altogether, as it was believed to have no political quotient whatsoever and was anyhow destined to disappear from history. Legal scholars, philosophers and historians may study religion for mainly antiquarian purposes, but its relevance for contemporary issues was nil. History, however, has refused to redeem secular promises and 'religion', as the refrain now goes, has returned to world politics with a vengeance. Secular theory, consequently, is fast going out of favour in the academy, and the affinity of religion and politics is no longer a shocking postulate in political science. Even philosophers with normative arguments for keeping the public sphere sealed off from religion, its language, symbols and political aspirations, have modified their stance, pleading that the politics of 'overlapping consensus' requires a coexistence of religious and secular discourses. Within the current intellectual debate on the relationship between religion and politics then, most of the ideological hurdles against the study of religion as a political phenomenon have disappeared. Rather, the relevant question for political science today is not whether religion and politics should interact but rather how they do so. It is in the pursuance of this objective that Ahmet Kuru's present work—ambitious, nuanced, empirically well-founded yet theoretically stringent—makes a significant contribution

The title of Kuru's book gives a fair indication of the scope and contents of his study, if not of its distinctive features. It makes a welcome addition to the growing corpus of scholarly works that engage with secularism in a spirit of critical inquiry rather than championing its cause. What is distinctive about Kuru's work is its focus on the politics of secularism in a comparative, not only trans-national but also trans-civilisational, context. Or, as the author himself points out, his book differs from 'sociological works on societal and individual religiosity', 'philosophical works on secularism as a worldview', 'critical works on the deconstruction of secularism as a discourse and as power relations' and 'anthropological works on secularism as an everyday practice'. Sure enough, this is a research monograph that relies primarily on 'original sources'—legal and political documents, personal interviews etc, but also on other printed material and other facets of the public debate, just as in its method it is rigorously academic in being descriptive and empirical, focussing on secular power that expresses itself through acts of public policy rather than by the nature of its ideological claims. Instead of becoming bogged down in normative controversies, Kuru attempts to apprehend secularism as governance, as ordinances, as legal framework for inclusion and exclusion. In short, his book is not a theoretical reflection on the meaning of secularism but a practical guide to its public manifestations in contemporary times. To suggest this, however, is not to minimise the ideational import of Kuru's work: his political scientist's approach yields theoretical insights aplenty. In fact, it demonstrates that secularism is not all form and procedure, a legal arrangement for the separation of church and state but, as José Casanova contends, 'a mode of state regulation of religion in society'.

Kuru's study reveals two different, almost diametrically opposed, policy trends towards religion in contemporary secular states. In the United State, he notes, official policies are 'generally tolerant toward religion in the public sphere', while in France and Turkey, the state, he feels, tries 'to confine it to the private domain'. In order to account for this inconsistency, Kuru advances a typology of secularism, classifying it into *assertive* and *passive* varieties (probably taking his cue from the French expression *laïcité de combat*, which captures laicism's 'jihadist' élan with Gallic felicity). Assertive secularism, in his own words, 'requires the state to play an 'assertive' role to exclude religion from the public sphere and confine it to the private domain'. Passive secularism, on the other hand, 'demands that the state play a 'passive' role by allowing the public visibility of religion'. Assertive secularism, he suggests further, is 'a "comprehensive doctrine", whereas passive secularism mainly prioritises state neutrality towards such doctrines'. Given this protean distinction, which is as obvious as it is circular, it is no wonder that Kuru is able to ascribe to every expression of the secular in public policy, whether in Turkey, France or the United States, some degree of 'aggression' or 'passivity'. Unfortunately, this listless and pallid terminology makes all distinction between observation and analysis redundant; what is being observed and what is being theorised are congruent. Its only virtue is political correctness: it avoids shrillness and polemics in today's incendiary ideological atmosphere. However, if Islam may routinely be described as 'fundamentalist', 'extremist', 'fanatic', why not secularism? Calling the assertive variety of secularism 'fundamentalist' and the passive one 'moderate' would be more apt, and, in fact, very much in accord with the political rhetoric of our times. In short, jihadist Islam and jihadist secularism should be spoken of in the same manner.

For all the discomfort of Kuru's politically correct and euphemistic terminology, we must take note of the two major strands of secularist politics that have emerged from different historical experiences. Two earlier attempts to theorise secularism and reveal its taxonomy are far more helpful for our discussion. The French sociologist (normally referred to as an 'Islamologue') Olivier Roy makes a similar distinction between *secularization*, whereby '*a society emancipates itself from a sense of the sacred that it does not necessarily deny*', and *laïcité*, whereby '*the state expels religious life beyond a border that the state itself has defined by law*'. Apart from the exemplary lucidity of these definitions, Roy's theoretical insights, drawing on the different historical experiences of France and Anglo-Saxon countries, do not simply reiterate the separation of State and Church thesis, but ultimately rely on the seminal (though not always clear) distinction between *state* and *society*. Anglo-Saxon secularism (the passive secularism of Kuru's theory) is a society-based approach that seeks conformity not through legal injunctions but through societal coercion and persuasion, while *laïcité* represents the French state-centred model (borrowed by the Turkish Republic) of rendering religion politically innocuous.

Roy's analysis of French *laïcité* is quite relevant to the Turkish experience, as the founder of the Turkish Republic did import 'the Jacobin state into Turkey along with its apparatus of legitimacy'. His insights are further supplemented by Kuru's analysis of recent French policies that have all resulted in the ban on certain Muslim practices. Nevertheless, his following statement certainly merits sober Muslim reflection: 'The state policies toward religion in France', he summarises, 'have been less restrictive than those in Turkey, despite the fact that assertive secularism has been dominant in both countries. The major reason for this distinction is the democratic regime in France, which has allowed critics to oppose assertive secularist policies, and the semi-authoritarian regime in Turkey, which had limited resistance against assertive secularism'. The clinching argument in this debate belongs neither to the assertive nor to the passive variety of secularism, but to democracy. A democratic political culture, and not any untouchable secular constitution, is the first prerequisite for the contemporary (Muslim) state's new deal with religion.

The second definition of secularism with a similar typology that is relevant to this discussion is by Elizabeth Shakman Hurd, who fully endorses the now commonplace secularism-laicism distinction, but gives it an American, Anglo-Saxon spin. The two varieties of secularism, according to her, are 'laicism and Judeo-Christian secularism'. 'The former', she claims, 'represents a separationist narrative in which religion is expelled from politics, and the latter a more accommodationist narrative in which Judean-Christian tradition is the unique basis of secular democracy'. The chief merit of this definition, in our opinion, is its rejection of secularism's claim to neutrality in religious matters and its putative universalism. Further, she is candid about the theological and civilisational moorings of this secularism in which the national Anglo-Saxon identity is subsumed by the more ecumenical Judeo-Christian one. Moreover, in this second trajectory of putatively Biblical secularism, 'Euro-American secular public life is securely grounded in a larger Christian, and later Judeo-Christian, civilization'. Following William E Connolly, she contends that this signifies a Tocquevillian approach to secularism in which Christianity does not need to be invoked that often 'because it is already inscribed in the prediscursive dispositions and cultural instincts of the civilisation'. According to this perspective, the uniqueness of the Western civilisation, even its secular ethos, is a gift of Christianity. For the specifically Western model of governance in which church and state are formally separated 'functions to soften sectarian divisions between Christian sects while retaining the civilisational hegemony of Christianity in a larger sense'.

Given these claims of uniqueness and aspirations to 'civilisational hegemony', it is not a mere sign of Muslim squeamishness to argue that secularism is not a self-referential, intra-Western or intra-Christian doctrine: 'Islam' as its other, politically theocratic and religiously non-conformist, is indispensable to the construction of secularism's self-image. According to all forms of secular discourse, either a country is pro-democracy, pro-Western, and secular, or it is religious, tribal and theocratic. The dismal fact is that 'Islam' marks the outer limit of secular 'tolerance', or of Christian ecumenism, and both varieties of secularism, assertive and passive, laïcist as well as Judeo-Christian, indulge in 'civilisational polemics' against it. Even Roy feels compelled to spell out that 'the critique of Islam is today a rallying point for two intellectual families that have been opposed to each other so far: those who think that the West is foremost Christian (and who, not long ago, considered that the Jews could hardly be assimilated) and those who think that the West is primarily secular and democratic. In other words, the Christian Right and secular left are today united in their criticism of Islam'. Even at the level of interstate diplomacy and international relations the image of Islam is equally bleak, as the following statement, made by a political scientist and a student of international relations, clearly testifies. Elizabeth Hurd feels that all her pleas and arguments for a transition to a more equitable and peaceful international order come to nought when they run against the spectre of Islam: 'A laïcist and Judeo-Christian secular West has been consolidated in part through opposition to representations of an antimodern, anti-Christian, and theocratic Islamic Middle East. Opposition to the concept of Islam is built into secular political authority and embedded within the national identities with which it is associated and through which it is expressed'.

It is to Kuru's credit that in his study of Turkish secularism, where he not only witnesses the arrogance of laïcist power at close range but also suffers the incredible banality and reductionism of its ideological discourse, he never allows his analytical vision to be blurred by soothing nostalgia and cultural despair, nor does he seek solace in the unredeemable promises of vacuous meliorism and supercilious modernism. The academic's text is, unusually for a Turkish writer, totally devoid of gratuitous rage or obligatory *hüzün*. In other words, Kuru remains forever critical and vigilant in his observation of secularism that expresses itself through legal injunctions and gleefully indulges in civilisational polemics but shows no signs of rancour or outrage. His scholarship is impressive, both in its summarisation of secular theory and its handling of the empirical data of secular practice, of secularism as governance if you will. The bibliography, citing all the relevant texts in English, French and Turkish, is extensive, just as the list of the scholars, politicians, writers and businessmen he has interviewed for his study is impressive. All this makes his book a welcome addition to the scholarly literature in this field and a competent introduction to the wider context of secular practice in three key secular states. Though scholars and general readers may benefit equally from its study, the transition from its conception as an academic monograph to its appearance as a culturally and politically noteworthy tome hasn't been as smooth as is generally the case with works with a wider appeal and a motley readership. It is full of tables and charts classifying and processing a lot of statistical data and other empirical facts, appropriate for a monograph but not for a general study. Turning every fact into a figure is a pretentious, and trivialising, gimmick of positivist sociology which is not to everyone's liking. The same is not true of Ahmed Kuru's work as a whole, however: it is informative, insightful, rewarding and very relevant to a crucial debate of our times.

And this brings us back to Turkey's peculiar dilemma with respect to secularism. That she is at the receiving end of civilisational polemics, Christian as well as secular, Rightist and Leftist, may be heartbreaking, but it has not weakened her resolve to work out her own pact with modernity and orientate her politics towards that goal. Nevertheless, it is no wonder that given the Jacobin nature of the modern Turkish state, the inner contradictions of her laicism had turned her politics into a game of musical chairs, or a roller-coaster for democratic hopes and aspirations. Fortunately the vicious cycle of civilian governments and army coups, the military's pretence to be the guardian of the laic constitution of the Republic, may be a thing of the past. Turkey under the AKP has achieved a perceptible degree of political stability and economic progress and is moving steadily towards a more democratic political culture and greater international respectability—all this within the framework of a secular constitution and without any inclination to follow the path of 'Islamist' politics that is the dissimulative slogan of many regimes in the region and the scourge of their citizens.

What remains unrecognised, or is wilfully suppressed in the ideological debates where Islam's incompatibility with secularism is an article of faith, is the unpalatable truth that neither *laïcité* nor secularism has much to do with the separation of the sacred and the profane, because in the end both realms lay claim to the same sense of the sacred. What modernity demands is a new contract between Church and State—something specific to the Christian tradition. If French secularism represents a *laïcité de combat*, marked by verbal violence and anathema, that is always censorious of a disfigured Catholic religiosity, and if American accommodationist secularism is a social contract with Protestant Churches (whose allegiance to 'Judeo-Christian' secularism may have been spurred by the all too worldly motive of blocking public funding to Catholic schools), it is quite reasonable to assume that the Jacobin model of laicism in Turkey fails to negotiate a fair deal with Islamic religiosity. However, it is already apparent to serious scholars that 'Turkey has turned toward a different trajectory of secularism that conforms to neither Kemalism (a Turkish version of laicism) nor the two prevailing versions of secularism, (namely) laicism and Judeo-

Christian secularism'. Little wonder that this Islamically motivated secularism (for lack of a better expression for 'worldliness') is perceived as a threat not only by the Kemalist establishment but other champions of laicism in Europe as well.

In the pursuit of a more viable future, Turkey has chosen to follow the modern path, but in her quest for a more authentic political existence she has also decided to adopt a secular constitution and a democratic way of life. A paradox or a contradiction in terms? Nonsense! Turkish Muslims have realised that a 'secular constitution', when properly construed, demands nothing more heretical than an acceptance of the reality of the territorial state and its commitment to the politics of citizenship and democratic rule—not by any means unacceptable propositions for a Muslim nation. What today is a cautious Turkish bid to become part of history may one day become a model for all Muslim states to emulate.

THE TERRIBLE BEAUTY
OF WIKILEAKS

Muhammad Idrees Ahmad

On 7 December 2010, Tunisian despot Zine El Abidine Ben Ali's regime blocked Internet access to the Beirut daily *Al-Akhbar* for publishing a US embassy cable which painted the dictator, his wife and her family in a deeply unflattering light. In the July 2009 cable, US ambassador Robert Godec had accused Ben Ali's regime of having 'lost touch with the Tunisian people...[tolerating] no advice or criticism whether domestic or international', and of increasingly relying 'on the police for control and focus on preserving power'. The cable mentioned the growing 'corruption in the inner circle', particularly around first lady Leila Trabelsi and her family, whom it said the Tunisians 'intensely dislike, even hate'. It finally concluded that 'anger is growing at Tunisia's high unemployment and regional inequities. As a consequence, the risks to the regime's long-term stability are increasing'.

Ten days later in Sidi Bouzid, 26-year-old street vendor Muhammad Bouazizi immolated himself in front of the local municipality building after his vegetable cart was confiscated by Faida Hamdi, a female municipal official who had then slapped him, spat in his face, and insulted his dead father. Anguished friends and sympathisers soon took to the streets to protest, and YouTube, Facebook and Twitter helped spread the fire further—the long deferred anger of the Tunisians had finally erupted. On 4 January 2011, when Bouazizi succumbed to his wounds, the 5,000 mourners at his funeral were heard chanting, 'Farewell, Mohammed, we will avenge you. We weep for you today. We will make those who caused your death weep'. Ten days later, as the protests reached a crescendo, Ben Ali and his wife hoarded their loot and decamped to Saudi Arabia. Some suggested that Wikileaks had drawn first blood.

However, neither Bouazizi's death nor Wikileaks' revelations about the ruling clique's rampant corruption would by themselves have triggered a revolution were it not for the vast pool of rage that was already bubbling. Dwindling opportunities for the masses juxtaposed with the 'great wealth and excess' of the presidential family had generated an explosive atmosphere waiting for a spark. A growing number of Tunisia's educated youth languished in hopeless unemployment, yet the embassy cable revealed that Ben Ali's son-in-law Mohamed Sakher El Materi, was serving dinners 'with ice cream and frozen yoghurt brought in by private plane from St Tropez' and holding for a pet 'a large tiger, named Pasha, living in a cage, which

---

Books and films mentioned in this review

Books

Daniel Domscheit-Berg, *Inside WikiLeaks: My Time with Julian Assange at the World's Most Dangerous Website*. Jonathan Cape, 2011, ISBN 978–0224094016, pp 304, £9.99

David Leigh and Luke Harding. *WikiLeaks: Inside Julian Assange's War on Secrecy*. Guardian Books, 2011. ISBN 978–0852652398, pp. 352, £9.99.

Micah Sifry, *Wikileaks and the Age of Transparency*. Yale University Press, 2011, ISBN 978–0300176766, pp. 176, £9.99.

Isikoff, Michael, and David Corn. *Hubris: The Inside Story of Spin, Scandal, and the Selling of the Iraq War*. Reprint. Three Rivers Press (CA), 2007. ISBN 978–0307346827, pp. 496, £9.23.

Films

'Wikisecrets', PBS *Frontline*, May 2011.
'Inside Wikileaks', Journeyman Pictures, December 2010.
'Information Wars', Al-Jazeera *Empire* (Panel discussion), February 2011.
'Wikileaks: Why it matters? Why it Doesn't?' Real News Network (Panel discussion), January 2011.
'WikiRebels', SVT Television (Sweden), December 2010.

consumes four chickens a day'. Something had to give—and along came Wikileaks and Bouazizi.

British journalist Gary Younge once quipped that the English nation only exists for 90 minutes during a game of football. As the webs of social relations that tied nations together have frayed under the neoliberal assault, societies have fragmented, existing only as imagined communities during spectacles, especially war and sport. The Wikileaks cables revealed little about Tunisia or Egypt that the individual citizen did not already know. But it was the spectacular manner of the revelations that turned a mass of atomised and jaded individuals into an angry nation clamouring for their dignity. As witnesses to the spectacle of the global phenomena that was Wikileaks and the local tragedy that was Mohamed Bouazizi, the Tunisians had coalesced into a community around the common source of their humiliation.

If Mohamed Bouazizi's spectacular act was born of desperation, Wikileaks founder Julian Assange's was born of ingenuity. By using the prestige and resources of five of the world's leading news organisations, Assange ensured a global audience for his revelations. In his earlier experiments he had discovered that dumping a mass of data online, however sensational, generated little public interest. Information, like any commodity, is also subject to the laws of supply and demand. Truth has never been in short supply, but it needs amplification to have an impact. An obscure website might draw those actively pursuing a story, but masses who are mere passive consumers of news will have little reason to upset the bliss of their ignorance. For it to have an impact the information will have to be thrust into people's faces.

That is what Nick Davies proposed to do. The veteran investigative journalist sought out Assange shortly after private Bradley Manning, the intelligence analyst who leaked the trove of military logs and diplomatic cables to Wikileaks, was arrested by the US authorities in June 2010. Manning had unwisely confided his role to a former hacker named Adrian Lamo who promptly denounced him to the military. The twenty-two-year-old soldier was arrested and put into solitary confinement where he has remained since in conditions which can best be described as near-torture.

Manning's epiphany had come after he was ordered to investigate a case involving fifteen detainees being held by the Iraqi federal police for distributing 'anti-Iraqi literature'. After having the pamphlets translated, Manning discovered that they contained a benign, scholarly critique of Iraqi president Nouri al-Malaki. But when he told his superior officer about this, he was told to 'shut up and explain how we could assist the FPs [federal police] in finding *MORE* detainees'. At that point, wrote Manning, 'I saw things differently...I had always questioned the way things worked, [but now] I was actively involved in something I was completely against'.

Manning's conviction grew stronger after he watched a classified video of an incident in 2007 where a couple of US Apache gunships had mowed down a group of civilians in Baghdad and bombed a building, killing between eighteen to twenty-six Iraqis including two Reuters journalists. One of the journalists was executed while crawling wounded on the floor. The helicopter also shot up a van after it stopped to assist the wounded journalist, killing the driver and his companion and seriously wounding the two children whom they were driving to school. But when Manning tried to look for media coverage of the incident, he found a *New York Times* report stating only that the attack had killed 'nine insurgents and two civilians'. That is when he decided to copy the video and other documents from the classified integrated military-diplomatic network and leaked them to Assange. Afterwards he told Lamo: 'I feel, for some bizarre reason, it might actually change something'.

On 5 April 2010, Wikileaks released the video of the helicopter attacks at a press conference in Washington. The video showed the slaughter being carried out to a soundtrack of casual banter which was inhuman in its unhurried and business-like detachment. The voices were calm and blasé, betraying no sense of threat—they seemed to delight in the act of murder. There was little remorse even after the crew was informed that their victims included children. The world was horrified.

Taking on the Empire

After a long search, Nick Davies finally tracked down Assange in Brussels and proposed an agreement. Wikileaks would give three of the world's leading publications—the *Guardian*, the *New York Times* and *Der Spiegel*—exclusive access to the documents provided by Manning and the papers will in turn ensure that the information would be given maximum coverage. Stories based on the revelations would be splashed simultaneously on the front pages of all three publications and Wikileaks would then publish them in full on its website. The deal would also protect Assange against prosecution under the US Espionage Act.

The US, unlike Britain, has no Official Secrets Act. In 2000, Congress passed one, but in a rare principled act, Bill Clinton vetoed it. The government has therefore had to rely on the 1917 Espionage Act, which it has hitherto used only sparingly. But the Obama administration, which has made a virtue of 'looking forward, not backward' when responding to calls for the prosecution of former Bush administration officials, proved perfectly willing to look backwards when prosecuting public servants who had exposed government wrong-doing. In an important expose in the *New Yorker*, investigative journalist Jane Mayer revealed that the Obama administration has overseen the most draconian crackdown on whistle-blowers in history—more extensive than Richard Nixon's—prosecuting more individuals under the Espionage Act than all previous administrations combined. Bradley Manning's prospects for now looked dim. But Assange could gain some cover by broadening the responsibility for publishing the classified documents to some of the world's leading publications.

The story of the deal and the subsequent fallout are told in a gripping account by David Leigh and Luke Harding in *Wikileaks: Inside Julian Assange's War on Secrecy*, even if the details of the deal are disputed by former Wikileaks spokesman Daniel Domscheit-Berg in his book *Inside Wikileaks: My time with Julian Assange at the world's most dangerous website*. Like Leigh and Harding, Domscheit-Berg appears torn between his admiration and his loathing of Assange, but he has only unreserved contempt for the *Guardian* and the *New York Times*, whom he describes as 'like dogs jealously guarding a bone', preventing Wikileaks from partnering with other media institutions like CBC and the *Washington Post* who were also interested in publicising the leaks. He also asserts that the idea of the partnership originated with Wikileaks itself rather than with the *Guardian* and Davies. His account of Wikileaks's modest origins and spectacular rise is more intimate and readable.

On 25 July 2010, Wikileaks and its media partners published the Afghan war logs—91,731 documents that covered the period from January 2004 to December 2009. They told a tale of extrajudicial murder, torture, indiscriminate violence, civilian deaths, and escalating insurgent attacks in clipped, sterile militarese. Many of these incidents were well known but where in the past it was possible for apologists to take refuge in ISAF's bland denials, now the horrors became irrefutable. The 'good war' turned out not to be so good after all. However, the logs were treated very differently in Europe and the US, highlighting the gulf between their respective journalistic traditions. Where the *Guardian* and *Der Spiegel* laboured to produce a meticulous picture of the everyday atrocities visited on the Afghans, the deferential US press confined itself to investigating the causes of US-NATO's failure. All attention focused on the evidence of Pakistan's alleged perfidy in repeatedly subverting US plans, the evidence for which was mostly derived from claims made by the Afghan intelligence service, hardly a disinterested party. Nevertheless, the leaks proved that despite their different political cultures, the US and Pakistan aren't that different after all: both aggressively pursue their respective interests with little regard for the interests of the Afghans.

The *New York Times* had been included in the cartel so it could publish minutes ahead of the others, thereby providing First Amendment cover to its foreign partners. The aim was also to protect Manning, who risked being tried for espionage if he was seen as having passed US national security secrets to non-citizens. But the paper balked and insisted that Wikileaks publish first. It also refused to link to the Wikileaks website. A disillusioned Assange then decided to expand Wikileaks's list of partners bringing in France's *Le Monde*, Spain's *El Pais*, Britain's Channel 4, and Qatar's Al-Jazeera. The original three were furious, and would soon retaliate.

On 22 October 2010, the Iraq war logs were released—391,832 in total. They documented incidents between 2004 and 2009. Torture, rape and murder of detainees; cover-up of civilian deaths; execution of surrendering insurgents; murder of civilians by mercenaries; murder of civilians by soldiers—Iraq, as some put it, was a 'hell disaster'. Operation Iraqi Freedom had taken a repressive and murderous authoritarian state and replaced it with a repressive and murderous authoritarian state, albeit under a more representative sectarian set-up. The US occupying forces it transpired had also adopted a formal policy to ignore torture and other forms of abuse by the Iraqi forces. Contrary to former US general Tommy Franks's assurances, it also turned out the US military did do body counts—and the logs yielded 15,000 more dead civilians than previously recorded. (The actual figure of course is much higher—somewhere between three quarters of a million to over 1.2 million—according to extensive studies carried out by the John Hopkins University and ORB. There have been no new studies since 2007).

On 28 November 2010, Wikileaks and its media partners started simultaneously publishing confidential diplomatic cables from 274 embassies worldwide, dated from 28 December 1966 to 28 February 2010. The 251,287 cables, which were to be released in trickles, were the biggest publishing sensation in history. They provided front page splashes for months, with candid diplomatic chatter providing plenty of sensational headlines. The colourful references to various world leaders and the frank assessment of their performance intrigued many. Some were gossipy, some of near anthropological precision. Most involved the kind of information collection that falls within diplomats' responsibilities. These were given prominence by the US media. But it was the frequent blurring of the diplomatic and clandestine functions that worried the rest of the world, some of which verged on criminality. Though Hillary Clinton was quick to denounce Wikileaks's actions as an 'attack on the international community', it turned out the US secretary of state had herself been leading a more sinister assault on international diplomacy. In breach of the Vienna Treaty which regulates international diplomacy, a cable bearing Clinton's signature revealed the secretary of state ordering diplomats to spy on foreign delegates at the UN, collect their encryption details, credit card transactions, frequent flyer numbers, and even biometric data. Diplomats were also ordered to spy on UN secretary general Ban Ki Moon.

There was a lot more to shock—and it wasn't just the US that came out looking bad. The cables reveal that China was allegedly making profits by reselling oil bought from Venezuela at the special rate of $5 a barrel, upsetting its benefactor Hugo Chavez. China was also described as less enamoured of its North Korean ally than it lets on in public, signalling its readiness to accept a unified Korea. The US attitude towards Britain comes across as condescending; the 'special relationship' treated as little more than a means to advance American interests. Vladimir Putin's Russia is described by the US diplomats as a 'virtual mafia state', in which oligarchs, public officials and organised crime were blurred into one. Gulf Arab leaders are revealed as even more venal, duplicitous and insecure than generally assumed. Many appeared busy scheming with US and Israeli officials against Iran. Some, such as Yemen's Ali Abdullah Saleh, were assisting US attacks against their own citizens, providing corridors for drone and cruise missile attacks, and then assuming responsibility for the attacks as their own. Equally treasonous were the Lebanese defence minister Elias Murr's comments in a meeting with US diplomats encouraging Israel to attack Lebanon and hit Hezbollah so as to strengthen the position of his March 14 Alliance. One cable likened Pakistan's Inter-Services Intelligences to the Taliban and Al-Qaeda, declaring it a threat to US interests.

The US government's response was predictably heavy-handed. The state department banned all its employees from reading or sharing the cables. Diplomats were not allowed to visit the website, even at home, or to search for their own names in the cables database. The cables could of course always be read in the *New York Times* thereby making the ban superfluous. Employees of USAID were also told to stay away from the website. However, more dramatically, on 30 November 2010, Columbia University's Office of Career Services warned students at the School of International and Public Affairs, a premiere trainer of future diplomats, to avoid linking to or posting comments about the diplomatic cables because they were 'still considered classified'. The email warned that talking about the cables 'would call into question your ability to deal with confidential information'.

After weathering intense denial-of-service attacks (an attempt to disable a website by digitally clogging up its servers), Wikileaks was struck the first blow when under pressure from Senator Joe Lieberman—a long-time proponent of limiting Internet freedom—and the state department, Amazon removed the website from its servers. Next Wikileaks's hosting company EveryDNS revoked its contract. Mastercard, Visa and Paypal were also induced to withhold their services from Wikileaks. Bank of America also closed its accounts. American Wikileaks volunteer Jacob Applebaum was detained and interrogated. Assange rightly denounced it as the 'privatization of state censorship'.

The reaction from the liberal intelligentsia was no less vicious. Wikileaks had given a lie to their self-congratulatory adversarial pretensions by showing the inadequacy of the methods through which they have channelled their dissent. The *New York Times* commissioned John Burns—one of that rare species of journalist who in 2003 actually saw Iraqis 'greeting Americans as liberators'—to write a sub-tabloid, sleazy profile on Assange which dredged up every rumour, unsubstantiated claim and allegation.

Editor Bill Killer did him one better by writing an 8,000 word piece extraordinary for its ad hominem malice. Nick Davies of the Guardian published an article in which he reproduced in prurient detail allegations from an on-going investigation into Assange's 'sexual impropriety'.

The left fared only slightly better. Unaccustomed to success, some Western leftists looked at Wikileaks's meteoric rise with suspicion. Some took exception to its partnering with mainstream media institutions like the *New York Times*, others questioned its decision to selectively release cables rather posting them in a single dump. A few wondered why the cables had so little on Israel.

Of course, there were always simpler explanations. There were no significant cables from Tel Aviv because the embassy there serves a largely symbolic function. Israel has never had to deal with diplomats because since its birth it has had direct access to the White House. This was impressed upon the US state department early when on 10 June 1949, future US ambassador George McGhee, who was responsible for the Palestinian refugee problem, met the Israeli ambassador in London to deliver a warning from President Harry Truman and secretary of state Dean Acheson that the US would withhold $49 million in promised loan guarantees unless Israel agreed to the return of at least half the Palestinians who had been ethnically cleansed by the Zionist forces. The Israeli ambassador calmly advised McGhee that he was wasting his time because his contacts in the White House had assured him that the decision would be overturned. Shortly afterwards, McGhee received a message from David Niles, the White House liaison to the Jewish community and a leading Zionist, informing him that the president had officially dissociated himself from the plan.

This of course is the tragedy of the Israeli-Palestinian conflict. Many of these diplomats are well informed and competent, but the US policy in relation to the region is not made by diplomats who are conscious of the US national interest but by Washington politicians who are conscious only of domestic electoral concerns.

Journalism 2.0

As an organisation, Wikileaks is slightly over four years old, but its impact on public discourse is already palpable. However, Michah L. Sifry notes in

Wikileaks and the Age of Transparency that Wikileaks 'is just one piece of a much larger continuum of changes in how the people and the powerful relate to each other in this new time—changes that are fundamentally healthy for the growth and strength of an open society. Secrecy and the hoarding of information are ending; openness and the sharing of information are coming'. But where Sifry's method is to work within the system, Assange's begins by questioning the very premises of its authority. As a veteran of the NGO world, Sifry's criticisms predictably hinge on process rather than outcomes. Though the successes of the movement he represents are impressive, none are as significant or world-changing as Wikileaks's.

Founded in 2006 by Assange and some hackers, mathematicians and activists, Wikileaks remains a work in progress, constantly in search of an effective and sustainable model. Conscious of the fact that it is venturing into uncharted territory, Wikileaks has continually revised and adapted its modus operandi. It began with the idea of posting large amounts of raw information on its website so that citizen journalists could parse and analyse the information and write articles based on it. It appeared few were willing to put in such effort. Only established media seemed to have the resources and motivation necessary for such a task—but few were willing to associate with or credit an unknown media start-up. Wikileaks next tried to serve as a publisher of last resort for information that powerful interests were trying to suppress through legal injunctions—a function it serves to date. Wikileaks has based its servers in various geographical locations and legal jurisdictions so that its operations remain un-censorable. If one is injuncted, others will continue to operate.

At one point Wikileaks even tried to auction some documents in its possession which would have given the successful bidder exclusive access to the material for a limited period of time. With the 'Collateral Murder' it tried to act as its own broadcaster but the impact was still limited. In its earlier days it had also partnered with individual journalists to publicise its data. With the Afghan and Iraq logs it entered by big time, entering into partnership with the world's leading publications, who were given exclusive access thereby investing them in the publication and promotion of the material. But both were single large data dumps and their impact only lasted a few days. With the embassy cables, Wikileaks hit upon a new model which would gain them maximum attention over the longest period of time. The cables would be released in a steady trickle organised around regions, issues or themes, thereby building anticipation and prolonging interest.

While the *NewYork Times*'s Bill Keller and *Time* magazine's Richard Stengel have both tried to dismiss Wikileaks as nothing without Bradley Manning, the organisation's achievements were considerable even before it received anything from the disgruntled soldier. Before the cables, before even the Afghan and Iraq war logs, Abu Dhabi's *The National* had reported that 'Wikileaks has probably produced more scoops in its short life than *The Washington Post* has in the past 30 years'.

After much effort, on 31 August 2007 Wikileaks's first successful media partnership came about when the *Guardian* published a front page story on corruption allegations against former Kenyan President Daniel Arap Moi based on a Kroll (an inquiry firm) report Assange had obtained. Next Wikileaks published a report on death squad killings in Kenya which also brought home the risks involved in such activism in a disturbing way when four of the individuals associated with the investigation, including the human rights activists Oscar Kingara and John Paul Oulu, were themselves subsequently murdered. The story was publicised by John Swain of the *Sunday Times*, and it won Wikileaks the Amnesty International annual journalism award. Later in November, Wikileaks published a March 2003 copy of the standard operating procedures for the Guantanamo Bay detention camp which revealed that contrary to its claims, the US military had kept some prisoners off-limits to the International Committee of the Red Cross.

In February 2008, Wikileaks published evidence of tax-dodging by the clients of the Swiss bank Julius Baer based on documents leaked by former executive Rudolf Elmer. The bank got a California court to issue an injunction against Wikileaks's domain name host Dynadot which took the website down. But in rehearsal of a tactic it would have to apply many times more in the future, Wikileaks activated several mirror sites in various countries. Several advocates of free speech, including the Electronic Frontier Foundation, the American Civil Liberties Union, and a journalist alliance including the Associated Press, Gannett News Services and the Los Angeles Times, rallied behind Wikileaks. It was a PR disaster for the bank, which soon withdrew its legal threats. Wikileaks picked up another award, this time from Index on Censorship.

Meanwhile, Wikileaks continued to serve as a publisher of last resort. When Barclay's Bank tried to bring an injunction against the *Guardian* from publishing its tax avoidance strategies, Wikileaks immediately hosted them in full on its website, rendering the gag superfluous. Likewise, when the oil trader Trafigura tried to suppress a damning report about its dumping of toxic waste in Ivory Coast causing great health hazards, Wikileaks, Greenpeace Netherlands and the Norwegian National TV all posted the report on their websites undermining the gag.

In August 2009, Wikileaks became a sensation in Iceland when the Kaupthing Bank brought the country's first and only injunction against state TV to stop it from broadcasting a damning expose minutes before it went on air. The bank, according to a leaked document, had given its partners and associates credit on extremely favourable terms shortly before it filed for insolvency. The producers of the show were outraged and they decided to bypass the gag by pointing viewers to the Wikileaks website where the bank's loan book was posted in full. The injunction collapsed, and Assange and his lieutenant Daniel Domscheit-Berg became minor celebrities. They used their fame to help pass the Modern Media Initiative in collaboration with Icelandic Member of Parliament Birgitta Jónsdóttir. The law, according to Jónsdóttir, replicates the Swiss banking model for information, enshrining source protection, free speech and freedom of information. It turned Iceland into a 'Switzerland of bytes [which takes the] tax haven model and transforms it into the transparency haven model'.

In March 2010, WikiLeaks obtained a secret 32-page US Department of Defense Counterintelligence Analysis Report with strategies for deterring Wikileaks and hunting down its sources. The report was produced in March 2008 showing that long before the Apache video, the war logs, or the diplomatic cables, Wikileaks had already been in the Pentagon's crosshairs.

These are only the highlights of Wikileaks's achievements. It has also released the secret manuals of Scientology; 6,780 Congressional Research Service reports; 570,000 intercepts of pager messages sent on 9/11; it leaked the US military's Human Terrain System handbook, a manual developed by embedded anthropologists to assist the military in pacifying occupied lands; and lists of forbidden or illegal web addresses for Australia, Denmark and Thailand which showed that parental guidance filters were being used to block political content. The effect of all the revelations has been explosive, and every news organisation worthy of its name is now playing catch-up. To stay relevant, several media organisations have announced their own drop-boxes for whistle-blowers. The results are mostly abysmal: *New York Times*'s drop box has yet to materialise months after the announcement; *Wall Street Journal*'s was soon revealed to be insecure, compromising the anonymity of the whistle-blowers. But there have also been some successes. Most notable among them is the Transparency Unit established by Al-Jazeera.

The Palestine Papers

Al-Jazeera's first scoop was not long in coming. On January 2011, Al-Jazeera partnered with *The Guardian* to release the Palestine Papers, more than 1,600 internal documents from over a decade of negotiations between the Palestinian authority, Israel and the US. These included records, minutes, notes and transcripts of meetings drawn up by members of the Palestinian Negotiation Support Unit (NSU), an outfit responsible for technical and legal backup head by Saeb Erakat, which is mainly funded by the British government. Some documents also originated with the Palestinian Authority's US/UK-sponsored security apparatus. They revealed large gaps between the public and private positions of the Palestinian authority and a degree of cooperation with the Israelis which verged on collaboration. They were 'as damning as the Balfour Declaration', wrote veteran Middle East correspondent Robert Fisk.

The Palestinian Authority, it emerged, had been ready to give up the 'right of return' of seven million refugees enshrined and protected by the UN General Assembly resolution 194. It had been willing to concede almost all of the illegal Israeli settlements in East Jerusalem—giving Israel 'the biggest Yerushalayim in history', according to chief Palestinian negotiator Saeb Erekat. Most shocking perhaps is the Fatah-led PA's willingness to cooperate with Israel to kill its own people. In a 2005 meeting the PA interior minister Nasser Youssef assented to Israeli defence minister Shaul Mofaz's suggestion to kill Hassan al-Madhoun, a leader of Fata's militant wing, the Al Aqsa Martyrs' Brigade. Four months later al-Madhoun was killed by an Israeli Apache gunship, and the next day Mofaz pledged concessions and a resumption of negotiations with Mahmoud Abbas. On another occasion the PA's Ahmed Qurei encouraged Israelis to reoccupy parts of Gaza to weaken the rival Hamas. The PA also appeared to have foreknowledge of the 2008–2009 Israeli assault on Gaza, a fact also confirmed by a June 2009 diplomatic cable released by Wikileaks. Most shameful by far was the PA's decision to join Israel and the US in sabotaging the Goldstone Report at the UN Human Rights Council, thereby eliminating any possibility of Israelis being prosecuted for war crimes committed in Gaza.

Albion's perfidies and Israel's sway over Western foreign policy were also in evidence. The most extraordinary perhaps was the British MI6's secret proposal to kidnap and detain Hamas and Palestinian Islamic Jihad members on behalf of Israel with the European Union footing the bill. The documents also reveal Britain's equipping and funding of the Palestinian Authority's notorious Preventive Security force and the General Intelligence Service. Tony Blair, it emerged, receives no more respect from Israel than he does from the rest of the world; even the Palestinian Authority considers him an ineffectual nuisance.

The practice of extensive record-keeping had started after the failure of the Camp David talks in 2000. Though Israeli foreign minister Shlomo Ben Ami would later confess that were he a Palestinian he would never accept what Arafat was offered at the summit, Clinton, the Israelis and ever-pliant Saudi Prince Bandar bin Sultan would all accuse Yasser Arafat of spurning a 'generous offer'. Indeed, Clinton went so far as to personally call cabinet members of the incoming Bush administration berating the Palestinians, and in the words of investigative journalist Patrick Tyler, deliberately 'poisoning the well'. One specific accusation against Arafat was his supposed lack of technical preparation and Palestinian leaders had therefore gone to some lengths to ensure that supporting documents would be drawn up in all future talks and the fullest records maintained. One member of the NSU entrusted with drawing up the records, the French-Palestinian lawyer Ziyad Clot, would later be revealed as one of the sources for the leak.

The composition of the NSU itself bears some attention here. Funded mainly by the British government's Department for International Development, the project is managed by Adam Smith International, a for-profit consultancy established in 1992 by the right wing think tank the Adam Smith Institute. The consultancy's British staff receive exorbitant salaries, a cause for much resentment among the Palestinians. But more serious has been the attempt to change the composition of the NSU staff in accordance

with the wishes of foreign donors so as not to risk funding. The best interests of the Palestinians are, in other words, subordinated to the profit
motive. Fearful of the Israel lobby's influence, the NSU leadership emas-
culated its highly able media and communications unit, which had
remained vulnerable to direct donor interference. It came under particularly intense assault for its work on the 2004 International Court of Justice
ruling on Israel's annexation wall. The NSU's Palestinian cohort had much
to resent.

Ziyad Clot would later explain his decision to blow the whistle as stemming from his disillusionment with the 'inequitable and destructive political process which had been based on the assumption that the Palestinians
could in effect negotiate their rights and achieve self-determination while
enduring the hardship of the Israeli occupation'. The 'peace process' was
'a deceptive farce whereby biased terms were unilaterally imposed by
Israel and systematically endorsed by the US and EU'. The Oslo process,
he added, 'deepened Israeli segregationist policies and justified the tighten-
ing of the security control imposed on the Palestinian population, as well
as its geographical fragmentation...it has tolerated the intensification of
the colonisation of the Palestinian territory... [it] was instrumental in
creating and aggravating divisions among Palestinians'. Clot expressed
outrage at the particular costs of the process for the Gazans, and the exclusion from it of the seven million refugees. He concluded that given its
structure, the PLO 'was not in a position to represent all Palestinian rights
and interests'. That is when he decided to blow the whistle.

The papers paint a damning picture. The Fatah leaders appeared more
concerned with preserving their authority over the pockets of territory
under Palestinian sovereignty than with liberating their people. Indeed, the
papers reveal a leadership perfectly willing to sacrifice its people in order
to retain sole control. The Palestinian Authority's first response was to set
loose its thugs on Al-Jazeera's offices and harass its journalists. But to its
great relief, the scandal was soon overtaken by events in Egypt. In the end
it decided discretion was the best part of valour: after its patron in Egypt
Hosni Mubarak was toppled by a popular revolution, Fatah agreed to reconcile with Hamas to form a unity government.

Democracy 2.0

As Iceland's Modern Media Initiative (IMMI) highlights, Wikileaks has already made a major contribution to the promotion and protection of investigative journalism. Excessive secrecy was one of the reasons why the lack of oversight over Iceland's banking sector became known only after the economy had collapsed. Leaks have also shown that in several states, including putatively democratic ones, Internet filters have been used to quash political dissent. Many people were struck by the banality of much of the material classified as 'secret', revealing how pervasively secrecy has been used by governments to limit accountability and oversight. A July 2010 investigation by William Arkin and Dana Priest of the *Washington Post* revealed that the culture of secrecy spurred by the events of September 11 has spawned a virtually unaccountable fourth branch of government which includes 850,000 contractors with 'top secret' clearance. Bradley Manning was cleared for the same access level as two million people, who all had access to the SIPRNet network. As Max Frankel, the *New York Times* editor who oversaw the publication of the Pentagon Papers, noted, any information shared that widely can't be considered 'secrets'. The function of such classification is simply to place some actions beyond the purview of democratic accountability.

The late Chalmers Johnson, author of the magisterial *Blowback* trilogy, recalled being asked by his wife while he was serving as consultant for the CIA, why so much of the agency's material was classified. Johnson replied that it would kill the CIA's mystique otherwise, if people found out just how banal most of its assessment actually is. This was brought home starkly when it was revealed that one of the sources the CIA had used in its highly classified October 2002 National Intelligence Estimate to support the claim that Iraq had links to Al-Qaeda was an article by David Rose in *Vanity Fair* magazine. The article was itself based on the testimony of a single Iraqi defector furnished by Ahmed Chalabi's Iraqi National Congress (INC).

But not all government reports are as useless as CIA estimates. The Congressional Research Service (CRS) has competent researchers with access to vast resources who produce meticulous reports at taxpayers' expense to inform congressional debates. Yet, for a variety of reasons, congresspersons' usually have them classified to keep them out of public view. Nearly seven thousand of them—worth billions of dollars in tax-payer money—were released by Wikileaks in 2009. This challenge to superfluous secrecy was a public service. As things stand, governments are able to classify any information as secret without having to offer a justifica-tion. This can only have a deleterious effect on democracy. Governments must only be allowed to keep the secrets that they can justify. The norm must be transparency—and in lieu of enforcing institutions, outfits like Wikileaks are necessary to ensure that government's compliance.

However, transparency cannot in itself be the end—and here Wikileaks has been legitimately faulted for some of its actions. As Wikileaks is itself now discovering, some degree of secrecy is necessary to the functioning of governments and institutions. Transparency must always have a public interest. True, the public interest can always be defined in a manner that justifies excessive secrecy (which is why some turn toward absolutist posi-tions on transparency). But if one were to accept transparency as an abso-lute, even organisations like Wikileaks wouldn't be able to function. Surely it would be inconsistent then for Wikileaks to keep the identity of its sources and funders secret. But that of course would invite reprisals and prosecution, especially in an environment where Wikileaks itself risks being charged for espionage. The answer to excessive secrecy therefore can't be absolute transparency. One must instead strive to democratise the defining of public interest so that it can be used as a touchstone for legiti-mate disclosure.

By this standard, much of what Wikileaks has done is legitimate and admirable. Wikileaks exists because public institutions have failed and lead-ers constantly lie. Most recognise the necessity of some degree of secrecy in diplomatic interactions but the cables are news only because citizens have long perceived a gap between the rhetoric and reality of American power politics. The cables were a confirmation. Leaking in itself is not a new phe-nomenon. Governments do it all the time when it suits their purpose. One merely has to read *Hubris: The Inside Story of Spin, Scandal, and the Selling of the Iraq War*, Michael Isikoff and David Corn's 2006 investigation of the Bush administration's strategic use of leaking to manipulate public opinion to know how pervasive this practice is. Journalist Bob Woodward has likewise written successive hagiographies of American presidents based on selec-tively leaked documents and official secrets. Wikileaks has overturned this control over the flow of information and undermined the cosy relationship between officials and the press. The leaks are no longer selective and few of them are flattering. Media gatekeepers are having a hard time spinning them and they consequently resent their diminished influence.

In 2010 *Time* magazine defied the judgment of its readers to select Facebook founder Mark Zuckerberg over Julian Assange as its person of the year. In a readers' poll Assange had secured 382,000 votes to Zuckerberg's 18,000. It had been some years since Facebook made a splash and most considered it yesterday's news. This led comedian John Hodgman to Tweet, '*Time* just named its Person of the Year 2007'. Forced to defend his choice, *Time* managing editor Richard Stengel confidently declared that 'Assange might not even be on anybody's radar six months from now…I think Assange will be a footnote five years from now'. This was a day before Mohamed Bouazizi set himself alight. It was also before Tahrir Square. It's over six months since Stengel's daring prediction yet Assange still remains on the radar and his list of media partners has grown to 63. Wikileaks still has at least two major leaks—on the financial sector and on the massacre of civilians in a NATO raid—scheduled for this year. It is safe to say that Wikileaks will be with us for some time to come. Given the present state of publishing, it is likelier that *Time* will be a footnote five years from now.

LYRICS ALLEY

Samia Rahman

With Sudan again hovering at the precipice of uncertainty and hope, and the Arab world writhing under the weight of popular upheaval, Leila Aboulela's dynastic novel *Lyrics Alley* (Weidenfeld and Nicholson, London, £ 12.99)—which unveils the tumultuous history of the powerful Abuzeid family alongside the death throes of imperial rule—could not be more timely.

It is the 1950s. Aboulela encapsulates the crumbling old order and the dawn of a new age in Sudan, Cairo and London. An age in which trajectories of faith, modernity and personal autonomy were as vital as they are now, played out by each character as he or she negotiates their own path to redemption.

Mahmoud Abuzeid is the head of the clan. A likeable, enterprising businessman, he commands respect, even deference. His family has flourished under British and Egyptian rule, culminating in him being granted the auspicious title Bey by Egypt's King Farouk. Yet there is a sense that he is very much a colonial construct, adhering to the conventions and hegemony of a dependent society. This is illustrated by his tireless fawning over the English couple the Harrisons, in order to secure a business loan.

Mahmoud Bey has thrived under the old order, the way things were, whereas his beloved son Nur represents a more egalitarian future. Mahmoud's hopes for his family are tied to Nur. Nur has been educated at a British boarding school in Alexandria and is set to study at Cambridge University. He has secured all the benefits offered by colonial rule and has a glittering future ahead of him. But then a devastating accident and his subsequent paralysis shatter every dream he had been brought up to believe he was entitled to realise. Love and marriage to his vivacious cousin Soraya, study and travel all are cruelly snatched from his grasp. The entire family is impacted. Nur sinks into desolation.

Yet his tragedy draws him to an alternate path. Destined previously to take over the family business and follow in his father's footsteps, Nur surpasses unutterable pain and despondency to discover a lyrical alley that would have once been closed to him: the life of a poet. Earlier in the novel his conservative uncle and Soraya's father, the humourless widower Idris, humiliates Nur upon finding a poem he has written. With the steady encouragement of his former tutor Ustaz Badr and the assistance of young Zaki, a poor relation who writes the words that Nur cannot, his lyrics resound across the airwaves on Radio Umdurman. His family overcome their misgivings. 'And with time, Mahmoud's reservations thawed. He still regarded Nur's lyrics as silly jingles, but he smiled when his friends and acquaintances mentioned that they had heard Nur's songs on the radio... anything was welcome as long as it kept the wretched boy amused and out of the pit of despair'.

Nur embodies the tragedy and the hope of Sudan as cessation from Egypt and Britain looms. His father had 'prided himself in harnessing both [Egypt and Sudan], in gliding gracefully between both worlds'. Yet we soon learn that Mahmoud Bey's own hybrid world is fragile. His fragmented sense of self is brought into sharp focus by his two wives. His sophisticated and beautiful Egyptian second wife Nabilah represents modernity and manners, while his Sudanese first wife Hajjah Waheeba is dismissed as ignorant, old and ridiculous. Waheeba is Sudan's past, while Nabilah embodies a glittering future.

The dichotomy exists within Mahmoud Bey himself, and its manifestation is complex and contradictory. Mahmoud supports Soraya's desire to continue her studies and allays the objections of her father, his brother. His progressive attitude and sense of moral justice prompt him to attempt to protect his daughter Ferial from the traditional Sudanese practice of female genital mutilation. He also takes responsibility for the servant Batool's marriage. Mahmoud Bey is a benevolent patriarch at ease with Egyptian diplomats and British bankers. Yet there is a deep-seated traditionalism within him that prevents him from turning his back on Waheeba when, in an act of spite, she lures Ferial to her hoash, leading her to be circumcised. This is Waheeba's victory over her husband's second wife. It is the pincer of a 'decaying past' that he cannot escape or deny. It is this part of him that Nabilah cannot understand.

Nabilah projects a perspective similar to that of the coloniser towards the colonised. Contemptuous and dismissive of the barbarity and vulgarity she perceives around her she even balks at the Sudanese traits in her children. She cultivates a world of Italian furnishings and Western etiquette in her part of the compound. Yet this home away from home, the exile's romanticised construct, is violated in the most horrific way by Ferial's circumcision. In simplistic terms Nabilah is the sneering, spoiled, figure of the imperialist. She is bewildered at Sue Harrison's enthusiasm for Sudan, for which she has nothing but scorn: 'The young woman was optimistic about her future in the Sudan to an extent that made Nabilah spiteful. Her warnings of perpetual dust, infernal heat and a host of creepy crawlies fell on deaf ears'.

Yet Aboulela does not depict caricatures. Through the medium of multiple narrators her characters are able to shape their own representation. Such insights into the private thoughts and whims of different protagonists enrich the narrative. The reader hovers above, observing events, listening in on ardent hopes and fears like a trusted confidante.

We learn that Nabilah is defiant because these are circumstances she did not choose for herself. She was only a young girl when her mother—seemingly anxious to rid herself of her overly attached daughter so that her own new marriage could receive her full attention—married her to the older Mahmoud Bey. Her understanding had been that she would continue to reside in Cairo. She had never imagined being re-located to Umdurman. As a result she builds a fortress of familiarity to insulate herself and her children from the unknown, and defines her identity in direct opposition to the 'other' epitomised by Waheeba. The first wife is a bleak figure mired in superstition who believes Nabilah has used black magic against Nur. Despite constantly reassuring herself that Waheeba is inferior in every way possible, Nabilah remains unsettled by the claim her husband's first wife has over him, a claim reinforced by Nur's accident.

Mahmoud Bey dictates the destiny of most of the women in Lyrics Alley. He arranges Fatma's marriage to his indolent and irresponsible eldest son Nassir, forcing her to abandon her education. He forbids Soraya from marrying Nur after his accident, and it is he who decides Nabilah will accompany him to London for Nur's operation, and not Waheeba.

Aboulela's representation of gender dynamics in Sudanese society in the mid-twentieth century and her powerful depiction of the spectre of female circumcision seem undermined by neat conclusions. Each female character is eventually reconciled to her lot. Bright and precocious, Soraya concedes that the love she and Nur share can only remain alive in the lyrics he writes. 'This... was where she belonged with Nur, right here, here in his songs'. He was once the one through whom she could glimpse the world of men, of literature, poetry, world affairs and knowledge. When her father refused to allow her to wear spectacles, Nur had a pair made for her. He was the progressive future she craved. Yet, even if fate had not interceded and crippled Nur, the reader is left wondering whether, compelled by family obligation and coerced by tradition, he could have ever satisfied Soraya's thirst for modernity.

Aboulela's evocative prose is most pleasing in her depiction of Badr. His is a voice that falls outside the upper echelons of Sudanese, Egyptian and British society. He is neither rich nor well-connected. An Egyptian teacher of Arabic and private tutor to the Abuzeid children, he is learned, wise and pious. Aboulela's characters reflect varying degrees of adherence to faith, and in Badr the concept of Muslim logic and spiritualised struggle is embodied. His gentle counselling brings Nur to a reluctant acceptance of his anguished state and a renewed interest in living. 'The Prophet Muhammad, peace be upon him, said, *When Allah loves a people, He tries them*. This is a trial, son, not a punishment'. Nur is moved by these words, comforted.

Aboulela quietly, without fanfare, illustrates the dignity of Islam. Faith permeates the novel as Qur'anic verse is interspersed with romantic poetry. Every character's heart is touched. Waheeba's clumsy and detrimental solicitation of a spiritual healer to help Nur reveals that the paralysed youth loves the rhythmic sound of Qur'anic recitation and the text's metaphoric language. Soraya, too, surrenders to the faith that Badr encapsulates, in spite of her unease with formal religion.

'Religious education... was a language she did not instinctively understand... She did not have an imagination for angels or devils but she was now sure—after Nur's accident—that people were governed by a will greater than their own'.

Aboulela does not idealise Badr, whose reveries balance both worldly and spiritual desires. The reader first meets him devouring with his eyes the furnishings and adornments of Mahmoud Bey's suite. He covets one of the state-of-the-art apartments that the Abuzeids intend to construct, the first of its kind in Sudan. He is described as being distracted by 'thoughts and half-baked schemes'. Badr's Islamic outlook, despite being softened by Sufi predilection, prompts him to welcome the increasing Islamisation of Khartoum and to lament, 'We could have done more... we could have spread Islam further, we could have squashed the seeds of religious deviations further'.

Disappointingly, Badr is depicted as a lustful man only protected from base instincts by the regimens of Islam. 'Badr needed his wife. He knew he had a weakness and a love for women. If the devil were going to tempt him he would tempt him with adultery'. Aboulela seems to give credence to the concept of the inherent lasciviousness of men. Although she strives to articulate the equilibrium characterised in Islam's gender roles, there is a sense that a woman is to be tamed. 'The sudden call to prayer from a nearby mosque jolted him out of his thoughts. It felt like a reprimand, a reminder of why he was alive... To fulfil and pacify [his wife Hanniyah], she who held his heart and was, so often, the cause of his disturbance'. Elsewhere, Aboulela writes: '[Badr] should say, 'Shut up, woman!' but instead he let her speak his mind. He unleashed her, she who was his inner self, his unrestrained half'.

Lyrics Alley is a rhythmic and evocative tale of idealised faith and romantic love. Its positive ending may be too romanticised for some, with almost every character experiencing some degree of deliverance from his or her personal anguish. This 'fairytale' conclusion is made all the more problematic by the lack of reference to the uncertain political future Sudan faces. The turbulence of Sudanese independence distantly looms in literary devices and background events, and although Nur's poem becomes an anthem for Sudanese independence, in reality the characters are barely touched by the political turmoil around them.

NEW MUSLIM COOL

Saffi-Ullah Ahmad

Being a hip hop junkie, I picked up this DVD begrudgingly, fearing a predictable story. I expected a sort of Muslim *8 Mile* meets (the awful) *Get Rich or Die Trying* in documentary format: gun-toting street hustler with a knack for rhyming finds Islam, leaves his old ways and becomes a local hip hop star who raps about emancipation. Brilliant viewing for fluffy liberals who have about as much knowledge of urban music and Islam as I do of water polo, but perhaps a boring watch for me. Prior to pressing the play button I'd even pondered a revised title: 'New Muslim, Not Very Cool'. Fortunately however, there is a lot more to this award winning documentary.

> *New Muslim Cool*, produced and directed by Jennifer Matorena, Co-produced by Hana Siddiqi and Kauthar Umar, distributed by Seventh Art Releasing, $19.95; www.newmuslimcool.com

New Muslim Cool is the sympathetically told story of a struggling Latino convert to Islam in post 9/11 America. Ignoring the old school Nike Air Max trainers, the opening scenes show a bearded, saintly figure who wouldn't look out of place in Biblical Jerusalem: long white robes thrown over his shoulder, staff in his right hand. Except he's in downtown Pittsburgh. Bells sounded in my ears immediately: convert overshoot syndrome. We've all seen it, right? Converts are often so strict they make Saudi clerics look like women's rights activists. I witnessed some striking overhauls during my time at university; from weed-smoking, bed-hopping raver who's drunk his liver to shrivelled oblivion to bearded literalist preoccupied with the *fiqh* of trouser length who won't be seen in anything other than a *thobe* (long white Saudi dress), all within a matter of weeks. The convert in our case—a Puerto Rican hip hop artist and former drug dealer from the mean East Coast streets of Boston—thankfully turns out to be fairly cuddly.

Prior to becoming Muslim, Jason Perez predicted two eventualities by the time he hit 21. He would either be languishing in jail or he'd meet an early death. Little did he know his life would be shaken that year when he came across a holy man. To the bemusement of his family, he would become Hamza Perez, the former crack dealing fiend gone clean. No more drugs, no more expletives, no more fighting.

Early on we receive a taste of the charismatic Hamza's passion for music. He and his more modestly bearded brother, Sulaiman, also a convert and hip hop artist, go by the stage name of the 'Mujahideen' or M-Team, with a distinctively Islamic touch to their style. Islam—whether stemming from Sunni, Shiite, or Nation of Islam sources, or newer factions such as the 5%'ers—has long featured in the lyrics of hip hop artists. It was this link that director Maytorena Taylor initially set out to explore. Knowing scarcely any famous Muslims as a child, I remember my friends and I becoming excited when we noticed Tupac's talk of going to the mosque in 'Dear Mamma', as well as Mosdef's introduction to epic pieces like 'Fear Not Of Man' with the words Bismillah-hir-Rahman-nir-Rahim. It might simply have been 'fast talking' to our parents, but to us fourteen year olds it meant so much more.

The Perez duo are first introduced on stage by Amir Sulaiman, now a big name on the Muslim hip-hop scene, who shot to fame some years ago on season 4 of Def Jam Poetry with such pieces as 'Danger'. On a local radio channel meanwhile, they're greeted by a cheery DJ who, acknowledging their Puerto Rican background, emancipatory lyrics and Islamic faith, jokes 'you sound like America's worst nightmare'. Although not explicitly about Muslim Hip-Hop, this form of music looms in the background throughout the documentary; new tracks are played almost as frequently as Hamza's beard pattern changes (from punk to full *tableeghi*, there isn't a style of facial hair Hamza doesn't embrace at some point or another).

A strong revolutionary hip hop scene remains, worlds apart from the garbage pushed by record companies. Whilst testosterone-overloaded 50 Cent, Dipset and Lil Wayne, pushed along by brain-dead DJ's like Tim Westwood, have rhymed boastfully about guns, drugs, pimps, 'bitchez', money and 'bling', the likes of Mosdef, Talib Kweli and Dead Prez have rapped about Malcolm X, illegal wars and occasionally even the objectification of women. With a longstanding problem for the latter group of artists being that decent lyrical content isn't very lucrative, increasingly rhymers like Immortal Technique—whose disturbing yet brilliant 'Dance With the Devil' is often dubbed on Internet forums one of the best hip hop songs ever performed—are dismantling the trend, for here you have an unsigned artist who's managed to rack up millions upon millions of hits on YouTube.

Disconcerting, however, is the penchant of 'alternative' artists for conspiracy theories, exemplified by the otherwise brilliant Jedi Mind Tricks and, unfortunately in our case, the Mujahideen Team who, alongside rightly slamming the Patriot Act and the Israel Lobby, talk of Freemasons and the New World Order. Oh, and they also wield machetes on stage.

The viewer can't help but warm towards Hamza and the tight knit community he finds himself among. *New Muslim Cool's* portrayal of the Muslim convert experience effectively counters stereotypes and generates warmth without overlooking the problems converts often face. Although grateful that he has left selling drugs and generally cleaned up his act (once described as a lost cause), Hamza's spiritual journey is hard for his family to accept and is marked by a clash of identities: Muslim, Puerto-Rican, American. Realising that it's more than just a phase, 'It's kinda confusing for us at times', his mother Gladys says. 'I brought the boys up in Catholic school'.

Hamza's religious development leads him to correct some of the wrongs he committed in the past. Working as an anti-drugs councillor, amusingly, he describes narcotics trafficking and selling in terms of 'pimps and hoes' to intrigued gatherings. 'I look at hustling like a corporation. Where there's crack, where there's Nike, where there's Wal-Mart, it's all pimping and ho-ing'. The dealers are 'ho-ing' for the police; an interesting twist of the belief held by some that law enforcement agencies profit from drug crime. Ideas relayed echo those put forward in the hit US series 'The Wire', whose director David Simon is troubled by the fact that state agencies commissioned to tackle drug crime across America work in terms of quotas and commissions. In situations in which the more drug dealers you lock up, the more commission you get, he argues bent officers recognise it isn't always profitable to keep drugs off the streets. There are no good guys.

Our protagonist also finds employment at the Alleghany County Jail, where with great pride he teaches multi-faith classes. 'I'm talking about the brotherhood of humanity', he tells receptive hoards of mainly Christian and Muslim inmates from a variety of backgrounds. Outside the jail, meanwhile, he preaches to non-Muslim gang members, advising them to leave their rotten ways and join him.

After meeting his wife to be, the level-headed Rafiah, on naseeb.com, they wed in a large colourful mosque, the sun glistening off its blue, yellow and pink tiles. With Rafiah, a headscarf-wearing African American in her late 20's, the tapestry of Hamza's identity becomes more complicated still. Amusingly, he uses the famous clash of civilisations line not in reference to politics or societal problems, but food. What would they cook on this momentous occasion?

With cameras following throughout, his wife smiles shyly as Hamza lovingly grabs her by the waist a short while after both have signed on the dotted line, for it is now halal to do so. Importantly, the viewer glimpses the couple's humanity and their ability to relate to their fellow country-men, whether Muslim or non-Muslim; characteristics often overlooked by the mainstream media which creates an air of paranoia and fear with regard to Muslims. The same daily struggle (albeit interspersed with prayers) as is no doubt replayed in countless households across America takes place at the Perez place; from schooling their children—both have children from previous marriages—and scraping money together to moving to a new house, the pair seem at the mercy of their ever changing but consistently challenging environment. Uninformed viewers will also come to realise that the much maligned term Jihad—regularly used by the pair in refer-ence to daily improvements of every sort—also has a friendly side.

'A Mujahid is someone who struggles in the path of Allah. That's what it is for us, it's a struggle to help revive the hearts of our people, kick Deen and raw lyrics that non-Muslims feel too. It's also a struggle spiritually because of all the diseases grabbing a mic can bring, like showing off, arrogance, conceit and so on', the M-Team say in a 2005 interview.

The local Muslim community in Hamza's part of Pittsburgh comprises of many who've strived to escape darker previous lives lined with drugs, guns and misery. Together they have a vision: to create a small mosque. Once it is seen through, it not only acts as a place of prayer but as a com-munity centre, one which on any given day one may enter and see groups of 30 people eating together on the floor and children singing Islamic nursery rhymes; I admit though, I felt sorry for the latter bunch upon hearing the Islamic version of Ring a Ring o' Roses, peaking at 'Sajda, sajda, we all fall down'.

As time progresses, the hardships associated with being Muslim in post 9/11 America become increasingly evident to Hamza. The spectre of the Patriot Act, which our central character refers to in his song lyrics in the opening scenes, looms over the small community.

When a camera is erected opposite the mosque—in precisely the opposite direction to where drug dealing is rife—worshippers feel uneasy. Tension reaches a high point on the evening of Friday 4 July, when FBI officers surround the area. A raid sees over twenty mosque goers lined up against the wall and questioned; with reasons initially elusive, it emerges after some time that the mosque was raided in connection with a convicted sex offender spending the night there. A local reporter however, highlights glaring inconsistencies in the official line, hinting ulterior motives to be the driving force, an excuse perhaps to see what the Muslim community got up to inside their new mosque.

Indeed the Patriot Act, an alarmingly illiberal and arguably unconstitutional piece of anti-terrorism legislation reauthorised numerous times, including by the Obama administration, has seen similar raids take place up and down the country. Enacted swiftly after 9/11 with little Congressional oversight or debate, it stripped away civil liberties like no prior act, granting a massive expansion of surveillance and investigative powers to domestic law enforcement agencies, including open interception of private communication and wanton issuing of search orders.

Sometime later, in true Patriot Act fashion, the FBI see to it that Hamza's clearance to enter jail in order to teach his beloved multi-faith classes is revoked. He feels angry, and although initially has no idea why this seeming injustice has taken place, it soon becomes evident that the authorities disliked an interview he gave some years ago on an obscure website (2003) in which he criticised the government. Intrigued as to its contents, although the documentary doesn't disclose much, an Internet search reveals the offending comments to indeed be quite distasteful. 'To all my Muslim immigrant brothers, stop bending over to our enemies out of fear of losing your status in this Dunya (temporary life). Stop collaborating and sleeping with the snake' (it goes on).

Undoubtedly however, by this point he has matured, becoming a better family man—as confirmed by a pleased Rafiah, who now works at a customer services desk at Comcast—and toning down his earlier more blunt ways. Referring to the controversial interview, 'I got a little raw. That's so young of me', he later recalls.

The M-Team's more recent lyrics—done more justice when performed, although admittedly not-spectacular—include: 'I live my life trying to be a humble slave, and find the answers to the questions in the grave/ That's how I spend my days, pretend I'm in the blaze, and when I bend and pray, I try to mend my ways/ I try to lower my gaze and stay modest, and life honest, tomorrow's not promised'.

His maturation leads him also to engage in laudable community projects such as collaboration between Jewish and Muslim poets. In scenes towards the end of the film, the camera follows Hamza walking alongside an elderly Jewish lady he has grown close to; a young, bearded, stockily-built rapper draped in basket ball jerseys, baggy jeans and bandanas, walking alongside a seemingly lonely, frail, upper middle class woman, both cracking jokes as the journey progresses. Speaking to camera, the woman says Hamza has for her dispelled many of the myths surrounding Muslims in America. Having won a variety of accolades including Aljazeera's Freedom Award, one can only hope Maytorena-Taylor's sensitive and quietly observational portrayal of Hamza's ongoing tale has the same effect on viewers.

The story, one of identity, discovery, and spiritual evolution in an increasingly hostile environment, has rightly been described by reviewers as uplifting. Towards the end of the 83min film, it is reassuring to know that although still struggling, our charming, joke-cracking central character seems to have found himself.

ET CETERA

THE CATALYST FOR KNOWLEDGEABLE GENERATION

SELANGOR FOUNDATION

For further details, kindly contact us at :

Corporate Affairs Unit
Menara Yayasan Selangor, No 18A, Jalan Persiaran Barat
46000 Petaling Jaya,
Selangor Darul Ehsan,
Malaysia.
Tel : +603 - 7955 1212
Fax : +603 - 7954 1790
Email : Info@yayasanselangor.org.my
www.yayasanselangor.org.my

CITATIONS

Introduction: Surprise, Surprise! by Ziauddin Sardar

On the special nature of contemporary times, see Ziauddin Sardar, 'Welcome to Postnormal Times', *Futures* 42 (2010) 435–444; and Merryl Wyn Davies, editor, 'Postnormal Times' *Futures*, special issue (2011) 136–227. Look out for *The Arab Spring: A Delayed Defiance* by Hamid Dabashi to be published by Zed Books in 2012. *13 Assassins* is out on DVD.

A Trans-Islamic Revolution? by Abdel-Wahab El-Affendi

The following works were have been used, and some have been cited, in this article.

Mehdi Abedi and Mehdi Abedi, 'Ali Shari'ati: The Architect of the 1979 Islamic Revolution of Iran', *Iranian Studies* 19 (3/4), (Summer—Autumn, 1986), pp 229–234.

Asif Bayat, *Making Islam Democratic: Social Movements and the Post-Islamist Turn*, (Stanford, Ca: Stanford University Press, 2007)

Asef Bayat, 'Democracy and the Muslim world: the 'post-Islamist' turn', *openDemocracy*, 6 March 2009, http://www.opendemocracy.net/article/democratising-the-muslim-world

Turki Al-Dakhil, *et al Muraja'at al-Islamiyyin*, Part I (Dubai: Al Mesbar Studies & Research Centre, 2009)

Abdelwahab El-Affendi, 'The Islamism debate revisited: in search of "Islamist democrats"'. In: Pace, Michelle, (ed.) *Europe, the USA and political Islam: strategies for engagement*. (London: Palgrave, pp. 125–138, 2010)

Essam El-Arian, 'Yawmiyyat Thawrat 25 Yana'ir-4' (Diaries of the 25 January Revolution', *Misress*, 6 April 2011, at: http://www.masress.com/almesryoon/53766.

and 'Yawmiyyat-5', *Misress*, 11 April 2011, at: http://www.masress.com/almesryoon/54610. And contemporary independent report on *Almasry*

Alyoum, 1 February 2011, at: http://www.almasry-alyoum.com/article2.aspx?ArticleID=287381&IssueID=2040.

Samer Frangie, Samer, 'The Arab Revolutions: an end to the post-1967 problematic', *openDemocracy*, 17 March 2011, at: http://www.opendemocracy.net/samer-frangie/arab-revolutions-end-to-post-1967-problematic.

Amr Hamzawy and Nathan J. Brown *The Egyptian Muslim Brotherhood: Islamist Participation in a Closing Political Environment*, Carnegie Papers, Number 19 (Washington DC: Carnegie Middle East Center, March 2010).

Youssef Michel Ibrahim, 'Democracy Be Careful What You Wish For', *The Washington Post*, March 23, 2003, http://www.cfr.org/world/democracy-careful-you-wish/p5747

Giles Kepel, *Muslim extremism in Egypt: the prophet and pharaoh* (Berkeley: University of California Press, 2003)

Abd al-Mun'im Munib, *Dalil al-Harakat al-Islamiyya* (Guide to Egyptian Islamic Movements) (Cairo: Maktabt Madbouli, 2010)

PBS *Frontline* (2011), 'What is the Muslim Brotherhood's Role in the New Egypt?', 22 February 2011, at: http://www.pbs.org/newshour/bb/world/jan-june11/frontline_02–22.html.

Carrie Rosefsky Wickham, 'The Muslim Brotherhood after Mubarak', *Foreign Affairs online*, 3 February 2011, at: http://www.foreignaffairs.com/articles/67348/carrie-rosefsky-wickham/the-muslim-brotherhood-after-mubarak?page=show.

Oliver Roy, 'Révolution post-islamiste', *Le Monde*, 14 February 2011, at: http://www.lemonde.fr/idees/article/2011/02/12/revolution-post-islamiste_1478858_3232.html.

Digital Revolution by Anne Alexander

A report on the efforts of the Mubarak government to shut down the Internet can be found on the *Wired* site: http://www.wired.com/threatlevel/2011/01/egypt-isp-shutdown/

The Officers For the Revolution are on Facebook:
http://www.Facebook.com/pages/%D8%B6%D8%A8%D8%A7%D8%B7-%D9%85%D9%86-%D8%A3%D8%AC%D9%84-%D8%A7%D9%84%D8%AB%D9%88%D8%B1%D8%A9/168595796526020?sk=info

BBC's Arabic website reports and testimonies of activists who had been tortured can be found at: http://www.bbc.co.uk/arabic/multimedia/2011/04/110401_egypt_torture.shtml

Ibn Khaldun and Arab Spring by Jerry Ravetz

The following works have been cited in this essay.

ibn Khaldūn, *The Muqaddimah: An Introduction to History*, translated by Franz Rosenthal, (London: Routledge and Kegal Paul, 1967)

Seymour Melman, *The Permanent War Economy: American Capitalism in Decline* (New York: Simon & Schuster, 1985)

Michael Lewis, *Liar's Poker* (New York: Norton, 1989).

Brian Martin, *Justice Ignited: The Dynamics of Backfire*, (Lanham, MD: Rowman & Littlefield, 2007).

Norbert Wiener, *The Human Use of Human Beings* (Boston: Houghton Mifflin Co, 1950)

The Turkish Model by S. Parvez Manzoor

The quotations are from Olivier Roy, *Secularism confronts Islam* (New York: Columbia University Press, 2007, p13, p54 and p ix.) Also mentioned are Elizabeth Shakan Hurd: *The Politics of Secularism in International Affairs* (Princeton: Princeton University Press, 2007, p7); and William E. Connolly: *Why I Am Not a Secularist*. (University of Minnesota Press, 1999. p. 24)

Café La Vie by Rachel Holmes

The details of the bespoke writer's courses, and student feedback, can be read at: www.palestineworkshop.org. Lubna Taha's full award-wining article for *Filisteen al Shabab* is available in Arabic at www.filistineashabab.com. Her translation of the article by Hussam Ghosheh, from Arabic to English, for the *Guardian* can be found at: http://www.guardian.co.uk/childrens-books-site/2011/may/03/jerusalem-palestine-festival-book.

Najef by Rose Aslan

Visit the English-language website for the Najaf 2012 Capital of Islamic Culture: http://alnajaf2012.com/en/index.php

TEN TOP TOWERING FATWAS

A spectre is haunting Muslims—the spectre of fatwas. All the powers of old Islam have entered into a holy alliance: to issue more and more fatwas, each as ridiculous as the other, and thus drown the Islamic earth in a pestiferous flood of fatwas. Muftis and Mullahs, on-line clerics and television preachers, bearded bovines and senseless Sheikhs—they are all at it.

So gather around, O believers! Here is a list of our all-time favourites.

1. The top place must go to the former Grand Mufti of Saudi Arabia, Sheikh Bin Baz. In April 2000, the Sheikh, an authority on the Qur'an and the sayings of the Prophet Muhammad, issued, after considerable study of the sacred sources, a fatwa entitled 'The Transmitted and Sensory Proofs of the Rotation of the Sun and Stillness of the Earth'. The learned Sheikh declared that the earth was flat and the sun revolved around it. Numerous Muslim scientists, who had measured the circumference of the earth correct to three decimal places way back in the eight century, immediately turned in their graves.

2. The Mullahs in the Deoband seminary in India are never far behind their Saudi colleagues. They have, however, introduced an innovation, and are now involved in a 'cash for fatwa' scandal. The going rate is said to be Rs 5000 per fatwa. Literally dozens of fatwas are issued by Deoband every week, like pork sausages coming down a conveyer belt, on a variety of topics—ranging from the use of credit cards to watching films (Both are *haram*, strictly forbidden, if you must know). But their divorce by mobile phone fatwa takes the biscuit. Issued in November 2010 by Darul Ifta, the fatwa department of Dar-ul Uloom, Deoband, it reads: 'Talaq (the word 'divorce') uttered thrice over a cell-phone by a Muslim man will be considered valid even if his wife is unable to hear it due to network or other problems'. They could have added: 'or if she is hard of hearing'.

244

3. But why bother speed dialling that number in the first place? You could send a text instead. In March 2007, the Grand Mufti of the UAE issued a fatwa urging the faithful to divorce their wives through SMS. 'Divorce through modern facility does not differ from divorce written on paper', the Mufti declared. He did not clarify whether you had to send three text messages or if simply one would do. However, he did emphasise that no one but the husband was allowed to send such a message. We hear that divorce by text has now become a popular pastime in Tajikistan.

4. But make sure you don't include those evil Emoticons in your text message. Emoticons, says Multaqa Ahl al Hadeeth, an Indian Internet forum for devout Muslims—that is, those who hate deviants and *ahl bidah* (people of innovation)—is the work of the western devils. The site, which describes itself as a 'meeting place for students of knowledge', asserts: 'Emoticons are forbidden because of its imitation to Allah's creatures whether it is original or mixture or even deformed one and since the picture is the face and the face is what makes the real picture then emoticons which represent faces that express emotions then all that add up to make them *Haram*'. That's devout logic for you.

5. Devout husbands must be eternally vigilant and careful, lest they accidently and unintentionally nullify their marriage. One way such misfortune could befall is by accidently seeing your wife naked during sex. According to a fatwa issued in January 2005 by Rashad Hassan Khalil, one time Dean of Sharia at that great citadel of Islamic learning Al-Azhar, 'being completely naked during the act of coitus annuls the marriage'. So cover yourself, O ye faithful!

6. What if the wife is dead? Well, that shouldn't stop you from having sex with her, at least according to the highly regarded Moroccan Islamic Scholar and a member of the country's religious hierarchy, Abdelbari Zemzami. He justifies his ruling, issued in May 2011, through an age old source of Islamic law—analogy. 'Since a good Muslim couple will meet again in Heaven, and since death does not alter the marital contract it is not a hindrance to the husband's desire to have sexual intercourse with the corpse of his (freshly) deceased wife'. So stop mourning and get on with it.

7. Dead or alive, do make sure that your wife is a real woman and not a 'tomboy'. Women who wear trousers, or behave in a 'manly manner',

according to an edict issued in October 2008 by the National Fatwa Council of Malaysia, are 'tomboys' and not women; and therefore *haram* (forbidden). So do make sure, O believers, that your wives do not have short hair, wear jeans, or speak too loudly.

8. Or do yoga. A month later, in November 2008, the National Fatwa Council of Malaysia identified Yoga as 'an aberration'. The *Iman* (faith) of a Muslim is already too weak, declared Abdul Shukor Husin, the Chairman of the august Council, to stand the onslaught of Hindu spiritual elements and chanting. Yoga 'can destroy the faith of a Muslim' completely! The Council is now working on a 'halal Yoga' so that 'more compliant Muslims would not be confused'. Presumably it involves halal necrophilia.

9. However, if your Yoga-practising tomboy of a dead wife wants to go out and work there is a handy solution to your problems. According to a fatwa by Ezzat Attiya, another genius from the Al-Azhar factory and head of its hadith Department, issued in May 2007, the rules forbidding unrelated men and working together can be easily overcome. The women should breast-feed their male colleagues. That, on the authority of some hadith or other, would make them kin, nearest and dearest who can work and hang out together.

10. In the end, as in the beginning. We return to Sheikh bin Baz, the late, lamented Grand Mufti of the Kingdom of unsoiled Muslims with perfect faith. Thanks to WikiLeaks we now know that it was none other than the blind Mufti himself who decreed, in a famous fatwa in 1991, that women should not be allowed to drive. The Sheikh declared, reads a cable, that 'allowing women to drive would result in public "mixing" of women, put women into dangerous situations because they could be alone in cars, and therefore result in social chaos'.

The man was right. The Islamic earth is really flat.

PAKISTAN

Aasia Nasir

Shahbaz Bhatti, the only Christian cabinet member in the People's Party led government in Pakistan, was brutally assassinated in Islamabad on 2 March 2011. The responsibility for the murder was claimed by the Pakistani Taliban. But what was his crime? He questioned the country's absurd blasphemy laws and championed the case of Asia Bibi, a Christian woman sentenced to death for alleged blasphemy. Thus a powerful voice of the religious minorities in Pakistan was silenced.

The following day, before the funeral of Bhatti took place, the House of Parliament paid respect to Bhatti with a two minute silence, with Members standing in Bhatti's honour. Four members of religious parties remained seated, thus not joining this mark of respect. Following the silence, Asia Nasir, a Christian and one of the few non-Muslim members of the Pakistan National Assembly, stood up to address the Parliament. She spoke without notes for 13 minutes, starting with a well known poem by the celebrated Pakistani poet Faiz Ahmad Faiz, Ham jo taarik rahon mein maray gaiy ('we who were executed in the darkest lanes'). Faiz himself was no stranger to either challenging the oppressive regimes of his time, nor to being a victim of their oppression. This poem was written on 15 May 1954, reportedly on reading the letters of Julius and Ether Rosenberg, executed in the United States (on 19 June 1953) for allegedly passing information about the American atomic bomb to the Soviet Union. At the time of writing, Faiz was in prison. Nasir concludes her speech with another Faiz poem: lahu ka suragh (sign of blood). This poem was written following the defeat of Fatima Jinnah by General Ayub Khan, in the rigged elections of 1963. (Nasir did not read the middle stanza which is included here for completion).

247

During her speech, Nasir mentions the 31 July 2009 Gojra incident in central Punjab, where Christians were attacked by Muslim fanatics, leading to around 50 Christian homes being torched, to 'avenge' the alleged desecration of the Qur'an by Christians. She also quotes another contemporary, left-wing Urdu poet, Sahir Ludhianwi. A member of the Progressive Writers' Association, Sahir moved to Lahore after partition. But his inflammatory poems, which had a strong communist message, led to an arrest warrant. He fled to Delhi in 1949 and then moved to Bombay, where he became a legendary song writer for Bollywood films. He wrote the songs for Guru Datt's 1957 film, Pyassa ('The Thirsty'), considered by many as one of the greatest films of the Indian cinema.

Following the speech, Nasir led a symbolic walk out from the House as a mark of protest. She was followed by almost every member of the parliament. The Pakistani government has remained silent since Nasir's speech and has taken no discernable action.

This is the full text of the speech, translated from Urdu for the first time.

> I longed for your lips, dreamed of their roses:
> I was hanged from the dry branch of the scaffold.
> I wanted to touch your hands, their silver light:
> I was murdered in the half-light of dim lanes.
>
> And there where I was crucified,
> so far away from my words,
> you still were beautiful:
> colour kept clinging to your lips—
> rapture was still vivid in your hair—
> light remained silvering in your hands.
>
> When the night of cruelty merged with the roads you had walked,
> I came as far as my feet could bring me,
> on my lips the phrase of a song,
> my heart lit up only by sorrow.
> This sorrow was my testimony to your beauty—
> Look! I remained a witness till the end,
> I who was killed in the darkest lanes.
>
> It's true—that not to reach you was fate—
> but who'll deny that to love you

was entirely in my hands?
So why complain if these matters of desire
brought me inevitably to the execution grounds?

Why complain? Holding up our sorrows as banners,
new lovers will emerge
from the lanes where we were killed
and embark, in caravans, on those highways of desire.
It's because of them that we shortened the distances of sorrow,
it's because of them that we went out to make the world our own,
we who were murdered in the darkest lanes.

Mr Speaker, through you I would like to request the House to give me their attention. Mr Speaker, through you today, I will address neither the Prime Minister of Pakistan, nor the 342 Members of this House. But Muhammad Ali Jinnah (the founder of Pakistan)! Today I address you. Because my brother has been slaughtered. Muhammad Ali Jinnah! You had invited us to join you, to build a home, that sacred home to be called Pakistan. And on that sacred land, there will be no Hindu, no Christian, no Muslim; under the shadow of its flag, we will only be Pakistanis. *Qaid-i-Azam*! ('The Great Guide', Jinnah's moniker) Today I demand to know, that after Pakistan was created, and we came to this our collective home on your calling, how have we been treated?

Mr Speaker, I demand to know from you, what crime had my brother, Shahbaz Bhatti, committed? Only that he wished to see Pakistan as envisioned by the *Qaid-i-Azam*? Mr Speaker, when we came to Pakistan, our forefathers decided to join Pakistan. When the Boundary Commission was deliberating, when Pakistan and India were being divided, few people would know that the Christians were considered for their own land, but the Christians declined their own land in preference for joining Pakistan, to be part of Pakistan. We came to Pakistan through choice. What kind of people are you, where is your humanity? When you needed our support for the creation of Pakistan, you were happy to welcome us. But once Pakistan was created, you turned us into minorities, our backs against the wall. Discrimination was heaped upon us. We became 'untouchables', pollutants. You wouldn't share eating utensils with us. You turned us into fourth grade citizens. At times, you destroyed our institutions. And sometimes you stole our Saviour from us.

Today, I want to know from this House, what is our crime as Christians? We have been, are and always will be loyal to Pakistan for we have shed our blood for this land, and yesterday, my brother [Shahbaz Bhatti] has shed his blood for this land. What was and is our fault for the discrimination heaped upon us? Now there will be speeches in this House, that 'minorities have equal rights'. I say to this House that for 65 years minorities have never had equal rights; we don't have equality now and we don't expect equality in the future.

When the Gojra tragedy took place, I said that I fear that our future generations may regret the choices made by our forebears, to join Pakistan. And yesterday, when my daughter screamed in my arms, 'Mom, let's leave this country', it became clear to me that our new generations will lament this decision. Mr Speaker, loyalty to Pakistan is second nature to us. I said to my daughter, 'No, my child, don't talk like this. This is your motherland. We won't go anywhere for we are of this land, we have grown up here, we are the children of this land. Even if we were to die for this land, shed every drop of our blood for it, we will not abandon this beloved country. For we are sworn to protect this garden'. [Clapping and banging of desks in support.]

Mr Speaker, Sahir Ludhianwi rightly said:

> Tyranny has its bounds,
> beyond a limit it self-destructs;
> blood has durability,
> if shed it leaves its mark.

My brother has shed his blood, not as a full stop to struggles but as the first letter of a new struggle. For you can try your utmost to silence the minorities or kill as many people as you like. Mr Speaker, yesterday, my brother was killed, next Asia Bibi may be hanged from the gallows, and you can riddle my body with bullets. You will not be able to silence the minorities. This struggle for our rights will continue.

Mr Speaker, the biggest sign of discrimination is that this House treats us worse than animals. Why only 'two minutes' silence for us? We are the believers of the God of Abraham, Jacob and Isaac, that Living God, who hears and answers our supplications. This is not the God of silence, deaf to pleadings. So why doesn't the House offer prayers for us? I want to know this, though the Prime Minister is not here. Yesterday, when one of your Party faithful sacrificed his life, yesterday when a People's Party Minister was brutally murdered in broad daylight, you continued with your Cabinet meeting. You should have postponed the Cabinet meeting immediately.

Mr Speaker, there is clear discrimination. Some ministers have more than one bullet proof car, but not Shahbaz Bhatti. This murder resulted from a security lapse. I personally spoke to Rahman Malik [Minister for the Interior], that we Christians have concerns about security. I was told by Malik that a bullet proof car had been given to Shahbaz Bhatti. I expressed concerns about security arrangements at Bhatti's house and was told that security had been provided. When I asked Shahbaz about this, he said that Rahman Malik was telling lies about providing security. Shahbaz had been asking for accommodation in the parliamentary enclave, but to no avail.

Mr Speaker, I want to say that the current government shares responsibility for Shahbaz Bhatti's assassination. For the Government had announced the formation of a so-called committee to review the Asia Bibi case [and to consider review of the blasphemy laws], but nothing was actually done. I used to ask Shahbaz to talk to the Prime Minister and the President about this, so that they could be challenged on not establishing this promised committee. No such committee has been formed, no meetings have been held. I said to him that he was being made a target [for opposing blasphemy laws]. No such committee was formed. Mr Speaker, the Prime Minister or the President have formulated no clear policy on these issues, formed no structures. Mr Speaker, I would like to make clear that my brother, Shahbaz Bhatti, had never uttered anything [offensive to the Prophet] for such behaviour does not befit us as Christians. We know well how to protect the honour of Prophets. No Christian or member of a religious minority would ever dream of insulting any Prophet.

Mr Speaker [becomes emotional and takes time to compose herself]. Mr Speaker, we condemn in the strongest terms what has happened. And we demand from the government; Pakistani Christians are outraged. But we will decide our plan of action after performing Shahbaz Bhatti's burial.

And if you are to form a committee, you should form a committee with cross party representation. And in that committee, you should decide who is and who isn't a citizen of Pakistan. And if that committee decides that Pakistan is an Islamic state, for Muslims only, for this is what the media portrays Pakistan as. Some extremist journalists repeatedly state that Pakistan is an Islamic state. But I want to tell you, that Pakistan is not just for Muslims. You have corrupted the history of Pakistan. People know that Christians sacrificed much in the struggle for Pakistan. On 14 August, the day of Pakistan's birth, a hundred Christian nurses shed their blood for Pakistan, on Pakistan's borders. You don't know this, because the history of Pakistan has edited out the contribution of Christians. The odd book acknowledges that those close to the *Qaid-i-Azam* included Christian leaders, but no one knows this today. Hindus had been on this land for centuries. But Christians came to Pakistan of their own volition. Why? To be murdered? To have our blood spilled on this land? To be regarded as 'untouchables'? To be classed as fourth degree citizens? Is this why you welcomed us into Pakistan?

Mr Speaker, today we Christians demand from the Prime Minister and the President of Pakistan that the culprits are apprehended and brought to justice. For we are not of some other land, not of America, not of Europe, but only of Pakistan. [clapping] And you must decide, if we are to gain equal rights, to gain equality, then we will remain in Pakistan, or tell us that there is no place for religious minorities in Pakistan and we will find another home for ourselves.

Mr Speaker, to end, I wish to say that we cannot condemn this event enough. Today we are shedding tears of blood. We have been given a clear message: that whoever raises their voice in support of religious minorities will be met by bullets. Mr Speaker, today we need a clear statement from the government; they must state their position on religious minorities. What are they doing to protect the minorities? We will no longer accept their excuses, lame excuses. The time of decision is upon the Christians of Pakistan: 'to be, or not to be, that is the question'.

Mr Speaker, to end, I refer back to my martyred brother, Shahbaz Bhatti; you clearly don't regard him as a martyr, but he is a martyr for us, among Christians, for he gave his life for the work of Christ the Messiah, and kept his faith to his last breath [clapping]. I salute this martyr, my brother, and praise his courage. Mr Speaker, I would like to finish my speech with these words from Faiz, so apt for this occasion.

No sign of blood, nowhere, anywhere
Not on the hands or nails of the assassin, nor on his sleeve

No shining redness on the dagger's lips, nor the tip of the javelin
No stain on the ground, nor the door frame
No sign of blood, nowhere, anywhere

[Not for the honour of service to the kings whose favours could be paid in blood
Not for faith or religion, a tax for eternal salvation
Not shed in battle, no glory gained
Not used to colour the battle standard, to achieve fame]

Kept crying for salvation, my guardian-less, orphaned blood
None heard its laments, gave it time or thought
No plaintiff nor witnesses, but verdict was passed
This blood of the wretched of the earth, has again irrigated the earth.
Mr Speaker, in protest at this appalling atrocity, I and other Members of this House representing religious minorities, are staging a symbolic walk out.

(*Translated by Waqar Ahmad*)

ON SAUDI WOMEN DRIVERS

Merryl Wyn Davies

It is a truth universally observed that women drivers exist to be scorned, belittled, demeaned and abused. I know—I used to be a woman driver! It is a fascinating curiosity that Saudi Arabia manages to conform to this principle by the singular expedient of preventing women from driving at all.

I have often wondered what it is about vehicular transportation that induces irreducible and ineradicable misogyny. In these sensitive days—post the men are from Mars, women from Venus debate—one is supposed to be more subtle than just to put it down to testosterone. If the androgenic hormone is not responsible, then what is it that makes the internal combustion engine the great redoubt and ultimate legitimisation of male supremacy?

Whatever the cause, it now appears that should this bastion of male pride be humbled in Saudi Arabia a new dawn of human liberty will be assured. Then the spring of Arab awakening will be made high summer by bevies of black shrouded women independently driving themselves to an infinite array of shopping malls or bustling around on a host of domestically-related tasks. This will be prelude to a new world order in the realms of social, economic and political power. Once this iconic pinnacle of indivisible liberty and human rights is secure then all manner of things will be well in the best of all possible worlds.

Actually, I beg to differ. While liberty may be indivisible, it is surely the case that not all freedoms are of equal moment. There are distinctions to be made concerning essentials. There are what might be termed required rights and those rights which are a nice bonus, should circumstances allow and make available their enjoyment. In other words some rights are contingent; they will inevitably follow if the basics have been put in place. In this order there is a battle cry of freedom, an inherent agenda. And according to this perspective the freedom to take charge of a motorised vehicle is, quite simply, tangential to human dignity, not least because it is entirely dependent on one's ability to afford a car in the first place—by no means a universal state of affairs. Where, I wonder, does it say that all people are created equal to own a motor car? God help the planet if they ever get round to legislating that clause.

There can be no question that the Saudi insistence on debarring women from driving is wrong headed. It relies on an infantilisation of women combined with a demonisation of their supposed sexual potency. In reality it is an empowerment of male weakness which actually sustains, nay encourages, positively unhealthy attitudes to human relations. A moment's reflection suffices to confirm it has nothing to do with Islam, except as a perverse misreading of Islam's inherent ethic of mutuality and balance in gender relations. It comes down to customary practise and an obscurantist inability to come to terms with change.

Once again Saudi Arabia and its peculiarities are being hyped around the world. It is not merely a question of the bizarre nature of this imposed and policed limit to freedom. It is a function of the global fixation with the fate and state of Saudi women. Muslim women the world over perennially find themselves caught in the crosshairs of this fixation. The supposed archetype of Islamic authenticity we are forever encountering is a stereotype framed by the idea of Saudi women. The sisters of Saudi have a lot to bear—but they also have a lot to answer for, to Muslim women who lead very different lives and struggle to vindicate very different attitudes and ideas about Islamic gender relations.

Clearly, I am in the category of one conflicted and unconvinced by the mould breaking nature of the 'day of rage'. According to the estimable Jason Burke in the *Guardian*, the outrage led some forty Saudi women to take the wheel. A breathless global media waited, watched and relayed more detail than seemed warranted.

Surely, I hear you think, my failure to rally to the spirited determination of these Saudi women verges perilously close to an anti libertarian stance. Once again I beg to differ. I am fully cognisant of the thin end of the wedge theory of freedom. Indivisible as liberty is, its course, so it is argued, must be inexorable, wherever one starts. Claim one liberty, no matter how small, and change will happen. A single blow for any liberty must eventually let freedom ring loud and clear everywhere. The trouble is I cannot think of or imagine anywhere or any time when this theory has been practised or put to the test.

My own experience of Saudi Arabia consists of being confined to what effectively became a *zenana* (cell) with some twenty Saudi women for the duration of a conference. Instead of discussing conceptual aspects of social policy and issues about broadcasting, as advertised and according to the papers I had prepared, at the behest of outraged members of the Saudi ulema I found myself discussing 'Women in Islam' with a hastily assembled gaggle of Saudi sisters. It was not a pleasant experience. I challenge anyone to have one single strand of escaped hair rudely pushed back under one's scarf while in the act of praying, because such flagrant disregard was supposedly irreligious, and not wonder who is victim and who willing, indeed zealous, collaborator with obscurantism.

In the privacy of our secluded conferring there was scant evidence of any questioning of custom and tradition, or indeed any thinking about the meaning and potential of interpretation of religious text. There was, however, a great deal of screeching, running, scrambling for shrouds and hiding whenever a waiter (male of course) arrived with our food. Using the hotel restaurant was deemed inconceivable by the Saudi ulema and, I must say, by my fellow conferees.

As a broadcaster commissioned to report to the world on the conference, my life was not made easy. I ended up luring the great and the good of the global community of Muslim scholars and intellectuals to my hotel room and sitting them on my bed to record interviews. Perversity has its rightful reward in the entirely contrary outcomes it produces. It is a measure of the regard for such nonsense that no luminary thought the location contrary to dignity or the decency of either party, and none therefore refused to be interviewed under these circumstances.

Nor would I try to suggest that all Saudis are clones of their ulema. Indeed, I came to suspect the Saudi organiser of the conference either had psychic powers of precognition or had fitted me with a GPS device years before they were invented. Whenever I made furtive escapes from the female quarters to go about my professional business I invariably encountered our host. He would plant himself resolutely in the middle of the corridor and engage me in loud conversation for as long as possible, interrupted as frequently as could be by introducing me to every passing notable. It was a heroic tour de force, only stopping short of challenging or indeed overturning the ridiculous ruling of the ulema.

And there you have my problem in a nutshell.

Today Saudi women are educated. Many further their education abroad in western institutions, just as Saudi men do. Saudi men and women travel extensively around the world. There is no lack of awareness of how different everywhere else is to Saudi Arabia. While women everywhere, in the supposedly liberated and enlightened West as well as across the diversity of the Muslim World, have endured and continue to endure discrimination and misogyny in multiple overt and covert ways, the difference in attitudes and outlook let alone custom and practise cannot be lost on any sentient Saudi. The willingness to frame their protest at the driving ban within the bounds of tradition, to stir without shaking the status quo is exactly what gives me pause.

Dedication to liberty and freedom does not just happen to counter inconvenience. Its surest hold on human aspiration is through reflection, analysis, and debate about the quality and condition of social, economic and political life. It is founded in moral force and suasion that is extensive and all embracing in its understanding and aspiration. Without such a context driving a car, whether the driver is male or female, is merely getting from one place to another. The resources to think and question are available in Saudi Arabia. Gradualism is a perfectly acceptable course of reform. However, gradualism shades into complicity with the comforts afforded by the system when it fails to entertain a general critique of the essential constituents of human dignity, liberty and freedom.

As things stand there is precious little evidence of a gathering groundswell of such thinking taking place in Saudi Arabia. Too little evidence, I fancy, to invest the actions of forty women behind the wheel of their cars as a harbinger of a new future. In the general scheme of things it is more of a distraction, and one that is not disinterested, from the serious life and death cries for basic and essential freedoms being undertaken elsewhere in the Middle East.

I was once a woman driver. I have foresworn the internal combustion engine on grounds of exorbitant cost and environmental detriment. I have opted for the inestimable pleasures of being conveyed door to door without the hassle of navigating through unfamiliar streets, finding parking spaces, paying parking fees and then walking half a mile to my desired destination. As a result I have been freed from the unprintable epithets hurled through passing windscreens and the unseemly gestures made in my direction. I have liberated myself from misogynist road rage and feel absolutely safe from any danger of thinking or acting like a Saudi woman. And that, dear reader, is why much as I urge them to freedom, I am not enthralled by Saudi women drivers as a rational summons to liberty.